THE POWER OF SUBMISSION

Foreword by Dr. Myles Munroe

KIM V.E. SANDS

All are scriptures taken from the King James Version of the Bible.

You can purchase this book directly from our website www.marriagemechanics.org.

(407) 385 8201

Kim Sands is an ordained minister and has produced this work under the inspiration of the Holy Spirit.

ISBN (hc) ISBN-10: 978-1-7362998-0-7

ISBN (e): 978-1-7362998-1-4

Printed in the United States of America

Marriage Mechanics Ministries, Inc. 11/05/2020

Contents

Dedication

To nine women that God has strategically placed in my life to help mold me into a vessel that he could use. To Ashleah and Krysta, My two daughters my angels, my daughter in law Frankayla, and my grand daughters Zariyah & Laurelle I cherish the treasure of you; you have truly helped to refine the gift that God has placed in my life. You have bought meaning and purpose in a way that only you can. My prayer each day is that God would help me to be a vessel through which he can channel his glory into your lives, and that you would become humble, yet powerful women of God. Valerie Hanna, Colleen Huffman, and Sandra Norris, My three blood sisters, Thank you so much for making my life exciting, our experiences together was a divine appointment. In the good times we've shared and the times when you wanted to squeeze my neck. For laughing and crying with me, I give thanks to God for you, I could not have asked for three better siblings. I love you! Continue to be empowered through obedience.

To Emma Hanna, My mother and best friend, you were obedient to God by constantly pointing me to him, instructing, and grooming me in the way that you did. Thank you for being what I needed at the right times in my life. You have truly been a vessel through which he has channeled his glory. I love you, my sister, and my friend. May the world see you as I do - a virtuous and blessed woman of God! And To the women of God the world over, my spiritual mothers, sisters, and children, accept the challenge, possess the power, and hold tightly the key to fulfillment, a sense of wholeness, destiny, and life. God is about to take you where you have never been before. Spread your wings and be lifted up... Through the Power of Submission!

Foreword

One of the greatest challenges of the 21st century is the gender war. Never before in history has the lines between male and female been so gray. During the last century the fight for equality between the male and female gender has taken conflict to another level. The declaration of the females right to participate in social, political and economic processes in societies throughout the world, have created a new equation for the value of the sexes in our post modern society.

The historical biblical record of the creation of the male and female and the establishment of the divine relationship structure between them as seen in the Holy Scriptures is clear. However, this book deals with all that and so much more.

Nowhere has there been more controversy over this issue than in the religious world. Churches, mosques, and synagogues have been the battleground for this conflict and many are still not sure the war is over. However it is important in issue to remember that no one knows the product like the manufacturer, and therefore when there is confusion about the functioning of a product we should refer to the manufacturer's manual.

In this work, THE POWER OF SUBMISSION, Kim Sands takes the reader back to the foundation of the relationship between male and female, the community, church, and nation. Her simply, profound style, leaps over the complicated theological boundaries to open the Word and reveal the principles of womanhood and the role and responsibilities of the Female. Her candid approach to the subject as a woman is just what men and women need to overcome the confusing alternatives of culture and social pressure. I believe this book will become a classic and should be read by all women and men alike. I challenge you to dive into these pages and let the power, truth and practical principles transform your concept and attitude of the female's role in relationships and life. Submission is finally being delivered from the shadow of fear and given its novel place in the plan of God for mankind. Read on and discover the hidden power of submission.

Dr. Myles Munroe

*Author of Understanding Your Potential & In Pursuit of Purpose,
International teacher, speaker, lecturer, and businessman, Founder of
Bahamas Faith Ministries International.*

A Word from the Author

For me, *"The Power of Submission,"* was an inspiring experience. Besides being one of the first books -that I have written, its message has helped to mature me from the newly married wife to the woman that I am today. This book holds some of the most treasured and sensitive moments of my life as well as the experiences and testimonies of other women that I have met through the years. The writing experience was soul searching and challenging at times as I came face to face with inner struggles and shared my victories, faults, and failures. Nevertheless it was rewarding and refreshing as well. It is not a storybook or a book to sit and read for pleasure. It is a message of conviction, revelation, and passion for women, men, and Christians alike. This book was meant to be read, put down, reflected upon, and read again. To the spiritually young it is encouragement and guidance. To the spiritually mature it is inspiration and truth. To all, it is understanding to walk with God in the life of His word through the power that comes with submission!

Many Blessings,
Kim Sands

I HAVE CALLED YOU,
CHOSEN YOU, ANOINTED,
AND APPOINTED YOU,
BUT I AM A GOD OF ORDER.

1

The Feminine Dream

*For the marriage of the Lamb is come, and His wife
hath made herself ready.*

– REVELATIONS 19:7

The clear sky blazes a rainbow of brilliance as the morning sun peaks over the earth. Birds are singing, and a gentle breeze perfumes the air with a blended fragrance of spring flowers. It is the dawning of a bright and beautiful day. Outside the church, a lovely young bride ascends the high steps, and enters through the broad wooden doors. Lively bridesmaids eagerly assist with her train of white pearled satin that trail royally behind on her way up the church steps. She cradles a bouquet of fresh cut red roses in her arms. A delicate pearl and diamond crown sparkles atop her perfectly coifed hair. Nestled in a soft, white, puffy veil of netting it covers her head and shoulders. She is a princess of regal beauty on this very special day.

Inside, she steps through the decorated doorframe of the sanctuary and takes her father's arm. The organ music begins; the guests' stand and turns in unison, all eyes now beholding the gorgeous bride. She lifts her eyes to the pulpit to see her groom waiting. His eyes alive with excitement as he watches his wife-to-be begin her journey down the aisle. Her heart races as she realizes that from this day forth, she will be with him for always, and together they will live happily ever after. This is the feminine dream.

Every woman at some point in her life, dreams of the day when she would find the man of her dreams and get married. From a very young age my mom would often speak of the day when we would grow up and be married as a special day to look forward to. My day began on a quiet morning on February 9, 1985. My mother awoke me at 4:30 a.m. to prepare for the 8:00 a.m. ceremony that would usher me into marriage. Twelve months before, I became engaged to a man I believe God brought to me and immediately began planning my wedding and building my hope chest. We had met in a bible college class six months earlier and knew right away that our future involved each other. This morning, I was excited that my day had finally come! As I stepped into the bathtub filled with warm water, bath oil, and scented soaps, Mom said to me, "Just relax, I will be back for you." I settled back and began reflecting on the eighteen months leading up to this day. I thought of how mom tried to talk my husband into a longer engagement. She wanted to have all her daughters around for a few more months. I smiled to myself. However between the two of us, we felt strongly that this was what we wanted to do. Neither of us wanted a long courtship, so we decided to get married and begin the process of getting to know each other after the wedding. This was our day!

The house was abuzz with activity. The young women that would stand beside me in my wedding were all at the house. Mom's hands were full. About thirty minutes later she was back with a lush white towel for me to step into. Then the real dressing began! There was the skin care, the hair designer, the photographer and videographer, shoes and clothing were everywhere. I was being adorned to meet my husband. Next, the dress was brought in - a pure white, satin gown that mom and I had designed together. Finally, when I was dressed, a white limousine awaited me outside my parent's home to take me to the church I grew up in. I was ready and on my way to be married.

Later, I watched my bride-maids walk up the church steps, while inside, the congregation prepared for the entry of the bride. The two trumpeters at the front of the sanctuary sounded their instruments announcing my entry as my father escorted me to meet my groom at the altar. I dreamt of this day for as long as I could remember, and it really turned out to be 'a dream come true.' Together, my husband and I had planned for months, to this very moment when everyone would see us, not as two, but as one. As we stood before God and our witnesses, my heart pounded within my chest, yet there was peace. I believed that I was ready to move from the protection of my parents and accept the headship of my husband. I felt assured that this was indeed God's will for my life. Yet with all that had taken place thus far, it was not until we accepted the responsibility of the covenant that we were divinely joined together by God. Caught up in the excitement and festivity of the occasion, we made our vows, signed the marriage license and were pronounced husband and wife as the congregation cheered. My husband and I individually made a vow to God that we would be one with Him until death. We were no more twain, but one flesh, husband and wife. Today, I look back and smile at the innocence and faith that propelled us forward.

As we walked out of the church, not much had changed physically, but everything was different spiritually. Two hearts and two very different lives were now one. I was not aware of it at the time, but my wedding day changed my life forever.

My Spiritual Marriage

As wonderful and memorable as my physical marriage was for me, equally glorious was the experience of giving my life to Jesus Christ. I was in the highlight of my teenage years and like most young people, I found myself searching for a personal identity. During this impressionable stage of life, I constantly battled against the powers of the flesh. I thought of doing some of the things that my friends were doing or experimenting with, yet at the same time, I wanted to live a life that would please the Lord. But I could not have it both ways. I could not hold onto my foolish desires with one hand and Jesus Christ with the other. Yet the tug of war continued and I battled with the fleshly desires and convictions of my heart. Thoughts that opposed God's Word were constantly seeking to dominate my youthful mind and I didn't understand God's purpose for divine order in my life. I remember in my early teens dreaming of how I would someday be on my own. I would have my own home, two beautiful children, and I would run things my way. There would be no husband because I did not want anyone to "rule over me." Then I surrendered my life to Jesus a few years later, met a young man that I thought would be my husband, and everything changed. At that point I now wanted a husband, but not one that would take away my individuality.

Today as I look back, I thank God for his divine destiny being fulfilled in my life. I now know that an independent heart will fight against the obedience of God. Obedience, which is the key to God's heart, matures into submission, and without submission, I could not fulfill the will of God for my life. It was a crucial part of my life, and ministry. Eventually, through the avenue of marriage, I would come to the point of understanding the need of dying to self so that God could minister to others through me.

One evening I had a dream that caused me to come to a definite conclusion of what was important to me. My heart was convicted and I surrendered my life to the Lord. That day Jesus Christ became my personal Savior. I will never forget the peace that filled my heart when I made up my mind that, no matter what happened, for better or worst; I wanted to completely surrender all to the Lord. Over time, I was able to turn away from what I thought was best for me and trust Him completely.

For each one that comes to Christ the circumstances may be different, however, one thing is certain, faith becomes a necessary requirement. Through the years Jesus Christ revealed himself to me as friend, brother, protector, provider, my lawyer, my doctor, the lover of my soul, and King. I understood that it was no longer my will, but his will being done in my life that would ultimately bring fulfillment. When I accepted Him, it required faith to believe that Jesus forgave my sin, and cleansed my life, and that He loved me more than life itself. I knew that if there had to be a parting between us, I would have to be the one to walk away, because He said, "He would never leave me or forsake me." I believed His word and accepted it.

> *... the breeding ground for*
> *submission is nestled in the*
> *marriage.*

In the physical marriage, even though I did not know everything about the man I was about to marry, by faith, I believed that when we made the vow to God, we were joined as one forever. I was in this for the long haul.

I was committed for life. He was mine, and I was his. We both understood that what we were committing to was lifelong union dissolvable by physical death.

In the spiritual relationship, this everlasting commitment was dissolvable only by spiritual death, not that the Lord would ever depart from me, but spiritual death will occur if I turn away or spiritually rejected him. To make it through either relationship, my humble obedience was crucial to the strengthening and endurance of both. Upon making the physical or spiritual vow of commitment, I was entering into a covenant with God that required total submission. The very basis of submission is found in the foundational scope of the institution of marriage. When we understand the purpose and depth of the marriage relationship, and the responsibility of the man and wife, then we will understand why the breeding ground for submission is nestled in the marriage.

What Is Marriage?

Marriage is a divine joining, welded in the spiritual, modeled in the flesh. It is holy, sacred, and it was established by God. Marriage is also the foundation of a brand new family. When God instituted this unique and powerful experience, it existed with a man and woman coming into covenant with Him. The man of his own will and the woman likewise accept a vow that would bring them into a covenant agreement with God. It is God who in agreement with the couple cements them together and ordains them husband and wife. He joins them as one, and only he can truly separate them again. The commitment of marriage takes a lifetime to fulfill.

When we think of marriage, we envision romance and beauty. We imagine flowers, soft music, beautiful attires, a ring, and a lovebird or two. These are only physical things that enhance the surrounding. The physical paints an awesome picture, yet it minimizes what is accomplished in the spiritual realm. The spiritual realm reveals to us the importance of a covenant.

There is a physical platform, but there is also an actual spiritual event that is not seen with natural eyes. Both platforms are essential to the marriage. It is not possible to partake of marriage and leave God out of it, because he is the only glue that can seal a marriage covenant. There are however, relationships that are not sealed by God, but band by civic law or the will of man.

When marriage was instituted in the Garden of Eden, it became a symbol of the Godhead, His image and His likeness. The Godhead consists of the Father, Son, and Holy Spirit; one God, three functions. Marriage is also made up of three as one; the man, the woman, and Christ. In the family, likewise; we can see three functions, the father (the head of the home), the mother (the divine assistant), and the children.

To look at what the marriage was created to be, we can look at the Godhead and receive a better understanding of a union or a united force. To look at marriages today, it might be difficult to truly understand this concept in light of the selfishness, division, and lack of commitment that plague so many relationships. Nonetheless, when we understand the love that Christ desires to share with his people, the relationship between a husband and wife becomes a spiritual symbol of this love. It is the kind of love that will solidify a union. A marriage between a physical man and woman is only as strong as the spiritual relationship between these individuals and God. This requires much more than a feminine dream.

The wedding day is one of the most exciting events in the life of any woman. Many women enter into marriage without realizing that they are entering a completely new runway of life. Without proper preparation and guidance the demands of married life will soon become a struggle. Indeed, there is a vast difference between the single life she has left behind, and the married life she has just entered.

The life of the single women, once symbolized an individual life that is devoted to God - one that embraces chastity, purity, and innocence. It demonstrates a life that is singled out and set aside. When the woman weds she takes on a completely new identity, one that will be symbolic of her devotion to God through the presentation of herself to her husband. It is identified by devotion, sobriety, humility, and unselfishness as her life becomes a demonstration of the joys and distresses of a life shared. Her devotion will bring fulfillment to her heart, satisfaction to her husband, and ultimately, glory to her God.

So many young brides enter marriage caught up in a world of fantasy and physical desire. Looking forward to spending the rest of their lives with the man of their dreams, few consider the seriousness and responsibility that comes with the covenant. All they can see is the "ship of love" waiting to take them to that joyful land of "Happily Ever After." Thus, they embark on this new journey with the misguided notion that their passionate love will conquer all, and that their marriage will be different from all others that have detoured off the path. To naive young lovers, marriage is a fairytale come true; it is Cinderella, Snow White and Sleeping Beauty all wrapped up in one.

The climax of their dreams is being whisked away to "Never, Never Land of Love" by their own Prince Charming. Of course, the beautiful brides-to-be never see the sequel to these fairy tales. They fail to realize that Cinderella had to run an even larger household than the one she left, and that her handsome prince became demanding and expected her to share in the responsibilities of running the castle - something she thought she was finish with. The stories never told how Snow White lost her figure and put on a few pounds after giving birth to her babies. When the prince began to object, she felt as if she was living with the varied characters of the dwarfs all over again. As for Sleeping Beauty and her prince, they had their first fight shortly after the honeymoon because he accused her of being lazy and sleeping too much.

Fairy tales rarely convey the reality of married life. In all reality marriage requires a leap of faith; it is a major faith walk. Anyone who has been married knows that being married is not a piece of cake. We are never told that our lives will change dramatically after the wedding and that for better or worse we must prepare to make major adjustments for many years to come. Nor are we told that marriage requires more "give" than "take." It is not until we enter the land of matrimony and that first overpowering rush of romance begins to wear off, that we truly realize the depth of marriage and how much more there is to ensuring marital success. Along with the love, there must be faith, devotion, trust, commitment, and more faith. These essentials make for a firm foundation. When we truly understand what God instituted through the marriage relationship, we will realize that the strength of the physical marriage (*man & wife*) is determined by the depth of the spiritual marriage (*Believer & Christ*).

From the beginning of time God admonished men of the importance of keeping a vow. Ecclesiastes chapter 5:4 states;

> *When thou vowest a vow unto God, defer not to pay it; For*
> *he hath no pleasure in fools; pay that which thou hast vowed.*
> *Better is it that thou shouldest not vow, than that thou shouldest*
> *vow and not pay. Suffer not thy mouth to cause thy flesh to*
> *sin, neither say thou before the angel, that "it was an error,"*
> *wherefore should God be angry at thy voice, and destroy the*
> *work of thine hands? For in the multitude of dreams and many*
> *words there are also diver's vanities, but fear thou God. (KJV)*

This powerful passage of scripture shows us the importance of making and keeping a vow or covenant. In the physical marriage, a man and woman are joined in a public manner. Here two individuals come together as one for a shared purpose. The spiritual marriage takes place when man becomes one with Christ through the born again experience. It is through the physical realm that the spiritual realm is often understood or revealed. In other words, the physical (*that which is visible to the natural eye*) is an indication of the spiritual (*that which is visible in the spirit realm*). In the spiritual marriage the bride is neither male nor female, but divine. Both types of relationships begin with a mutual agreement and divine acceptance.

The first physical marriage was consummated in the Garden of Eden when God brought them to each other and Adam accepted Eve as his wife. Adam spoke the first vow saying to the woman, "You are now bone of my bone, and flesh of my flesh." They became one flesh through a mutual covenant.

Marriage is a platform for service. It is a life of continual sacrifices. The man commits to doing all he can to help the woman and the woman also commits to doing all she can to help the man. For without sacrifice, can it be considered a marriage? What is a marriage if there is no need of sacrifices?

Marriage is also an establishment of domestic order. Within the domestic setting the platform for service is exemplified by the sacrificing of the life of Jesus Christ. The sacrificing of his life opened the door for man to experience an eternal relationship with the Father and redeemed man back to God. The giving of oneself totally to each other models the sacrifice of Christ, and opens the door for us to reveal to a lost humanity unselfishness, loyalty, and trust. It is the relationship Christ desires to have with his people. In depth the marital relationship becomes a platform of continual service that surpasses physical imparting, progressing to the point where both parties will give willingly and without fear, for the betterment of the other. It is in this level of sacrifice that submission is begotten, fertilized, and given physical expression.

God's plan is that marriage would consist of two heart that will willingly walk the runway of life, hand in hand, for better or worse, for richer or poorer, in sickness and in health, for as long as both of them are alive, (Romans 7:2). An intricate part of this promise is love and obedience, complimented by the act of submission. Submission is an aspect requiring humility and honor, first to God and his Word, then from the man to Christ and from the woman to the man. It gives us a platform to fulfill the great commandment of loving the Lord with all our hearts, and loving another as we love ourselves. This was the design of God from the beginning.

The Beginning

The sphere was nothing at the beginning except blackness, nothingness; an empty vacuum that swallowed up existence. Yet it prompted God to speak life to the vast vacancy, and everything changed! Out of the dark vacuum arose radiance, substance, and exuberance to showcase the excellence of earth. It was a display of divine power.

When our minds reflect on power, we think of a level of control and domination. When we seek to envision true power our finite mind is forced to look to the revelation of who God is. He is ultimate, divine, untainted Power, he is the creator of the heavens and the earth, the ruler of all things, the vision of majesty and authority! As the supreme one who delegates power, He puts it where he wants, when he wants, and to whom he wants.

He created and multiplied himself into mankind, a bi-fold human race and declared that they will reveal his image and his likeness. God gave them dominion over every earthly living thing. Now the power of God would be ultimately displayed in the masculine and feminine makeup, their dominion to be made stable by the power of submission.

The masculine and feminine natures were furnished with the responsibility of headship in the male, and the essence of a quiet strength in the female. With authority the way was paved for direction, guidance, leadership, shepherding, and governing. This type of power is usually very appealing to all, it is the kind of power that most people recognize, admire, and seek after. However, in order for authority to be genuinely effective it must be embedded with humility. Humility, in itself is a soft but potent kind of power that is almost always overlooked. For as grand as authoritative power may be, it is inadequate without submission, the facial side of humility, supported and strengthened through service.

From the beginning, all God desired was for mankind to embrace submission. Submission to his will, his word, and his way. But mankind sought worship, turned away from this beautiful form of humility and sought authority instead. What many failed to notice both then and now is that submission unlocks the gate to authority. Submission is the basic establishment of order. Together, authority and submission in their intended purpose would not only create a foundation of stability, but they complement each other, and become a force expressing unity, oneness, and completeness. This divine unity is witness in the Godhead that gave birth to the awesome creation of the sphere we know as earth.

Authority and submission are both empowered by humility. Just as they are modeled in the character of God, we can see them in the handiwork of his creation. As God took dust and filled it with his breathe, He burrowed into man's soul a characteristic that when committed to him, was powerful enough to lead, yet humble enough to follow. He gathered them together and nestled both into the dual human hearts of the male and female. In the male, authority was dominant; and in the female, submission was dominant. Here authority and submission was given a dynamic platform in the formation of the marital relationship. When God brought the man and woman together and united them as one, the basic form of relating was unfolded in the institution of marriage.

There these two forces were made to work interchangeably to show forth God's glory. For there was no other earthly relationship that would model the divine concepts of authority and submission as perfectly as the marriage relationship, and no other creation of God would model the purpose and wealth of submission as perfectly as the woman.

Marriage is the most challenging of relationships, yet the most rewarding. The principle of this relationship paves a pathway for every other relationship when demonstrated in the way we live. Unless one is willing to give all and hold on to nothing, there will be no true marriage. Marriage requires two, each giving one hundred percent into the relationship. Anything short of this will feed division in the marriage. The challenge becomes greater when we enter into a marriage covenant ignorant or in denial of the Word of God as it applies to the marriage. Marriage is a walk in faith which requires the grace of God and two committed hearts.

When the husband and wife team has a personal relationship with Jesus Christ and submit to the challenge of living their lives according to the will of God, regardless of what comes before them, this is where the journey to submission begins in the physical marriage. It stems from a willing heart, the innermost depth of an individual soul, desiring to be presented as an offering unto the Lord.

One day soon, the spiritual bride like the physical bride will prepare for the greatest wedding ceremony that eyes will ever behold! Each and every day, she moves forward to make herself ready. The experiences she faces are sometimes difficult and overwhelming, but diligently she presses on, driven by love and anticipation. The groom remains still, but watching. He is aware of her every step. His hand is not relaxed, but ready to reach forth and catch her lest she fall. He is available at her every beck and call, and looks forward to the day when he will claim her as his own and take her away to the home that he has prepared for her.

Everything will be ready in anticipation of this feminine presence, but until then, he eagerly awaits the arrival of his love. Excitement is in the air. Indeed, the audience that will witness this grand, once-in-a-lifetime occasion is already assembled to cheer them on to victory. Soon the bride will look back, happy that she was faithful. She will finally be in the arms of her groom and greatest love, the one and only Jesus Christ. She had made herself ready by truly embracing obedience with a willing heart. It is when the physical woman reaches this point of acceptance that she too is equipped and ready to display the awe-inspiring character of a woman, as *God's Model.*

2
God's Model

"And the rib, which the Lord God had taken from man, made he a woman, and brought her unto the man".

– GENESIS 2:23

Adam sat down on the rock. It was just one of the many beautiful spots in the garden where he loved to go and rest. The bubbling stream and the clouds glazing across the sky were glorious. At times, he would let his feet fall into the water, or he would dip his hand into the stream and let the water trickle through his fingers. It felt wonderful! This was usually the way he began most of his mornings, roaming through the garden, sometimes walking, other times running as the gentle breeze caressed his face. Just the sight of the beautiful flowers all around him, mixed with the sounds of the singing birds and the gentle kiss of the wind inspired him to praise his Father God over and over again.

As Adam walked through the tropical forest, today seemed different. There was a brand new feeling in the air. The flowers in the garden bounced about as though delighted, and the wind whistled through the trees. The whole earth bustled with expectancy. Adam thought to share his sentiments with his animal friends. As he moved over by the large oak tree, there perched on a solid limb was the parrot, his feathers a radiant display.

Its attention, however, was captivated by a smaller, less colorful rendition of his species, grooming itself on a branch one step above. Adam's heart was warmed when the female looked up and gave her male counterpart a "come hither" glance. The male parrot quickly joined her and the two flew away together into the deep lush woodland.

It was a joy to watch the animals relate to each other. The two dogs that had become his best friends play tag for hours in the green grass and the squirrels chirped excitedly to each other as they flicked their tails. Two leopards half hidden in the shadows rolled on the ground, wrestling playfully. Even the whales in the water seemed to rejoice as they dipped in and out of the ocean. Adam smiled. Everything around him was perfect. He made a mental note to talk with some of his other four-footed friends, but right now he was feeling rather sleepy.

Spotting one of his favorite resting places, Adam lowered himself onto the comfortable patch of soft grass. Amidst the pink and yellow flowerbed, with the warmth of the sun on his face, he leaned up against one of the large trees. "Ah ha," he said, with much joy and satisfaction in his heart, "This is good!" The soft clapping sound of water running up against the rocks soothed him like a lullaby. He thought of all God had taught him in the cool of the day, and the communions that had become the highlight of their afternoons. How fulfilled I am, Adam mumbled, as his eyelids drooped closer and closer together, and before long he had drifted off into a deep sleep. Little did he know that his Father, God, was about to introduce something new into his existence, and when he awoke, life as he knew it would be changed completely.

As effortlessly as he had drifted off to sleep, Adam woke up. How long he slept, he did not know, but as he became conscious, something caught his attention. For a moment, he was unable to move as his eyes beheld the figure before him. As he focused on this mysterious creature, his whole body felt overwhelmed. He jumped up and stumbled backward with a sense of carefulness. The entity in front of him moved ever so slightly. At first, Adam thought it might be an illusion, or a dream, so he pinched himself just to be sure that he was awake. Staring straight into the creature's eyes, he became mesmerized by the two deep indefinable, radiant orbs gazing back at him. Oh how captivating, he thought, how simply divine was this countenance!

The entity slowly moved in toward him before reaching out. Where did it come from? Adam wondered. Deep within his spirit, Adam sensed a connection. He knew with an inner confidence that something as magnificent as this could only be from God. Studying the creature carefully, he could see the image resembled his own reflection that he often glimpsed in the ponds and streams throughout the garden. Yet, the shape was more elegant, delicate. The body flowed in symmetrical curves, and the features were radiant. The skin appeared soft, supple and glowing - so much so that he wanted to reach out and touch it, but he didn't dare. He felt compelled to pick this creature up and hold it in his arms forever. Captivated by the sight, his legs became weak and wobbly. He could feel his body tremble. His eyes traveled the breadth of the creature - he could not get enough. He wanted to touch the curly strands of silk on top of the head that flowed and rested softly around the creature's shoulders. Adam felt a sense of excitement building deep within his being. Somehow, he knew that from now on things would be different.

Suddenly, he felt a soft, warm flutter on his temple, and looking up he saw that the radiant image had moved closer in. She touched him. That's when he noticed that her hand felt like the touch of cotton against his face. Instantly and impulsively, his cheek flushed. Adam wondered why his body was responding in this manner! He had never noticed these feelings before. He backed off, resisting the urge to pull the image unto him, knowing he would not be able to let go. He looked around for his Father, knowing that this was definitely the work of His hands. Adam had become familiar with his father's pattern of creativity, perfection, and excellence. And then he saw Him. As he looked into the eyes of God, all of his questions were answered. God had given him a help meet. Tears filled Adam's eyes. Until then, he had not been aware of what he needed, or that he was somewhat incomplete. But his Father had known and brought to Adam the feminine side of himself that would compliment and complete him.

She was an integral part of God's magnificent creation. Already, Adam noticed how her feminine heart gave ovation to the masculine traits that identified him. She was a part of him, yet, separate unto herself. What captivated Adam most was the fact that somehow she knew him; she really understood who he was, and what he felt. This was divine. Right away, he knew he had found a loyal friend. He touched her, his hand moving over the contours of her face and down over the soft suppleness of her body. "Wow," he said, "another just like myself." His mind raced as he once again took in the beauty of the figure beside him. He was searching for just the right expression, but his lips preceded his mind as he uttered these words; "This is now bone of my bone, and flesh of my flesh, she shall be called "woman" because she was taken out of man," (Genesis 2:23).

As they stood together for the first time, Adam felt whole. Looking at her again, he noticed the smile on her face, a glow that mirrored the joy that they both felt in their hearts. They were so happy. As she touched his belly, Adam was filled with joyous laughter, much like what he shared with his Father. Truly delighted, Adam rejoiced, realizing for the first time that this was what the animals enjoyed with each other. Now he would have a companion all his own.

Eve, on the other hand, felt a warm glow in response to Adam's reactions. She stood before him, the first woman, the first wife, the perfect companion. Before, the elements that strengthened him had come from within his being, but now she possessed them in her heart along with the ability to bring satisfaction to his physical soul. Looking at, and watching Adam, it was obvious that she was created differently. She was aware of how important this difference was to the magnificence of her creator. Her capabilities, though different, were very important. Already, it enabled them to assist each other. Over the next few days, Eve watched as Adam's spirit soared to new heights. They enjoyed the time they spent together and this new relationship that neither had ever known. Above all, their intimate moments with God at the end of each day strengthened their relationship. There was always something from their relationship with him that they were able to implement into their own. There was so much of His nature in both of them. His character, thoughts, and personality were wrapped up in their being.

There was a divine unity, perfect love, and trust in their relationship that Adam had never seen amongst the animals. She joyfully assisted Adam in his chores around the garden, and oftentimes prepared a fine meal of fruits and vegetables that they enjoyed together. It brought her satisfaction to encourage his heart and motivate him as he fulfilled his God given duties. Together they would roam the garden as Adam basked in the physical admiration of the woman. Everything was beautiful. Adam felt needed and Eve knew that she was wanted. They were on their way to accomplishing the divine mission of God as man and wife.

The Woman of God

When God created the woman, he created a model; one that would avidly walk the runway of life to showcase the very character of His being. In today's world, a model walks a runway to display a product or item. The woman has been chosen to walk the runway of life to reveal the aspects of God's character that is feminine. Every woman has the potential to be a woman of God, a female who has determined in her heart that she will walk in obedience before God. When this decision is made it brings her closer to God and to his ultimate desire for her life. It is here that divine purpose will be brought to light. The closer we come to his divine purpose the more fulfilling our destiny will be.

Every soul is created with a purpose to fulfill on the earth. In the beginning when God created Adam and Eve (Genesis 1:27, 2:1,) He created the entire human race, and Adam and Eve were the first man and woman to be brought forth. As time progressed, God brought forth other, like Abraham, Lot, David, and the prophet Jeremiah to whom he said, "From before I formed you in your mother's womb I had a purpose for you, (Jeremiah 1:5)." It is God who designated whether we would come forth as male or female, black or white, tall or short. He alone decided whether you or I will grow up in an African, Asian, European, or West Indian culture. It is he who called forth Thomas Edison to create the light bulb, and Martin Luther King Jr. to fight for the rights of all men, regardless of color. It is he who brings forth a baby boy or girl and positions them in a family. It is God who chooses presidents and leaders like George Bush or Saddam Hussein. He lifts them up and takes them down. Everything will come to fruition in the fullness of time, because God has the world in his hand, and he is always in control.

And God in his wisdom gave birth to the woman. To look at her with physical eyes only reveals what human flesh and blood portrays, but spiritual the woman is so much more than eye can see. She is the feminine nature of the Lord concealed within the female. When God created the woman she was not bought forth haphazardly, but she came forth with three distinct purposes: to model the feminine nature of God, to support the masculine nature as a divine helpmate, and to aid in reproduction of mankind. She was fearfully and wonderfully made. Every inch of her being was perfectly designed and set in place. Her soft skin, her features and curves, her personality and emotional temperament, God knew exactly what he wanted in this vessel. As the first spirit being to inhabit a feminine body, she was called forth to give expression to womanhood. It was not her choice who or what she would become, it was God's. Like the male, she too, was made in God's image and in his likeness.

As individuals, we are given a free will to make choices. The woman too must make the choice to walk in the fullness of God according to her make- up. When she accepts, she comes closer to God's intended purpose for her life and matures into the woman of God. Like her creator she becomes gentle, humble, wise, and virtuous, (Genesis 1:26). Now he can use her, move within her and through her to accomplish His will as the feminine image of God is given physical validation through her obedience. When she walks in obedience, she releases God's desires for her life. She will enhance, beautify, nurture, and protect that which has been entrusted to her.

Every woman can attain this place of honor. However, it requires a submissive heart. Her carnal nature or flesh cannot hold on to, or even reach such virtue without the Spirit of God. When she walks in obedience, she models the excellence, wholeness, and humility of the Godhead. She brings to the masculine nature, the assistance that he needs to accomplish the mission that God has purposed for the male. When she rejects this, she moves further away from her truest purpose. When she permits the Lord to pour his glory into her, it is then that she is transformed through His nature, his Word, and true obedience to His will. As she humbles herself to accept the provision of God through her husband, she will thereby help him to walk in the will of God for his life, that of loving and caring for his wife and all that is around him. In helping her husband, she enables him to attain his destiny and walk in dominion upon the earth.

From the time of deception in the garden, the position of the woman has been under attack. The wounds from this attack has shaded and almost blinded her to her divine and awesome purpose. When her heart was rocked by deception, this opened the door of disobedience in her life. As a result, submission became a challenge and a struggle. The woman had to fight the urge to cater to the desires of her flesh daily. When she sought to serve only herself, this hindered her from walking in the purposes of God. When she fulfilled the desires of her flesh this caused the model to stumble and even fall on the runway.

The only way to get up on her feet again is through total dependence on the Lord. When Jesus Christ came to earth in the flesh he came to show mankind the way back to God, but that was not all. He also came to clear the pathway for the women to embrace humility and be restored to her divine position of power. Before he departed the earth he said, "I will send the Holy Spirit, he will lead and guide you into all truth." When the woman of God allows the Holy Spirit to lead and guide her, she will enter into divine truth. It is divine truth that will open her eyes, helping her to see and understand who God has created her to be, and aid her in walking the pathway of destiny the he has prepared. This is the only way that she can truly become God's model in every facet of her being. The powerful nature of God that gives her dominion through submission is the same power that dwells in the masculine gender enabling him to walk in dominion over the earth. The power in both, though manifested differently, ultimately belongs to God. This power, which was demonstrated in the life of Jesus Christ when he walked the earth, aided in his spiritual submission to the Father. This same power waits to radically affect everything upon the earth when we too unite as one with the Lord.

In the first days of creation, everything was completed before God rested. God brought forth man from the dust of the ground and man became a living soul, complete with a body, soul, and spirit. The male and female nature of God enveloped one body, that of the male. But in the fullness of time, God reached into the male and brought forth the female and joined them together as husband and wife. In him, they are one unit; physically they were two complete individuals.

The woman was not brought into existence just for companionship, but together they would represent the oneness of their Creator. As a unit, the man and the woman would multiply and replenish the earth physically and spiritually. Each had a responsibility and a purpose to fulfill. Eve's fall was the result of her disobedience to God, not to Adam. When she stepped out of the will of God, it was then that her divine purpose was contaminated. When Adam joined his wife their unified purpose was corrupted and they fell out of unity with God and each other.

Fulfillment was lost with the entrance of sin into the lives of mankind. However, much of that which was lost can be recovered through the redemptive grace of salvation. Through salvation today's woman is able to recapture much of what was forsaken before the fall by allowing God to model the feminine nature through her. It is important that women understand that the only way they can bring change is by submitting to the Lordship of Jesus Christ. Submitting is the essence to how a woman functions. It aids in her spiritual relations but also in her relationships with her husband and children.

If a woman never marries, bears children etc., just walking in her calling as an individual devoted to the Lord in spirit, is a ministry in itself. It is in this capacity that she will surrender herself to the Lord with all her heart, as well as focus on her spiritual life and Christian duties. The single woman is readily available for many demands that will present itself with the commitment of Christian ministering. Developing these qualities will greatly prepare her for another level of ministering – that of marriage. Ministry is an outlet for Christian service, and marriage is also considered ministry. It is yet another phase of life and obedience. In the marriage relationship, she ministers to God through serving her husband. Here she can model the love of Christ by giving herself for the uplifting of another. If her heart is not willing to serve as a single woman, it will not be willing to serve in marriage. In just these two levels of ministry, singleness and marriage, the greatest commandment and law of life is expressed; that of loving God with all our hearts, and then loving another as we love ourselves, (Matthew 22:40). Serving her mate becomes her focus, her joy, her life. It is not a task or duty but an accepted commitment.

The blessing of marriage for the woman is motherhood, which is yet another facet of ministry as she gives birth. New life begins with the giving of oneself. As she becomes one with her husband, the union is rewarded with offspring. When they are fruitful and begin to multiply righteous seed to be offered back to the Lord, the earth is replenished. They continue this replenishment through the rearing and training of their children. Just as God had taught Adam to groom and nurture the earth, in motherhood the woman will do the same with her children. Her natural tendency to nurture is an essential part of her make-up.

The nature of God which is often compared to the lamb can be seen in the nature of the woman. It is impulsive, gentle, attentive to the detail, compassionate, and humble. Contra-wise, the side of God that is characteristic of the Lion is firm, restrained, keen, inflexible, and authoritative. This can be identified in the man. However, all of these characteristics in both man and woman have been defiled by sin, thereby hindering each from exhibiting the untainted and true glory of God. Like the masculine gender, the feminine gender was fashioned with the instruments necessary to enhance and fulfill her destiny.

The will of God for her life
depends much on her desire to be
a help meet for her husband

As she walks in the divine purpose of God she exemplifies the glory of her Creator, showcasing His strength and beauty through her life living, and the unity of Christ and His bride in the spiritual marriage. Before the fall, Adam and Eve possessed direct access and responsibility to God. As a result of sin, the man was made to cover his wife, and the woman to subject herself to the headship of the man. Her purpose was not taken away, only redefined. What was done willingly was now a necessity. Now the will of God for her life depends much on her desire to be a helpmeet for her husband. Her desire to help him was only attainable through her willingness to humble herself under his covering.

Many women may ask, "What does it mean to be a helpmeet?" A helpmeet is a co-laborer, an aid, one who assists in the completion of a duty or task. Whoso findeth a wife, findeth a good thing and obtaineth favor of the Lord (Proverbs 18:22). In marriage, it is the heart of the female to assist her husband. In the working relationship between a man and his secretary, the responsibility of the secretary is a good physical description of a helpmeet. A biblical show of help can be found in the story of Moses and Aaron in Exodus 17. When Amelek came to fight against Israel, Moses told Joshua to go out and fight while he stood on the mountaintop with the rod of God in his hand. Moses sought the help of Aaron and Hur to hold up his hand when he became weak. When Moses' hands were raised, the Israelites would conquer, but when his hands fell, the Israelites would lose. Therefore, the help of Aaron and Hur was instrumental in the victory. Moses was not fully equipped to fight by himself because of the weight of the battle. The same is true with the man and the women. Eve was placed at her husband's side to hold up his hand. She would be a source of strength to him when he was weak, but in order for her to divinely assist, she must walk in submission to God. There are times when a woman might misinterpret the word help. She may oftentimes interpret "help" as relieving her husband of the task completely. However, when Aaron and Hur helped Moses, their assistance was limited to simply holding up his hand at that particular time. They were not required to take the rod or and hold it up for him, but to stand by him, becoming the help that he so desperately needed. As helpmates, we too, can learn from Aaron and Hur. The position of a help meet empowers her husband, enabling him to fulfill his purpose according to God's direction.

When women today understand and accept the will of God for their lives, they will bask in the divine purpose of God for the female, and renounce the feelings of unworthiness brought about as the result of disobedience. I remember the moment when I realized that God had indeed called me to ministry. I looked within myself for the ability to sustain the call, but I came up with a limited supply. Of course, this led to insecurity because my concerns were 'me.' Then the Lord showed me that it was not about "me" but all about 'Him.' The choice was all his, and none of mine, John 15:16.

He had not chosen me because of my appearance, personality, up bringing, teaching ability, or anything else that we so often feel qualifies us for the many calls of God. It was for His Glory, and the many souls that would be reached through what He has deposited within us through His Spirit.

Oftentimes, we become prideful when we obtain accomplishments or are called to Christian service. Presumption tells us that there must be something special about us that have enabled us to reach a plateau of success. Sometimes we may think that it is because we are so precious in the sight of God that he would rest his hand upon us. When the angel came to Mary with the news that she would give birth to the Christ child, the first thing she said was, "How can this be, seeing I know not a man?" She too, was drawn to the flesh before realizing that what was about to be done in her was a spiritual work and completely out of her hands. The Angel of the Lord quickly informed her that she was about to experience a transformation by the Holy Ghost, who would overshadow her by the power of the most high in order to fulfill the Lord's will.

We could never make ourselves eligible for anything apart from God. A woman would allow the enemy to make her feel unsure of her womanhood, not realizing that she did not choose to be a woman, but it was indeed the plan of God for her life. He called her woman for a purpose, placing in her everything that was needed to fulfill her purpose and display his glory. Likewise, all that has been placed within us is there for the glory of God. It is not about what we look like, what we know, what we need, what we have, or what others think about us. All things were given to us, set in place, planted, and brought forth to enable us to reach a place of excellence in Him. As freely as God has given to us we receive and give to others. It is through this process that we grow and gain strength, encouragement, maturity, vision, and peace.

As the man receives, he would be empowered to strengthen, encourage, construct, perfect, envision, and receive peace from God to give back to his wife and family. His devotion would enhance her femininity. Her humility would stimulate his masculinity. This position of the woman is so important. When Eve fell she weakened her husband to the point of his destruction. With the cords of trust broken, ruin was evident.

Upon entering the 21st century, women of God everywhere are admonished to cast off the old robe of complacency and return to His original plan for their lives. Embracing submission will evoke a major change in this day. God is bringing women to a place where they will stand side by side with their husbands. This will enable them to divinely move in the awesome calling of God for their lives. However, this will not be accomplished in her own strength, through selfish motives, aggression, intellect, or special abilities. It will be a willingness to obediently follow the Lord that will allow His mission to be fulfilled through human vessels.

God is calling His women to excellence. Our obedience will not only release the power within our hearts, but it will release the power to bring change outwardly as well. It will give birth through the floweret of a humble heart that is teachable, yet humbled by the unmerited favors of God. It will bring change to governments, nations, and the lives of common men, young and old alike.

God's women and chosen vessels that will carry this awesome power and grace will seemingly appear out of nowhere, to revolutionize the earth before the coming of Christ. Single women that are living pure lives before the Lord, married women who revere the authority of God through their husbands, widows and grandmothers, will all burst forth with a confidence that touches lives everywhere. Married women who have been made to live the life of the single woman because of separation from their husbands, but who have fully committed their hearts to the master, will do the same. These are the end time lanterns that will carry the fire of the anointed one, brought to life simply by uncovering the beauty of submission.

3

Uncovering the Beauty of Submission

"Except ye be converted and become as little children,
Ye shall not enter into the kingdom of heaven."

– MATTHEW 18:3

In today's changing times, with its many compromises in moral and biblical values, submission has become quite a controversial forum. Its reputation has been tortured, abused, raped, falsely accused, and left for dead, yet it lives on. It rests, grows, and is nursed in the tender hearts of many sensitive consciences the world over. Submission has been passed on from generation to generation and just when it seemed it would recede, it has sprung to life again. It is adorned and compared to the spirit of the dove.

The dove is one of nature's meekest species. This bird is known for its comely countenance, softness of eyes, and sweetness of voice. When God chose the dove to work with Noah after the flood, it was because he knew that this animal could be trusted. It was the dove that God also sent to rest upon His Son at the baptism in revelation of a Father that was well pleased. This bird that is often used as an emblem of peace holds a true resemblance to the beauty of submission.

Submission is the humble response to divine authority. A gentle sense of obedience, it calls for the willing surrendering of the heart. Many classic dictionaries define submission as passivity, subservience, bondage, or even inferiority. Yet nothing could be further from the truth. These harsh words are extremely damaging to the true concept of submission. There are many opportunities for submission, yet the most rewarding occurs when mankind humbles himself and bow in submission to the divine purposes of God. Therefore, according to God's word submission is power!

When man yields to God, he makes himself available to His perfect will. Submission calls for both humility and obedience. When mankind responds to God with an attitude of total surrender, his heart genuinely says, "Here I am Lord, available to you, use me as you will." He embraces the spirit of the dove and a workable relationship is unveiled. Every man or woman of God that has experienced any level of victory did so because of a humble heart that responded in obedience. Noah could never have built such an edifice, or gotten all of the animals into the ark, without divine leadership and instructions. Joshua would definitely had been defeated at Jericho had he not embraced submission. Elisha, Jeremiah, or any of the prophets would never have triumphed, had they not allowed the Lord's power to flow through them. Jonah fought against God before coming to a point of total surrender, and when he did, he was released from the mouth of the whale. When Jesus walked upon the earth in human flesh, he said these words, "The works that I do are of my Father, He sent me," (John 15:10). The same is true of us today. We can do nothing except we submit to Christ, who submits to the Father. Any level of success in areas of our lives that we might attain is determined by our willingness to totally and completely embrace submission.

When Jochabed, the mother of Moses placed her baby in the river, I could imagine how her heart raced within her breast. She needed to preserve her baby's life, but she didn't know how. She could hear the cries and midnight mourning of other mothers whose babies had been murdered. As she held her son to her bosom, it felt as if her heart was being pierced. The soldiers were getting closer to her house, and soon there would be a knock on her door. As she looked at little Moses, now making baby sounds and beginning to recognize her face, joy filled her heart. He was growing so well. She loved touching his fat little cheeks, his little hands and legs were getting stronger each day. She knew it would be hard to continue to hide him. Surely the men would soon realize that there was a baby in the house.

Finally, when it seemed the burden was too much to bear, she responded in total surrender, "Lord," she cried, "My hands are tied, I don't know how to save him and I don't know what else to do. You gave this baby to me, now I give him back to you and submit to your will for his life, I accept it, whatever it may be." Jochabed embraced the spirit of the dove. Then God spoke! Make an ark of bulrushes; daub it with asphalt and pitch. Put the child in it and lay it by the reeds of the river. Immediately her hands were at work. Hope leapt in this mother's soul. Peace filled her heart. Excitement and determination motivated her as her fingers moved quickly to protect her growing baby. This is the awesome result that transpires when there is submission. God came to her in the form of Wisdom; He told her what to do. What would have happened had this young mother not completely surrendered to God's instruction? What if she had only done a part of what she was told? Suppose she had said, "This is stupid. I will not put my baby in that dirty river!" Where would her baby be if she had not humbly submitted and allowed God's will to be done through her? The truth is her baby's life would have been lost.

Submission, which is the mature state of obedience, must become a way of life or a lifestyle if we are going to follow Christ. It is often associated with the responsive reaction of a wife to her husband. While this is the basic pattern of establishing order in the home, it is also the foundational illustration of how the feminine adjusts to the masculine in all things. If we can grasp the submission of a wife to her husband, then we will understand what Jesus Christ expects of his people, his Bride, and what he models in the relationship with His Father. Submission acts like a revolving door, it strengthens authority, which in turn, breeds and stimulates submission. This can be demonstrated to us in many facets of life.

1. In the humble response of children who is secured and confident of a parent love. With willing obedience they generally accept what is poured into their lives by their parents.

2. In the relationship of a laborer and supervisor, reverence is mutual as they work together for a common goal. Authority is expected and freely accepted.

3. Watch it dance in a wife who has accepted the divine purpose of God for her existence. As she allows the Spirit of God to mold her into what he needs, and what is needed from her for the betterment of her husband and children.

4. Standing strong in the life of a man whose heart is humble and void of pride. It is he who seeks spiritual guidance through which he will govern his life and home.

5. In the purest form, we can find it cradled in the heart of Jesus, as he surrendered his will to His Father. Without any resistance, he submitted his life for the sins of the world, shedding his heavenly robe, out of love and obedience to the sovereignty of God. This is the crown and beauty of submission.

The attitude of submission is nurtured through love, trust, faith, and belief. In a spiritual context, it resembles a heart in the hands of the Master, just like clay in the hands of a potter. When mankind submits to God, he allows God Almighty to transform the very being of the heart in pattern after the character of God. One of the greatest spiritual truths of submission is that it gives us unlimited access to the throne of God.

Submission is a prerequisite for every level in life. In the day that we destroy submission, we will dissolve order and eradicate authority, because submission does not exist without authority. Likewise, if there is none to submit, what is the purpose for the position of authority? In the book of Ephesians, we are exposed to the truth that in every segment of society there is a need for authority and submission. In the Church, the nation, the workplace, and certainly in the family, there is a chain of command through which one will be called to submission. We are taught from a young age to respect authority, or face the consequences. If you break the law you will go to jail. If you fail to adhere to the regulations of your employer, you will be fired. Yet all over the world it is with little or no regard that we demand the right to reject authority in our homes. The marriage relationship, which is the foundation of the family, the fabric of the nation, and the breeding ground of submission, is presently crumbling before our very eyes because of a blatant disrespect of authority and rejection of submission.

Submission by force is not
submission at all.

So, why is it so hard to accept the principle of a wife submitting to her husband? Because when we hear the word "submit" we think of bondage, injustice, and abuse. We associate it with the battered woman, the molested child, women in foreign lands all being forced to resign themselves to oppressors in the name of submission. With this misconception, we reject it, unaware that submission cannot be compared with abuse. When a person submits, it is their consented agreement that lays a foundation.

When the response of submission is forced, it ceases to be submission because it must be a willing act from the heart to make it genuine. Therefore, submission by force is not submission at all. Satan has sought to present it as degrading, damaging, and repulsive, because he knows it is an essential requirement for establishing order. So often, those in leadership who rule with pride instead of humility do not help to dispel the myths that surround submission. But in the hands of God, submission is power to aid divine leadership, an honorable position, a channel by which nations, homes, and lives will be brought to a place of divine destiny. A surrendered life whether, rich or poor, small or great, of the greatest intelligence or none at all, can be used of God when submitted to his will. When submission and authority come together in unity anything is possible. The Word of God tells us, "With God all things are possible." When mankind humbles himself to be used by God he will move mountains. If we desire to see God's view of this level of obedience, take a good look at the life and ministry of the Lord Jesus.

A Perfect Example

When we seek the perfect picture of submission, where every glint of art comes together in unison to form a platform of excellence, our finite minds race to retrace the footsteps of Jesus Christ. None reveals the spirit of the dove as flawlessly as He. From the embodiment of human flesh to the cruelty of the cross, his existence portrays a presentation of submission wrapped up in total obedience. He was the Son of God, an equal part of the Godhead, yet he never sought to defend himself on the way to Calvary. With humility and honor, he accepted the position given to him and walked in the will of his Father. Here the attitude of submission was displayed when he laid down his life. This level of obedience and trust resulted in great and mighty works that was done in the earth. If we ever desire to understand what submission entails, look no further than the baby in the manger to the crucified Savior for a model description.

His most powerful life example showed us how his greatness was demonstrated through humility. In John 12:49, Jesus spoke of his submission to authority.

*"For I have not spoken of myself; but the Father which sent me, he
gave me a command, what I should say and what I should speak.
And I know that His commandment is life everlasting: whatsoever
I speak therefore, even as the Father said unto me, so I speak."*

Jesus submission allowed the power to flow through him that he might fulfill the will of the Father. All through his ministry here on earth, Jesus would constantly go to his Father in prayer for instructions and guidance. When he took on human flesh until his death on the cross, He and the Father were one. Even though he came forth in the physical, everything Jesus did was of the Father, whose hand was clearly seen in the works of His Son. Submission to the Father brought about total obedience. It is through this obedience that he was given the power to serve all men. When his disciples quarreled over who was the greatest among them, Jesus taught them that greatness is birthed in humility rather than pride. In Luke 22:25-27, Jesus explained how those in authority governed in pride, but this was not acceptable for his people. He said unto them,

*"He that is greatest among you, let him be as the younger and
he that is chief, as he that doth serve. For whether is greater,
he that sitteth at meat, or he that serveth? Is not he that
sitteth at meat? But I am among you as he that serveth."*

In essence Jesus was telling his disciples that the blessing is in giving not receiving, in serving and not being served! Again, humility is indeed the door to true greatness and the life pattern of Jesus that all should follow.

As I was reading my bible one morning, I came across a familiar passage of Scripture in Philippians Chapter Two. I had read the words many times before, but this time the words rested in my heart. I had been seeking a deeper understanding of humility and submission and as I read this passage, I knew I had found my answer. Not only did I receive a revelation of submission, I also got a closer view of Jesus.

"Let this mind be in you which was also in Christ Jesus: Who, thought it not robbery to be equal with God, but made himself of no reputation, and took upon him the form of a servant, and was made in the likeness of men, and being found in fashion as a man, he humbled himself and became obedient unto death, even the death of the cross, (Philippians 2:5-8).

As I read the words I began to pray silently that God would help me to humble myself especially when it seems the situation might be unjust. I thought of how hard it is at times for us as human to not respond in defense. Our fleshly minds constantly look for an opportunity when we can be exalted or establish a reputation. I thought to myself, "Is this why the message of submission is seemingly so ugly? Could this be why so many want no part of it? What would happen if we allowed nothing we did to be done through strife or vainglory? If husbands and wives in lowliness of mind esteemed the other better than themselves, would there be so many broken relationships in our nations." My mind reflected on a chorus we sang at church. The words were:

> *I want to be more like you,*
> *Jesus, I want to be more like you,*
> *I want to be a vessel you work through,*
> *I want to be more like you.*

I thought to myself, if I really want to be like Him, then I must embrace a submissive spirit, because that was the character of Jesus. It causes one to esteem another better than oneself. This is the attitude that enabled Christ to give his life as ransom. When we esteem others better than ourselves, children will honor parents; the employee will provide honest work to his employer. Wives will reverence their husbands, and husbands will love their wives like they love themselves! A submissive mind seeks to uplift another, rather than focusing on how it can be uplifted. In the spirit of meekness, we will give, seeking nothing in return. We will forget about self, and securing the better part, but be ready and willing to offer up our best. This is the platform to greatness, the heart that is worthy of exaltation, for which the Father will reward with eternal life.

The humble act of Jesus Christ today remains an example for all to follow. In Ephesians 5:24 the body of believers, also known as the church or the bride of Christ, is admonished to submit to the groom, who is Jesus Christ the Lord. Except we embrace submission, we will be overtaken and destroyed by pride and rebellion. It takes more than will power to bring one's flesh into subordination. It takes the power of God! This power was given to us through the victory of Christ on the cross. When he said it was finished, the power became ours, now we must accept it.

In times of temptation, Jesus stood strong knowing that his obedience was the key to our deliverance. He was tried, tested, bearing the thorns, and withstanding shame, to overcome triumphantly. His ultimate desire was to come into the obedient will of his Father. Submission brought about his exaltation, for now the world must bow at the mention of his Name. What Jesus did was not for vainglory, for he loved us enough to be belittled, scorned, dragged in the street, and killed so that man would have a way of escape. He walk the earth seeking what he could do for man, never what man could do for him. He had a purpose to fulfill and he fulfilled that purpose. He became what was needed to redeem man back to God. His submission to the Father opened the door for restoration. Now his life has become our perfect example, a life that reaches out to bring healing, deliverance, revelation, and newness of life. This entire act was done in spite of the fact that man deliberately went against His Word, yet He never held it to his charge

Let us do as he did, all things without murmuring and disputing; that we may be blameless and harmless sons of God, without rebuke in the midst of a crooked and perverse nation, among whom we will shine as lights in the world, (Philippians 2:14-15). Jesus prayed that we would be one as he and the father were one, and when we follow his example, the glory that was given to him, would become ours as well.

Men & Submission

For some time the discussion of submission was considered a message just for women. Many overlooked the part of submission that involves the men. Today, it is becoming clear that submission is for everyone, and yes, men must also submit. In fact, he more than anyone, must embrace the spirit of the dove because of his designated position of headship in the home. But to whom must he submit? The answer will determine whether he will become a vessel of honor, or bite into the apple of deception once again.

I met a gentleman one afternoon that was a guest speaker at a local church. As we got into a conversation about that evening's topic he related how the man ought to submit to his wife out of reverence to God. His biblical backing was Ephesians 5:21, "Submit to one another out of reverence to God." Long after our conversation my mind continued to replay his words. I began to wonder, "Could that be true, can it work?" Yet, in my spirit I couldn't digest it. Once again I reached for God's Word and went directly to the Scripture to read it entirely. This time I read it from an authorized King James Version. The words and implication were different from the earlier quotations of my friend.

> *Submitting yourselves one to another in the fear of God.*
> *Ephesians 5:21 - KJV)"*,

It was so clear "one to another." Not that I was to submit to him and he submit to me, but I submit to him, and he submit to Christ. I reached for another Bible with eight different translations and read each.

TEB - Submit yourselves to one another because of your reverence to God.

NIV - Submit to one another out of reverence to Christ.

Jerusalem Bible - Give way to one another in obedience to Christ.

NEB & RSV - Be subject to one another out of reverence for Christ.

Living Bible - Honor Christ by submitting to one another.

Phillips Modern Bible - And fit in with each other because of your common reverence for Christ.

I discovered the difference between submitting "one to another" in contrast to "one another." Just a simple rearrangement of a few words altered the meaning. However, the way it is presented cannot erase its true meaning because submission is only necessary when authority exist. For one to submit to a rank lower than oneself is condescending. The text in no way exhorts that the woman submits to the man, and the man to the woman. It does, however, counsel that we submit to the ordinance of authority designed by divine order, the man to Christ, the woman to the man, children honoring parents, and servants submitting to their masters in the fear of God!

Immediately, I began to understand why sometimes as Christians our messages appear contradictory. It is important to read the Word and pray for revelation. I began to pray in my heart, "Lord show me the truth of your word." I jumped out of bed a short while later, awoken by a thought that filled my mind. "Every man who submitted to his wife paid the price." I was taken back by the thought, because it seemingly came out of nowhere, and was so potent. I began to analyze it. I paced the floor as the thoughts continued to come. Look at Adam. Remember Samson? Consider Abraham. These men had all yielded to the voices of their wives over the voice of God. While the woman will model submission for her husband, it is not the woman to whom he must submit. As man is the head of his wife, and requires her submission, so Christ is the head of the man, and also requires that the man adhere first to him above anyone else.

Abraham was a man strong in faith (Genesis 17). God promised him a son by his aged wife, Sarah. He knew that this could only be accomplished by the hand of God because his wife was past the flower of her youth, and unable to give him children. Because of his faith and relationship with God, Abraham believed and accepted the promise. Time went by, he and his wife grew older, but no baby came. Abraham loved his wife and desired to please her. His heart ached seeing the tears Sarah cried at night as she yearned for a baby to cradle in her arms and call her own. When Sarah suggested that he lie with her handmaid, his heart turned toward his wife with compassion, and he submitted. Abraham loved and respected his wife, all of which God required of him. However, Abraham made a crucial mistake when he submitted to the voice of his wife instead of to God. God had told him to wait for the promise. As a result, Abraham reaped anguish that affected his life and the lives of generations to come.

What about Samson? He fell in love and lost his life (Judges 16). As he laid in the arms of his wife, many nights she would run her fingers through his hair and sing lullabies in his ear. He had the answer to a secret that only he and God knew, but the enemy wanted it and sought to obtain it through his wife. It was the secret to his strength. However, when he submitted to the subtle manipulation of his wife, instead of standing strong in obedience to God, he was destroyed forever.

As for Adam, he was cursed and removed from God's presence because of disobedience. God said to him,

> *"Cursed is the ground for thy sake. In sorrow shalt thou eat of it all the days of thy life. Thorns also and thistles shall it bring forth to thee, and thou shalt eat the herb of the field, in the sweat of thy face shalt thou eat bread, till thou return unto the ground, for out of it was thou taken."*

Why did this happen? It happened when Adam hearkened unto the voice of his wife, over the voice of God (Genesis 3:17). That was his first mistake, not that he listened, but that he heeded when he knew it was against God's Word. It's a sad commentary, but the more I searched, the more I found. Had any of these men consulted God first, their family outcomes would have been different. Here lies the importance of men and submission.

When a man submits to Christ, he opens his heart to supreme guidance from the Lord. It is through Christ that he lives, moves, and has his being. He cannot do it of himself, but as he opens up to the will of God; a pathway is constructed through which God can operate. There is nothing easy about loving another unconditionally, but with Christ, the man is empowered by the Spirit to not only love, but to lead his family and indeed the world back to God. In Corinthians 11:3, we are told that the authority of the woman is the man, the head of the man is Christ, and the head of Christ is God. This is the divine ordinance set up by the Godhead through which man is called unto the obedient order of authority. All authority is set in place by God, whether good or evil, and for this reason must be given honor. The book of Ephesians establishes the foundation of submission for every level of relationship, whether in the home, workplace or nation, we are called to respect those with authority in the fear of God.

The discussion of men and submission is crucial to the family structure. In order for his family to reach their destiny, the man must submit himself to God. God has positioned both the man and his wife to fulfill his mission on earth, but it is the male who has been given the task to shepherd, govern and rule in earth's most treasured establishment, which is the family (Genesis 3:16). The word "rule" here makes many women defensive. I remember one day thinking, "But Lord this just doesn't seem fair." However, at that time, I did not have an understanding of God's divine ordinance. I could not see where submission, according to my understanding could uplift me. My confusion to the purpose of authority, in the marriage relationship, caused me to respond in defense.

When I came to understand the male and female purpose within marriage, I began to understand why it was so important to both persons that the man walk in his purpose and the woman walk in hers. Through submission to Christ, a man is given access to all the tools necessary to establish, maintain, and repair what God has placed in his care. As he humbles himself in obedience, the Spirit of God comes into his life and co-ordinates the ability through him. He is now empowered to love his wife as Christ loves the church, to provide direction and leadership for his children, to walk in dominion upon the earth. Now, he can do all things through Christ who strengthens him, when he realizes that it doesn't begin in him, but in God.

Failure to submit brings destruction because he has to rely on flesh and flesh cannot give access to this type of power. It is the spiritual power of God that gives life to man. When he rejects submission, he stops the divine flow of the Spirit that gives him life. His tools begin to rust, because he has no oil. His wife becomes vulnerable, his children displaced, his home becomes a wreck, and he feels lost. In desperation, he seeks another source usually the person who is closest to him. In most instances this is his wife, his divine assistant, his helpmeet. One might ask, "Why is that so wrong, wasn't she given him for this purpose." Yes, she was given to Adam a helper, not an instructor. When a man comes to the place of depending on his wife, not only is this a subtle form of idolatry, but it is totally against God's order in the home. It is he whom God has elected to lead his family, and he will be held accountable. His total dependency must always be on the Lord to lead him through whatever channel he chooses. When a wife comes to her husband with a matter, it is his responsibility to consult with God for ultimate direction or confirmation whether he agrees or disagrees with her.

Example:

Wife: *John, I think we need to sell this house and move to a larger one.*

Husband: *That sounds like a good idea Barbara; it will solve some of our problems.*

One of two responses may follow. Either the husband and wife will proceed with their plans, or the husband will say:

Husband: *I want to pray about this first, just to make sure that we are moving in the right direction.*

Wife: *Alright John, I will be praying with you as well.*

Or it might even be the wife who might say, honey, let's first pray about this to make sure that we are moving in the right direction. By doing so she encourages her husband to submit to Christ and strengthens her home. His wife may motivate him, but Christ will instruct him. Anything other than this is bound to bring the type of results that Adam reaped.

This is not to say that a man is never to listen to his wife. It is the divine purpose of the women to assist her husband in everything. She will offer suggestions, to assist her husband in various situations. In many circumstances, God will use her to speak to her head. It is a wise man that hears, responds to, and is able to distinguish the voice of God through his wife. Remember Pilate's wife who motivated her husband to take his hand away from the killing of Jesus? God had already spoken to her by way of dreams, and she was able to assist Pilate in his decision. Pilate, after much resistance from the people, washed his hands of the situation declaring Jesus an innocent man. When a man honors his wife as an accepted part of himself, he is not intimidated but he will benefit from the voice of wisdom spoken through her.

Women must continually encourage their husbands to embrace submission, even when she desires to have him do things her way. She must fight her fleshly mind and compel him to totally submit to Christ. A wife's constant pray that her spouse would be sensitive to the voice of the Lord and not be confused or hindered by the work of the enemy, is his greatest source of support. He could easily be tempted with the spirit of independence, a kind of pride that keeps many men today from allowing their wives to be one with him. The only effective way to combat this spirit is through humility. A woman might have a more committed relationship with the Lord than that of her husband. God will use her to impart wisdom and instruction to her spouse. A woman is naturally intuitive and apt to influence. God will use these gifts to inspire leadership in her husband. This is how she retains her blessing. She must want to see her husband submitted to Christ and receiving direction. Because the man is the head of the home, does not suggest that he alone would make every decision, or that God would only channel his message through him. Both the man and his wife are vessels of God to be used for his purpose. Had Moses resisted the help of Aaron and Hur (Exodus 17:11), Israel would have lost the battle.

There are times when God will use our children, or he might use another member or believer in the church to bring a leader to a place of accountability, as he did with King David when Nathan the prophet confronted him. All God requires is a submitted heart through which he can speak. And he is not a respecter of persons. It is important that those who are used by the Lord also give respect to his divine order of authority and walk in humility. A husband or father in personal relationship with God is the greatest asset of a family. He can make the difference between ultimate success, and total failure, because just as God imparts for righteousness,

Satan imparts for wickedness. Knowing Christ and being directed by his spirit hinders men from being easily deceived by the enemy, and propels him towards excellence. By submitting to Christ, he opens himself to being filled with the wisdom and divine insight of God. He can then be filled with the love, creativity, and compassion that Christ possesses and that his wife and children crave. When God is allowed to manifest himself through the submissive man, he will be well able to lead his home, community, church, and nation to the bosom of the Father.

Many men shy away from the mere mention of submission, because so often they are made to feel chauvinistic by admitting that a woman should submit to the man. Because submission has been blown out of context, many in society, and indeed the church, ignore the topic for fear of rebuttal. When a man does not understand the purpose of his wife's submission, he cannot understand his submission to Christ. The enemy deceives many men in this area by hindering them as providers, thereby weakening their ability to lead. They depend on their wives, mothers, or reasoning minds, rather than depending on God. When times of difficulty arise, instead of looking to Christ for guidance, they may look within themselves for a solution. There are many who may be ignorant of the fact that in order to make it daily they must allow the Word of God to guide them, and this must come as a result of personal seeking. Therefore it is wise for one who finds himself in the position of a leader to cast himself at the Master's feet for complete guidance and direction in everything he does. Man cannot rely on any other source or security; he must seek Wisdom for himself.

When a husband comes to the place where he is totally dependent on Christ, God will show him how to lead and guide his family and his affairs. He will become a vessel ready for the master's use. This is often an area where men and leaders are greatly challenged, because their typically independent mindset makes it difficult for them to let go of their will completely and allow the help and support of others. When he comes to a place where he can relinquish his hold and allow his heart to trust freely, it will take him to a place of freedom. No longer will he be doomed to suffer in silence and defeat, but he can put his hand in the hand of the man who stilled the ocean and be led by that hand. He will become a wonder worker, not only in the things of God, but in everything that his hands touch. Just as Jesus submitted to his Father and became the servant of all, when the man submits to Christ he becomes a provider not only of the physical things, but, that which is spiritual as well. With God, the Word declares, nothing shall be impossible!

But if any provide not for his own, and specially for
those of his own house, he hath denied the faith,
and is worse than an infidel. 1 Timothy 5:8.

God will not compromise his Word. Just as a child is to honor his parents, not vice versa, the wife is to submit to her husband and her husband to Christ the Lord. God is a God of Order!

Women & Submission

When the Lord began relaying the message of submission into my heart, I thought it was so that I could become a better wife. Little did I know that not only would it bring me closer to my husband, but revitalize my relationship with Jesus Christ. In Ephesians 5:22, Paul admonishes the wife to submit to her husband. Many balk at such a notion. A lot of women have admitted to being insulted or offended by the mere mention or concept of submission and associate it with feelings of worthlessness and insignificance. This could be because of the way submission was communicated to us. Few viewed it as a key characteristic of power and authority designated to the feminine creation. There is nothing shameful about submission. It is designed to liberate a woman to the destiny to which God has called her.

One day the Holy Spirit spoke into my spirit, "Your submission to your husband is a physical indication of your submission to me." Immediately, I was taken aback. I knew and recalled many times when I was less than submissive or respectful. And to think that my actions toward my husband, was an indication of my spiritual attitude to the Lord was disturbing. I prayed silently all day, convicted by the words I heard in my spirit. I knew this could not go on, there had to be a change. I wanted to live by what I knew was right. In answer to my prayer, the Holy Spirit began to teach me this essential side of humility.

The relationship between the man and woman is the basis for all existence in the human race. When God required that the wife submit to her husband, it had nothing to do with the issues of value or equality. It is through her submission that she becomes a vessel through which the glory of God will flow, making her actions a model behavior for all living things. When a woman is submitted to the will of God and walks in obedience to His Spirit, He will teach her how to submit to her husband. Of course, it will not happen over night. The woman will not get up from her knees and suddenly begin to submit completely, but perfection will come over time.

It is the power of God invested in her that will move her into the position of the divine assistant. This is a side of the woman that a man desperately needs to accomplish God's vision upon the earth. He needs to constantly see submission in his wife and know that God expects the same action of him. Together, they have been given the responsibility of bringing the earth back into submission to God. As she begins to move in the power that makes her the woman of God and supports her husband, she will unveil the value of obedience before her children.

The act of submission was a restoration of defied authority as a result of man's rebellion in the Garden of Eden. Before the fall there was divine unity. External borders were not needed because the man and his wife were submitted to God and there was divine order. Through the sin of disobedience this was destroyed, however, God restored order, and the man and woman were both placed under authority; the man under Christ, and the woman under the covering of her husband. When either walked in obedience, they displayed the originality of divine order, the woman to the man, man to Christ, Christ to God. (1 Corinthians 11:3)

Growing up in the 70's and 80's, a time when the feminist movement was drastically gaining ground, I did not hear much about women and submission. Women were moving in circles, which years before, would have been unacceptable. Domestic commitment was not something that the feminine gender was gravitating toward, but drifting away from. Little girls began to play with Barbie dolls instead of baby dolls. Young women were being encouraged to take over the work market, instead of focusing on being homemakers, wives, and mothers. Caught up in the same mindset, I was working as a trainee draftsman and preparing to become an architect, with hopes of owning a firm someday. But in my heart, another war was going on.

My biggest dream was to be married, and fill my home with children. Somehow, I had to bring these two dreams together and make them work. I never realized the architectural goal, but God did give me the husband I prayed for, a man whom he would use to not only fosters my desire for womanhood, but who instrumentally motivated me in becoming a woman of God. Within months he captured my heart, and we were married. Then I became aware of another war raging within my soul.

After the vows were exchanged, I began to settle into a new way of life. I began to unpack my things unaware that there were some other bags as well. One of the bags contained my strong will and challenging nature. The need came to open this bag about three weeks into the marriage. We had just returned from a beautiful honeymoon in the Pocono Mountains of Pennsylvania, back to work, and just beginning to enjoy our life together. I began yearning for some of the familiarity that I had left behind at my parent's home, especially the close relationship with mom. One evening I came home from work, and hurriedly prepared and served dinner. All day I had planned how after dinner I would visit my mother; sit on her bed, and talk.

Soon Lambert and I were finished eating. After tidying up and making sure that everything was in place, I prepared to leave. When he asked where I was going, I told him I wanted to visit my mom for a while and would return in an hour or two. Coming toward me he said, "But Kim you were there yesterday, and the day before that, why don't you stay home this evening? You don't have to go up there again." I tried to explain that I had only stopped in passing, or to pick up little things that I had left behind, and both times she wasn't even there. This evening, I wanted to spend some quality time with her, but he wouldn't hear of it.

Very quickly I became defensive and told him, "This is what I had planned to do this evening, and that is what I am going to do." He continued to insist that I should not go out, but I boldly replied, "My mind is made up and my decision is final." Nobody is going to stop me from seeing her, not even you." With that I headed for the door, but he persisted as he pulled me by the hand. "Kim, you are no longer a single woman. In married life, things are different. I understand you may want to go back up there, but if I ask you not to go you should respect my request." "I do," was my reply, "But it's not like I am going to stay. Why would you want to stop me from going by mom's house?"

In my mind I felt as if we were defining turf. He was testing the waters of authority to see how much I would yield, and I wanted him to know that marriage did not mean that he should control me. "I will respect you, but not everything you asked me to do I would agree with, I stated. With this in mind, I was out the door, leaving him standing there. I felt justified that I was not letting him 'rule' me. Shortly thereafter, I was on my way to the place that for so long had been my home.

As we sat and talked that evening, I began to tell my mom how I had to push my way to her house because Lambert didn't want me to come. I thought I would receive her approval, but I was dead wrong. "Kim," she began, "I am happy to see you, and have you with me, but not at the expense of your marriage. Lambert is now your husband and you were wrong for the way you handled things tonight." At first I argued, but Mom stood firm, and instructed me from the Word. "As the church is subject to Christ, so let the wives be to their own husbands in everything. If I were to tell you differently," she said, "I would be giving you unbiblical counsel that would eventually bring destruction to your relationship." I said to her, "But Mom, this was something that I really wanted to do. It's not like it was wrong or dangerous. There was no reason for him to hinder me." Still Mom came back, even stronger! "If you were still at home and had asked Dad to go out somewhere, and he had objected, even though you might not have agreed with him, you would have respected his authority. Now the authority has been changed, and your husband is the authoritative figure in your home. If your husband wanted you to stay home tonight, I would have understood, and would accepted this no matter what I felt."

As I drove back home, I felt a bit angry. I thought that I was trapped under authority for the rest of my life if this is what submission was truly all about. My thoughts wandered back to our pre-marital counseling sessions when my pastor read the Scriptures that pertained to the submission of the wife. As far as I was concerned at that time, submission would not pose a problem. I was in total agreement. In my heart, I wanted to be obedient to God's Word, yet when the time came I flunked drastically.

There is an attitude and response that comes as a result of honoring your husband and at that time I did not have it, nor did I understand it. Back then, I was totally unaware of the fact that my insurrection to my husband was indicative of my response to authority in any form, physical and spiritual. Equally, I was not aware that through submitting, I was positioning myself to be used of God to reach my husband in areas that I could never otherwise easily accomplish. Additionally, I would be able to affect my children, co-workers, and nation. When a woman truly has a servant's heart toward God, there is also a level of respect that will manifest itself. She not only accepts authority but she comes to reverence it. Many women out of respect and a godly fear would never stand up to their employer. It is in like manner that she ought to regard the authority of her husband.

I soon realized that due to lack of knowledge and spiritual understanding, I became prey to carnality. In my mind, I tried to justify my actions. A battle raged in my head, "Why should you have to stoop to that? You are an intelligent, young woman with the ability to make your own choices. You do not have to embrace submission!" Yet in my heart I knew that in order to please God in this marriage, I had to be willing to humble myself and allow him to use me to physically live His Word.

When I got back home that evening I was embarrassed, yet as we settled down to talk about it, I found myself still trying to justify my actions. I began to explain to my husband that, "I was not prepared to be controlled. That he should not expect me to just adapt my life to his." The truth was that being able to adapt, was the catalyst of a right relationship with my husband, which required humility. Unless I was willing to adjust my life to that of my husband's, my marriage would go nowhere. There had to be some changes, some rearranging, less resistance, and a mind of submission, or our union would be fruitless.

I had to trust the Lord and submit to my husband. The spiritual part of me desired to conform, but the natural side of me resisted. However, the Lord had planted a seed of wisdom through my mother that evening, which took root and began to grow. I was on my way to understanding the value of humility in a marriage.

Today I look back and thank God for his grace to grow and mature and for mercy when what I was doing was wrong. Had I continued that course of action in our relationship, I might not have had a marriage today. Over the years there were moments when I still struggled and wondered why I had to be the one submitting? Why couldn't we both walk in the position of headship? My questions came when I thought my husband was making a bad decision or didn't trust his judgment. Like many women, I began to look for loopholes, asking, "What does submission really entail? How much are we expected to give up?" The answers to my pondering came swiftly, 'Submission requires a sacrifice and you are expected to give up everything.' I fought with this in my heart until the Holy Spirit began to give me divine understanding. I watched as God instructed me and then used the submission to my husband to teach him submission to Christ. At first, I had to humble myself before I was ready to walk in this level of grace. It was then that I realized that what I thought was too much to give up was really nothing at all.

The truth of the matter is when we accept Jesus as our Savior we give up everything. It is our human flesh and limitations that seek to hold on. Nevertheless, the more we submit to the Lord, the more our vision is enlarged as to what true submission is, embracing the spirit of the dove. Jesus Christ has already lived the example for us. When He submitted to His father this was only the beginning. His submission resulted in blinded eyes being open, the dead coming back to life again, the sick healed, and ultimately man's ability to live eternally. When an individual submits to God it will result likewise with the manifestations of the power of God in that life. Remember Jesus did say that we would do even greater things than he, but this will not happen without submission!

When God created the woman, he endowed her with the power to affect change. Submission was never meant for punishment, but for purpose. Mankind would learn how to respect authority of every kind just by watching the relationship of the woman to her husband. It is through this that children understand how they ought to respect their parents. It begins in the home, that's why submission in the home base is so important. From here it filters to the outside, in the workplace, church, and nation. Lack of submission will bring confusion into the lives of the very ones to which she was called to minister.

Submission is a direct command from God, and not the husband. It places the woman on a pedestal that can only be given by God. Except a woman is willing to submit, she cannot receive the blessing in her marriage and family that God has made available to her. I soon came to accept the fact that submission had nothing to do with disgrace, shame, or forced subjection, but it is a personal choice of the woman to make herself a willing vessel. The woman who is obedient will find that submission also brings spiritual maturity and prosperity as it ushers her to a place where she can be used of God to glorify his name.

Because our nature is sinful, submission does not come automatically. Our fleshly nature refuses to come into subjection. Romans 8:3-4 tells us "What the law could not do, in that it was weak through the flesh, God sending his own son in the likeness of sinful flesh, and for sin, condemned sin in the flesh; that the righteousness of the law might be fulfilled in us, who walk not after the flesh, but after the spirit." The reason submission is often difficult is because so much of the world's mindset has severely penetrated the church; so much so, that many are left pondering whether submission of the wife is from God or the Devil. When this level of deception takes root, individuals will find themselves rebelling against any level of authority. Until the time that we come into a personal relationship with the creator, we will not be able to understand submission inspired by the love of Jesus. Through the Holy Spirit, we can walk in his example; submission will become power rather than bondage. A woman must come to the realization that it is not a great career, fame, fortune, or love affair that will exalt her, but humility. The more she humbles herself, the more God will exalt her. The more she is exalted, the greater the power to change situations that surround her. In fact when the world looks at the godly wife, they should be reminded of the spiritual bride of Christ.

A lady, I will call Brenda, told of how she lost her job. She couldn't find another one right away so she stayed home for a while. It resulted in a complete change in her life. For the first time in 14 years of marriage, she had to look to her husband, but at the same time the Holy Spirit showed her the true meaning of submission to the Lord and to her spouse. She had to commit to trusting both of them immensely. There were times when she felt afraid, wondering how the bills would be paid. To find some kind of peace, she would fall to her knees in prayer. This brought strength with which she was able to encourage her husband. With only one paycheck, there was no "my money, your money," and the financial battles ceased. Together they began to budget and plan the little that they had. There were times things became tight as the money ran short, but they found that coming together in agreement to God's promises was far more rewarding than the way that they had handled things before. As she humbled herself, she watched her husband become confident, strong, and responsible as he arose to defeat the challenges that confronted his family. For the first time during their marriage they were on one accord. Unity took on a new meaning in their marriage when they came together in agreement. Amos 3:3 questions, "Can two walk together except they agree?"

When we seek to become independent, we awaken the threat to true unity. Everyone wants to feel in control and in charge of themselves and the things that belong to them. We run from dependence not realizing that we are running away from the doorway to humility. Mankind was not created to live independently of each other. In the book of John chapter 15, Jesus shows us the significance of dependence through the illustration of the vine and branches. Together they represent life and unity. In like manner, when a husband and wife come together in the bonds of love and divine unity, there has to be a change, something has to happen. In fact, their oneness is the desire of the Lord.

Children & Authority

The life of a child is the most powerful arrow with which one can pierce the future, because what is stored in it will eventually affect tomorrow. It begins at the threshold of life, when a newborn baby is placed into the hands of the father and mother. It is here that the lesson of submission and the power behind it comes into effect for that individual. Paul admonished children in Ephesians 6:1 to "Obey your parents." The Word of God instructs parents to "Train up a child in the way he should go, and when he is old, he will not depart from it," (Proverbs 22:6). It is through the life patterns of parents that a child should first become acquainted with the spirit of the dove, in the interchanging of authority and submission.

When parents strive to give their children a godly heritage they are giving them one of the greatest gifts of life. The admonition to train up children involves two very important aspects; that of instruction and example. Psychologists tell us that a child's intellectual potential is pretty much set by the age of seven. In the Bible, a little boy by the name of Joash became King at the age of seven.

The role of the father and mother is to plant the proper seed of preparedness into the life of the child. In demonstrating to my children one afternoon the importance of a mom and dad in the lives of children, I ask each to cover the left eye, and tell me what they saw. Each responded that they could see the things on the left side of the room. Then we covered the other eye, and they could only see the right view of the room, but when they looked with both eyes uncovered, their view encompassed the entire room. I explained to them that Daddy alone might instill commitment, and Mommy might instill trust, but together we help them to build character. It is best when children see their parents as a united front instead of two forces.

It is for this reason that the marital relationship is so essential to the lives of children. When we came into the world we were empty, knowing nothing. As we grow, our parents will teach us many things that will ultimately affect the rest of our lives. David said in Psalms 51:5, "Behold, I was shaped in iniquity, and in sin did my mother conceive me." Mankind is born into the world with an inherited sinful heart. At birth we are naked and rebellious. A parent's submission to God opens the doorway for us to walk in obedience. This is one way that God provides guidance and direction to children.

The child that you hold in your arms and call your own came into this world with a destiny. I believe before each child is conceived in the womb, he or she exist in the spirit realm and is known of God. This individual was given an identity through the DNA of its parents, but before making entrance into the world he or she, Like Jeremiah, has a divine purpose to fulfill, (Jeremiah 1:5). This is why children are referred to as the reward of God. Many parents or guardians are not aware of what is being placed into their hand when they accept the responsibility of parenthood and the charge to rear the child in the fear of God. In your hand is a seed with unlimited potential. Your submission to the will of the Father can make a vast difference that will effect generations.

Long before a child comes to accept and understand who God is, they are given a view of Him through their parents. In the parental relationship they are exposed to authority and the masculine and feminine natures of God just by looking at mom and dad. The dominant expression of authority in the father and the dominant expression of submission in the mother, will ultimately unveil their understanding of the Godhead.

The parental relationship also holds lessons in life that are relevant to equip, empower, and bring children to adulthood. Such lessons, which include instructions in leadership and authority, obedience, love, forgiveness, trust, respecting others, and showing compassion is endless. It will not only build character, but it will lay the groundwork for the duration of life. On the contrary, if a child is constantly exposed to dishonesty, strife, rebellion, selfishness, hatred, and un-forgiveness, these traits will eventually embed their way into the child's soul. This will result in confusion and rebellion; weapons that become Satan's doorway to the destruction of the mind. These are the issues that later in life must be purged so the individual can be free to do the will of God. One of the primary responsibilities of parents is to protect the pure hearts of their children. This can only be done through the wisdom and divine direction of the Lord.

Because the lessons that one will learn from their earthly guardian will assist them throughout life, the relationship of the parents is considered the most crucial in the life of an individual. The responsibility of protecting the pure hearts of children serves as a covering and filter against the evil that exist in the world. This is done through helping them to understand the Word of God and applying it to their everyday life. So it is in the spiritual relationship of Christ and his church. The oneness of God the Father and Christ the Son holds all the lessons relevant to equip, empower and bring maturity to the believer. Their examples of authority and submission lay fundamental grounds that will lead us to perfection.

When children rebel and flee this covering, or when parents refrain from covering and safeguarding their children, they leave an opening for the enemy to attack. It is intended that a child will move from the covering of parents to the covering of the marriage, (Matthew 19:5). Within the marital relationship, there is additional covering for the woman by the headship of her husband and for the husband by the headship of Christ. Together, they make up the covering head for their children. As a direct act of rebellion against authority many children flee the home of parents to live on their own even before marriage. Just as fleeing the nest prematurely can have devastating consequences; equally as damaging is the rebellion of parents who fail to adhere to God's mandate for the home and in the rearing of their children.

How do we cover our children? The most effective way is through prayer and instilling godly wisdom. As a young girl, it was always comforting to hear the prayer coverings that my mother draped over her children. Many times, I would awake in the night to the sounds of her prayers. This encouraged me as a mother to do the same for my children. I realize that I cannot always cover my children physically, but I can cover them spiritually no matter where they are. For it is when I have placed them in the hands of the Lord that they are totally protected.

At the age of accountability, the child will exercise the free will given by God to decide whether he will serve God, or mammon. If he chooses to submit, when he leaves the comforts of his parents to cleave to a mate, his submission to God will ultimately determines the success of his future. It will mean the difference in a submissive or rebellious wife or husband, a joyous or sad marriage and family life, success or failure in secular accomplishments, to the rise and fall of nations. A young man who is not submitted to the will of God cannot submit his life to the total development of his family. The Word of God instructs him to love and cherish his wife like himself, unconditionally; to provide, lead, direct, and govern his family in the ways of God (Titus 2:6-8). If he refuses to submit to this, he will eventually weaken the spiritual strength of his family.

The same result is accomplish when a young woman is admonished to devote, esteem, love, and befriend her husband, to provide love and care for her children and keep her home (Titus 2:4-5). Many young couples enter marriage unaware of the fact that the success of the relationship does not lie in how well they know and love each other or how much money they have saved. The richter scale for success does not measure victory according to who the parents are, how well the wedding was attended, or the perfect plans for the future, but it depends totally on the strength of the spiritual foundation and the individual's twofold commitment to God and his Word. The wealth of their relationship depends largely on their understanding of obedience and submission.

As in any other relationship, this submission must proceed out of a willing heart. It cannot be compelled even from children. As a parent, I too, made this awful mistake, time and again in order to generate a desired response. I used control to bring forth obedience, rather than teaching the children truth. This appeared to work in the younger years, but as the teen years approached this method became ineffective. It was then that the Lord began to instruct me to reach my children by speaking to their conscience instead of the carnal nature, taking into consideration their ages and maturity. Soon the attitudes began to change, on both sides, as we began to better understand each other. I remember telling my teenagers that this was a new experience for me as well, I had never parent teenagers before, but I was willing to learn. As God guided me, I was able to foster and cultivate a better relationship with my children.

I understood why control and domination would kindle rebellion or defiance, driving children away from submission. We have seen it so often - a parent forbidding a young person from developing a premature relationship. When it is done with force, instead of concern and compassion, it seems the young lovers are that much more determined to stay together choosing rather to rebel. "Ye fathers provoke not your children to wrath," is Paul's advice to parents in Ephesians 6:4, "but bring them up in the nurture and admonition of the Lord." We ought to enrich their lives with loving edification mixed with godly wisdom. Just as King Solomon asked wisdom to lead the people of God, we as parents must desire wisdom to rear our children. Yes, we will all make some mistakes, but even our mistakes can serve as valuable lessons. By not being afraid to show frailty of self, but total dependency on God, we can greatly affect the lives of our children. When we allow the Lord to order our steps we will not only teach them the power of submission, but the importance of accepting and respecting divine authority.

Submission in the Workplace

The opportunity to serve is indeed the true test of leadership. It takes nothing to sit back and have someone cater to you, but it takes everything to relinquish self and serve another. First and foremost, it demands humility, which yields a submissive spirit and a heart that seeks to honor others. This is the attitude that we ought to adopt as we give service to those around us, and in authority over us. The workplace is indeed the greatest forum for this concept.

Whether your workplace is in the home, at church, in the super market, or in a major Corporation, your aim should be service. 1 Peter 2:17 sums up submission of servants by saying, "Honor all men, love the brotherhood, fear God, honor the King!" The Word of God admonishes us to submit to every ordinance of man for the Lord's sake. It goes on to tell servants to be subject to their masters with all fear, not only to the good and gentle, but also to the froward. These words not only speak for themselves, but also send a message that redefines order, and demands respect for leadership. In our modern world many find this task distasteful, unreal, and oppressive. They are not aware that in the context of scripture it is potentially an open door to promotion.

In the community there is a part we all have to play. Through working together we build society. Your job or career is your way of giving back to community and serving each other. This includes the doctor, the teacher, the landscape guy and the butcher. Also the policeman, the accountant, the waitress, and the sales manager must each use this opportunity to serve the other with gladness. We all need each other and the sooner we understand this, the stronger and healthier our communities will be. In the workplace, you are not your own, you are there for the good of the people. Your responsibility is to serve honestly and faithfully, not to fight to get into the top seat. Genuine service and the right attitude will eventually lead to personal success.

Consider this: You graduate from college and find a job. Today is your first day at work. You've been introduced to the company's president, managers, supervisors, and fellow workers before being shown your office. The rules, regulations and stipulations pertaining to the job and company is outlined for you, all of which you willingly accept. From the moment of this mutual acceptance, you are to conform to the laws of the company. You are told the company's lunch hour is at 1:00 p.m. for everyone, but this time is not suitable for you. You talk it over with your supervisor, but is informed that it is the policy of the company.

The fact of the matter is that whether you have to pick up the children at three, or pay a bill at eleven is not their concern. You are to bring yourself and your time into subjection with the company work hours. If you cannot submit, you will have to leave.

I recall a situation on my job some years ago. I had gotten to work late one morning. Even though the office was given a five minutes grace period, I was still three minutes tardy. When my supervisor brought this to my attention, I began to explain how my parking space was taken and I had to drive around a second time to find another. However, she refused to hear it, as far as she was concerned, this was not her problem. I immediately became defensive, wanting to know why she was reacting in this manner. "I have said all that I am going to say, Mrs. Sands," she said, "as much as we need you here if you can't comply, maybe you should leave." Needless to say, I took my seat. My pride was hurt, but I had only been married a few months and I needed my job. Later on during the day, I realized that my supervisor had a point, and besides she was only enforcing the rules of the company. After that incident I paid more attention to avoid being late no matter what the circumstances.

The Word of God demands that you comply to authority with reverence and peacefulness. If a policeman stops you on the road, this is neither the time, nor the place to challenge him. When the pastor corrects you, it is rebellion if for revenge you leave the church. This type of action is a corruption of the heart. There is a right and a wrong way to handle conflict. How tedious are the struggles of those with delegated authority, as daily they must deal with attitudes, damaged spirits of hurt, pain, and rebellion in the lives of those under authority. Parents, supervisors, teachers, ministers, and lawmakers can all identify with the monotonous task of leading the rebellious.

> "Servants, be obedient to them which are your masters
> according to the flesh, with fear and trembling, in singleness
> of heart, as unto Christ. Not with eye service, as men
> pleasers, but as the servants of Christ, doing the will of
> God from the heart. With good will doing service as to
> the Lord and not to men, Knowing that whatsoever good
> thing any man doeth, the same shall he receive of the Lord,
> whether he be bond or free," Ephesians 6:5-8. (KJV)

Eye service is the epitome of corrupted service

Eye service is the epitome of corrupted service, because it is offered void of real interest and heartfelt devotion. How we respond to those in authority over us is indicative of our response to the authority of God. Whether in the workplace, in the church, at a meeting, or at the stoplight, it makes no difference because God rules through delegated authority. Those in the highest office who have been given authority must also embrace submission or answer to God. Young ministers and workers must be able to submit to the spiritual authority over them, regardless of their education or experience. Your supervisor may be younger, and not as mature as you are, however, his position of authority deserves respect. When one is able to comply, it is also a sign of genuine maturity.

There was a young minister that I knew very well. During his teens, God began to use him in the ministry with spiritual gifts and signs following. As a crowd grew around him he decided it was time for him to open a church ministry. An older pastor approached him, and offered the young man the opportunity to sit under him for a while longer, but the young minister refused. "He didn't need him," he said. He left to begin a church ministry and within months his ministry became one of the largest in the city, but the people never stayed very long. Within years, the church attendance dwindled considerably forcing him back to the elderly pastor for advice.

A good leader must first learn to submit. Ministry is not having a large following or a big congregation. Neither is success measured by how much you have or know. Submission is extremely important in the business world. Your expensive education, seniority, or know-how will not give you the right to rebellion or cause disorder. Imagine if soldiers in the military refused to submit to those above them. What about if every teacher in the school decided to do their own thing and disregard the principal? If the receptionist demanded the right to rebel again her bosses, the office would be out of control and the business eventually destroyed. Our lives, schools, churches, and business all require order. Overall success is wrapped up in serving the people, our community, our nation, and our God. The higher we desire to go, the lower we must humble ourselves to serve others as we embrace the spirit of the dove. For it is when we can reach the youngest, the lowest of the lows, or the most ill informed, that we are truly ready for a promotion.

So often we pay the price for disobedience and arrogance, even though we see the blessing of God in our lives. We begin a job, and immediately demand special treatment because of "Our degree", or in the church because "God is using me." Authority was not given to us to generate pride, but to lead the way to maturity. It was not intended for control, but to model the pathway of humility. When we come up against authority, we come up against God himself, for he is authority. It is he who puts governments and kings, presidents and prime ministers, religious leaders, husbands, and parents in place. The more that is given, the more will be required of you. The higher up you go, the more you will be tested.

Many times the test may seem difficult, and often humbling, yet it paves the way to growth and development. When we refuse to accept this chastening, we will remain stagnant or find ourselves coming face to face with the same task over and over again. Eventually we will get the message, one way or the other at the risk of being broken or destroyed, (Isaiah 1:20). The worker that embraces submission can be spared the consequences of tough love by simply submitting to Christ on the job. When we sit at our desk or report to work on Monday morning and prepare to work as unto the Lord, it is then that we are ready to serve. Whether management says "Good morning" or not, should, not determine how well you work during the day. As you allow the Son to shine through you and minister through your occupation, both you, and those around you will be inspired.

Whether your boss is in the office or not, your work ethics should remain unquestionable. As a willing servant in the work place, be mindful that you were placed at this post not only to receive a financial reward, but to become a channel through which the Lord can reach out to others. It is God who ultimately provides that job and everything else that comes with it at the end of the day. Work as unto him, and know that your dedication on the job in many ways is a sharp physical indication of your intended service in the kingdom of God.

The Church & Submission

We have been called to the work of the kingdom, chosen by the Master's hand, anointed and appointed to do his biddings, yet with all our gifts, callings, and talents, order and submission will play a major role if we are going to walk in the power and authority of the Lord. In the home, community, and even the church, order is needed, and submission is required. Except we come to this place of humility, we will not see the glory of God in the church.

The model of submission by a man and his wife can reveal to the church what is expected of them spiritually and relationally. God has called the Church to submit to his Word and His Will. This is the only way that we can be prepared for the battles that confront us daily, and fight the good fight of faith. We are about to enter into the hottest part of the conflicts. We need to be prepared for war, and our level of winning calls for us to be in position. As a body of believers, the church must get into a place where the divine instruction and directions can flow through every area of the body, in every nerve, limb, organ, the entire vessel. Except we line up to receive from the Master, the bride of Christ will be caught unprepared with no oil in her lamp.

We are at a place, where ministry houses seem to be idle and ineffective. It appears the churches that sit on the corners, or line the streets are not affecting local areas. Like the church of the Laodiceans (Revelations 3:14), we have become more concerned about being increased with goods, than how we appear in the eyes of God. It is sad that young pastors today are seemingly more focused on building a mega church and having a television ministry than building lives and allowing God to meet the needs of those in the congregation regardless of size. Having a ministry is looked at as having one's own business, and the job of the minister has been reduced to that of a CEO, sitting back in easy chairs during the week, and preparing a speech to present at the pulpit on Sunday. Meanwhile, the body is weak, wretched, blind, naked, and miserable. Family problems have escalated; covenant relationships are becoming a thing of the past. Our hearts are no longer satisfied with the pure old gospel, and keeping the ministry members interested is a minister's biggest task. Blatant sin is being accepted as, 'modern living', and revival has become a taboo word. We are anxious for the crown, but we have turned a blind eye to the cross. Is the church submitted? As things seemingly fall in shambles, God has put his foot forward to declare divine order in his house.

Just as the physical family is made up of the man, woman, and children with varied purposes and responsibilities, so is the family of the church. As the headship in the family is singular, so is the headship in the church. Regardless of who stands behind the pulpit, Jesus Christ will always be the designated head of the Church, just as the husband is head of the home no matter who brings in the bacon. When we talk about the church or spiritual bride we refer to the born again believers found in every nation of the earth.

Just as our body functions to enhance life, so should the spiritual body. The brain, the heart, the liver and lungs, the digestive system, they all work together to keep the body operational. Likewise, everything else that God as created whether in the physical or spiritual, it is set to work together, especially his children. When we look at the denominations we can see so many beliefs and this is the basis for division among us. Jesus Christ is the foundation of the Christian church. Among many religious denominations there are some practices that are beneficial to the Christian church.

For example, the Catholic Church's commitment to charity, the Jehovah Witnesses devotion to witnessing daily, the Seventh Day Adventist honor of the Sabbath day to keep it holy, and the Pentecostal Movement with spontaneous worship and holiness in lifestyle. Nonetheless, except we can stand together and allow the word of God to be our rule of faith, practice, and discipline, we will not be effective in winning the world to God. God is not coming back for denominations and practices, but a people of faith, united by his love. There must be one mind, and one heart, and one Lord of our lives if heaven will be our eternal home.

Like the natural physique with a head, body, and functioning parts, receive command from the brain, unity must flow from the head of the church which is Jesus Christ to those called to spiritual authority. He has designated the body to flow symmetrically through divine appointment, gifts, and callings.

And he gave some apostles, and some, prophets, and some, evangelist, and some, pastors and teachers; for the perfecting of the saints, for the work of the ministry, for the edifying of the body of Christ. Till we all come in the unity of the faith, and of the knowledge of the Son of God, unto a perfect man, unto the measure of the stature of the fullness of Christ. Ephesians 4:11-12

In the set up of the church, there is a designated order, which begins with the ministerial body. I like to think of it as the heart, pushing and pumping to ensure that life continues. Nevertheless, by itself it cannot do the job; every organ must do its part. Like the liver that purifies the blood so that the heart can work it throughout the body, other gifts and callings sheltered within God's people are there to work and minister for the divine will and wealth of the entire ministry. Within the nucleus of the ministerial body, order continues. In the forefront or shoulder of the ministry is the ministerial team. They are set in place to ensure perfection, ministry work and edification of the entire body. These make up a very vital part of the ministerial body. Firstly, the ministry of the apostle, secondly the prophet, thirdly the teachers, after that miracles, gifts of healings, helps, governments, diversities of tongues. When the ministerial headship can embrace the spirit of the dove and become one with the rest of the membership body, together they can fulfill the will of God for the Church. This begins not man's order but divine order in the house of God.

Divine order sets the stage for unity, servant hood, and humility. Contra-wise when carnal men set up order the focus is on partiality, selfishness, and pride. This we must be very careful of. When there is no order, or when the body is not functioning properly this spurs chaos. In the physical, it looks like an epileptic seizure where every organ is doing its own thing. When a part of the body is not functioning it can be liken to a retarded body, limited by a handicap, the Spirit is alive inside but the physical body is limp. Contra-wise when the body is in order and every part is functioning as it should, there is life and replenishment. If we look at the purpose and responsibilities of the husband and wife we get a glimpse of the home and how the family fits together. The same is true of the church. When the church is submitted to the Word, she will bring forth children, righteous seed that when added will grow and mature into the body of believers with specific gifts and callings according to their divine destiny. Let's look at the work of the divine leaders.

Apostle: Anointed to walk in divine leadership the Apostle brings order and dispels error. This ministry is unique because in addition to walking in the apostolic calling, it is prophetic, evangelical, pastoral, and apt to teach. It is equipped in this way to birth, groom, and grow other ministers and ministries. So often when we look for the apostle, we look to bishops, senior pastors, or ministers with strong influence, but in heart the Apostle is a humble individual that is called to expound the Word of God concerning order, structure, and administrative discipline. He is powerful enough to walk in this office, yet humble enough to stand back for the operations of the others.

Prophet: The prophetic ministry, also known as the eye of the eagle, is gifted with vision. It forewarns and forearms the ministry. Like a watchman who senses or becomes aware of danger, and heralds to others, "Trouble is coming, get armed and ready," the prophetic minister does likewise. He sees and brings warning that alarms the church of God. In addition, he also perceives the gifts and talents that are buried within the hearts of God's people. In the Old Testament, the prophet was also referred to as a 'seer,' and God's mouthpiece. Amos 3:7 tells us, "Surely the Lord will do nothing, but he revealeth his secret unto his servants the prophets." This ministry is of extreme necessity in the administration of the church. It will keep the body sober, vigilant, and on guard so that it is not easily destroyed by the craftiness of the adversary.

Evangelist: The mouthpiece and motivator, this minister is anointed to speak stirring words that will cut to the very heart piercing asunder to soul and spirit. Dead, dying, and weary souls are energized, built up, made stronger, and brought back to life by the water of the word that flows with life giving power. His work will venture near and far to bring souls into the kingdom.

Pastor: The shepherd, he leads and loves the body. He will give his life for the sheep. You will know him by his heart to serve, protect, provide, and love the people of God without hindrance. Many may pastor, but it takes a true shepherd to lay his life on the limb for the sheep. This comes almost natural to this minister who soothes and protects those who are often so vulnerable.

Teacher: This ministry is one of illustrative instruction. It is called and anointed to prepare and show the body how to live effectively using the Word of God. This minister unveils truth and brings clarity to the darkest of understanding helping the church to apply the Word to everyday life. Through eating, drinking, and daily washing of the word, believers will affectively blossom, bloom, and grow in the knowledge of the Lord.

This leadership team stands together as a foundational front for the edification of the body. Each has been equip with responsibilities that would operate as an immune system, protecting, shielding, building, enhancing, and equipping. It is through this avenue that life and progress comes to the church. If any particular one is missing in ministry, that church can be considered handicap and open to attack through the neglected area because a door has been left ajar. They work together in the position of leadership not to use others to exalt themselves or be worshipped by others, but to become a stepping-stone to propel the people of God back to Him and into their rightful positions. Their focus is not what you can do for me, or what can I do for you, but what can we do for Him. This becomes the foundation for real ministering.

Like the male and female, no one person, calling, or position is more important or valuable than the other. The principle difference is function. Both the husband and wife are needed to run a home effectively. Even the husband who prides himself on being the head of the home must admit that without his wife, a house is not quite a home. The same is true in the house of God, every gift and calling comes together to bring edification and maturity. **"Ye have not chosen me," Jesus said, "but I have chosen you."** The ministerial body should not exalt themselves in pride because of their divine responsibilities, because the callings are distributed by God and has nothing to do with the minister's earthly abilities.

But now hath God set the members in the body as
it hath pleased him, 1 Corinthians 12:18.

Each of these ministries is desperately needed to feed the body of Christ. One cannot function effectively without the other. Everything else that is needed can and will be found in the membership body of believers. Like the wife who helps her husband run the home, the body of believers helps the ministerial body to accomplish the work of the ministry. The word of wisdom, word of knowledge, faith, gifts of healing, working of miracles, words of prophecy, discerning of spirit, tongues and interpretation of tongues, all worketh by one spirit. There shall be no schisms or divisions, but equal care one for another. If one suffers, then all suffer. If one be honored, then are all honored. There is no one person designated to do the work of God independently, we all move interdependently with each other.

In the book of Acts when the apostles and others came together, they enquired among themselves whom it was that God had given a message. In doing this they allowed others that were used of the Lord to freely operate in their calling. There were no big shots, or controller of the ministry. This may seem strange to say the least today because we have strayed so far from submission to divine order that the church is seemingly experiencing an epileptic seizure. Prophets are operating as Apostles, Evangelist is doing the work of the Pastor, those called as Psalmists are now taking over churches, etc. In many ministries or churches we find a total absence of the ministerial team. There are no apostles, prophets, evangelist, pastors, or teachers working together to perfect the saints.

This end time find spiritual leaders running the church independently. For many leading a church has become a personal business venture. Some pastors have employed their spouse as partner in the ministry regardless of whether or not they have been called by God to that place. Not only is this very dangerous spiritually, but it leaves little room for real accountability. Together they become the apostle, prophet, evangelist, pastor, and teacher to that ministry. The detriment of this was seen in the divorce case of a pastor and his wife. When the couple separated members watched as the church and everything in it was divided or sold. Members were scattered and the ministry disassembled. This is not to say that a husband and wife team can not lead a ministry providing they are divinely equipped to do so. Nonetheless, we must understand that the way the kingdom of God is set up, no man or human is an island. It is not about what we like, what we want, or what we dream up. It is what the Lord Jesus wants to do, and how he desires to do it. We are the servants, we follow His directions.

This personal ownership of the Lord's house also opens the door of pride and domination. Few individuals can resist the temptations of dictatorship when placed in a position of authority. This can be compared to a home where the husband or wife rules with an iron rod of fear and control. The other spouse and children are like servants instead of valued members of the family. In a number of ministries and homes this has become the accepted way of operation. The children of the house though gifted, sit dormant and unused because a lack of spiritual vision on the part of the leader. When Jesus began his ministry and chose his helpers, he never operated in this manner. He never sought the center stage; in fact, except one was an ardent follower they did not automatically know who was who amidst the men. Jesus never ruled by dictatorship. He sent his disciples out, trained them, and gave them opportunities to follow his lead, but he always led with a servant's heart.

Why is it that in peering through many of the fancy stain colored windows in today's ministries, it appears as though church houses are fast becoming models of a traditional slave quarter. There is also a misinterpretation of submission. Like many husbands who demand submission from their wives, many pastors and church leaders have adopted the same attitude toward their members. Their attitudes declare, "You had better submit to me!" Under the disguise of spiritual father, set man/woman of the house, God's man/woman of the hour, First lady, or God's anointed, many are leading people away from a direct relationship with Christ to a remodeled relationship that resemble the Roman Catholic priest and the people. Individuals are more fearful of displeasing the pastor than displeasing God.

I was at a church meeting where the passionate leader at the front began to inform the people saying, "God expects you to submit to me as the set man in this house. Whatever I say you must do because as the leader of this church, God speaks through me. To disagree, or reject would be interpreted as a lack of submissiveness, and will result in a loss of your holding any positions in this church." The quiet congregation said nothing, and the meeting went on. I was shocked and sat quietly to see how the meeting would unfold. Sure enough, everything the pastor put forth was readily accepted. No one dared to go against the commands set forth for fear of rejection, or so called spiritual discipline. The reason for this concept is because in the church world the pastor or leader has assumed the position as the head, with the laymen positioned as the wife instead of Christ as the head and the pastor and laymen as the wife. Therefore you submit to me instead of we submit to Him has become the order of the day.

But is this what God intended for the church? What is the Church? She is the body of Christ, His bride! Does that include leaders and laymen or just laymen? No, that includes every born again believer as laborers with Christ. A married man and his wife are one before God, so is the church leaders and the members. When God set up his church, he laid the foundation on which the church would be built, His Son, Jesus Christ. In the Old Testament, God spoke and led through appointed leaders, which consisted of godly men, prophets, kings, priest and the like. One of the greatest leaders was Moses. Even with his faults and failures his life and ministry gave us a remarkable example of how God leads his people. When Jesus came, leadership was presented differently. No longer was there a designated man, but men in union led by Christ.

This does not mean that there is no respect for church leadership. We are taught in God's word to submit to those who have the rule over us. Just like any position of leadership, we must give honor where honor is due. In 1st Timothy chapter five we are told to, "Rebuke not an elder, but entreat him as a father and the younger men as brothers, the older women as mothers, and the younger women as sisters, with all purity." What we must understand even in the church is submission to leadership by force is not proper leadership at all. A few verses down in this same passage of scripture it reads:

*Let the elders that rule well be counted worthy of double honor,
especially they who labour in the word and doctrine, for the
scripture saith thou shalt not muzzle the ox that treadeth
out the corn. And the labourer is worthy of his reward.
Against an elder receive not an accusation, but before two or
three witnesses. Them that sin rebuke before all, that others
also may fear. I charge thee before God, and the Lord Jesus
Christ, and the elect angels, that thou observe these things
without preferring one before another, doing nothing by
partiality, lay hands suddenly on no man, neither be partaker
of other men's sins, keep thyself pure. I Timothy 5:17-22*

Again, like the man and wife both functions must be respected as the wife submits to her husband and the husband submits to Christ. She honors him enough to not disrespect him, and he loves her enough to honor her as a part of himself. The same order stands amidst the people of God. The pastor even though he is in a position of authority loves the people and honors them as part of Christ and therefore a part of himself. Likewise, the members honor and respect their minister and the position he has been placed in by God.

The first thing Jesus did as he entered into ministry was to appoint a governing body - his twelve disciples. As time went on, others joined the lineup, but there was still one leader, one head, which was and still is the Lord Jesus. He asked Peter, "Who do men say that I am?" Peter responded through divine revelation, "Thou art the Christ, the son of the Living God." Confirming Peter's words Jesus stated, "Upon this rock I build my church." What is the rock; it is the truth and knowledge that Christ is the pillow of the Church. Not man, but the Son of God. Many Christian or church folk may say, "Well we know that!" And many do, but do we understand what this means? Looking at the present day set up of churches is quite different from what is set forth in the New Testament. From as young as I could remember, my family was always in church and it has always been set up the way it is even now. The pastor is the designated leader of the church and everyone else follows. However, upon looking into the Word, where the title of a pastor is mentioned only a few times, I wonder why this position in contrast to the others has gained such prominence.

What we have today is so far from what the apostles had that it is almost frightening. As a result the manifestations of the power and presence of

God is almost nonexistent. Most churches are started with a man and a vision, securing the position of a pastor. In due time, or as the church grows he is elevated as the supreme leader of the ministry. Survey have proven that most pastors today came out of other churches where they were hurt or discouraged, and began what is termed 'their ministry!' Eventually pride sets in and it really becomes their ministry in that they hold the reins of control and selfishness lined with self-righteousness. Set up as the ultimate vessel to be used of God, eventually he is set on a pedestal to be worshiped. There is little accountability, if any, so the pastor very likely does what he wants, how he wants, when, and where he wants it. The apostles, prophets, evangelist, teachers, and other pastors, if present, are subject to him. He may appoint elders, deacons, and other ministers, but often they must become 'yes men' that are also subject to him. They must stand by and support him and his vision or be rejected or even removed. This is the typical present day status in the body of Christ, but it is totally opposite to the will of God for his people.

A man that is called to an apostolic position must be a man of humility, pliable in the hands of God to be used to set the body in divine order. He must be willing to accept the gifting and callings of others as God reveals. If God says that the usher at the door has the message for the church on any given Sunday morning, then the ministerial body or individual over the flock must be humble enough to submit to this. His ultimate desire must be to adhere to the desires of God's heart and not his own. He seeks out the gifting not only in his physical children but also his spiritual children whom God has placed in his care. He must be sensitive to the Spirit of God and the Holy Spirit speaking through the ministerial team and others around him so that he is not easily deceived. His prayer and hearts desire must be, "Thy will oh Lord, be done." It is then that God is able to guide this vessel that is void of self, to help eradicate the spot of sin and the wrinkles that come through disorder. The body of Christ is much too heavy to be carried by an individual man or woman. The wisdom of God is too vast to be stored in a single human mind. Therefore God has placed gifts and calling in the body as he see fit. He is not a respecter of persons, his call is to whosoever will, let him come. He has set in place instruments of every kind to produce the symphony of sounds that will bring music to his ear.

Yes the church is out of order, but God is about to restore both order and submission. Jesus said that the last generation shall do much greater works. First, she must be humbled so that she can accept it. Pride and arrogance must be done away with so the pure light of the Word can fill

God's vessel. Those of us who make up this bride must come together to be one with Christ, the brain of the body. The shoulder, bodice, hands, and feet, has to be connected that the blood may flow throughout and bring forth life. In a physical sense when obstruction prevent the brain from communicating to the body then retardation or death results. When all is in place and working well then the entire body will be strong and fit to accomplish its purpose.

When this is accomplished in the foundational stage, all the other disorders and schisms cease or fizzle out and the body begins to function properly. Solutions to problems that seem too difficult to handle or deal with will be boldly confronted and conquered through humility and prayer. We will not have so many social, emotional, spiritual, financial, and relational issues. We will understand what it means to submit to Jesus just as he submits to his Father. We will commit to giving our all like a humble servant, and pass the test of true leadership. With our hearts surrendered, and our minds renewed, we will be ready to affect the world, empowered by submission.

Submission & the Nations

History has a way of repeating itself. As our minds span back through generations, one thing is certain, nations that have not honored God, eventually fell to swift destruction. We look at the nations today, from the United States of America to the United Kingdom. We look at Europe, Asia, the Middle East, to Haiti and the islands of the seas. Are nations today embracing submission? Even though we may all agree on principles and politics that govern our world, the thing that divides us most is our reference to the Almighty God. Just as mankind rise and fall according to his obedience or disobedience with God, the same has been true of nations. The nations whose God is the Lord is blessed. It is His righteousness that exalts a nation and makes it successful.

As we look at the nations within the continents, hardly can we point out nations that are submitted to God. In the nation of Africa, North & South Americas, Europe, Asia, Australia, Antarctic, there is a struggling with major issues of morality according to the Word of God. Yet, even though there are many within these nations that have committed their hearts and minds to God, it does not constitute submission on the part of the entire nations, until proclaimed by a designated leader. We can see wickedness penetrating the boundaries of many lands. There are wars and rumors of wars, famine and pestilences, earthquake and natural disasters as God himself calls lands of people to repentance. Lawlessness is the result of disorder and anarchy, but what is expected of a nation when it embraces the spirit of the dove and walk in submission to the Lord?

Let us look at the story of Nineveh, a people who had become arrogant, rebellious, and marked for destruction. God was about to destroy Nineveh, but mercy was extended when he used the prophet Jonah to give the people a warning. When Jonah did, all the people and even the animals submitted and repented in sack cloth and ashes and God gave them grace.

So the people of Nineveh believed God, and Proclaimed a fast, and put on sackcloth, from the greatest of them even to the least of them. For the word came unto the king of Nineveh, and he arose from his throne, and he laid his robe from him, and covered him with sackcloth and sat in ashes. And he caused it to be proclaimed and published through Nineveh by the decree of the king and his nobles, saying, Let neither man nor beast, herd nor flock, taste anything, let them not feed, nor drink water: But let man and beast be covered with sackcloth, and cry mightily unto God, yea, let them turn everyone from the violence that is in their hands. Who can tell if God will turn and repent, and turn away from his fierce anger that we perish not? And God saw their works that they turned from their evil way and God repented of the evil, that he had said that he would do unto them and he did it not. Jonah 3: 5-10

The king of Nineveh knew that God was his only hope. He saw his human frailness, and stepped down from his throne, laid his robe aside, and humbled himself before God while demanding that the people do likewise. This leader submitted and found grace in the eyes of God, personally and nationally.

It begins with the father who is leading his family. His family is a part of the community that yields a leader, who ultimately represents the people that makes up the nation. When a nation refuses to honor God, it becomes open to lawlessness, disorder, and every violent sin. In Psalms 33:12, scripture reads, "Blessed is the nation whose God is the Lord, and the people whom he hath chosen for his own inheritance." When a nation fears God, they inhabit the blessings that are promise to his people, contrawise, when they denounce God or have other Gods before him, the enemy is given entrance and makes his haven in the nation where God and his Word is not honored. The call to repentance is a call to submit. To turn away from what appears to be right in your own eyes, and humble yourself before God that he might hear from heaven, forgive the sin, and heal the lands.

It is obvious to all that the Nations of the world are spiritually sick. Even though many nations continue to prosper and have wealth, just like the church at Laodicea (Revelations 3:14), that was wretched, blind, poor and naked. There appears to be no real power or spiritual success anywhere, and moral decay is rampant. The leaders put on a good face to the people, but behind closed doors they are walking the floor in hopelessness and frustration. The people are looking to their leaders whose powers are limited, oblivious to the fact that it is God who ultimately rules over the nations. All of the nations of the world are dealing with major issues. The continent of Africa which is seen as a part of the world that is economically impoverished, or Asia, while experiencing rising economical wealth, is still seen as a land of social poverty. It stands side by side with the United States of America - one of the richest nations of the world, yet poor in morals and values. With all its wealth it is also known as the divorce capital of the world – a nation eroded by the spirit of division. If we were to take a closer look at the nations, we would see that none is more profitable than the other. They are all suffering because of rebellion and disobedience at one level or another. Nonetheless, the word of the Lord saith, even to the nations, "Behold, I stand at the door and knock, if any man hear my voice and open the door, I will sup with him and he with me. The call to the nations is a call for submission!

The prophet Habakkuk understood the need for national submission in his day and time. His heart grieved for the violence and contention that had surrounded him. Both violence and contention stem from disobedience, lawlessness, and a selfish heart. At that time, Jerusalem was being destroyed under the hands of the Babylonian. The wicked was apparently destroying the righteous. As a result, not only was there disorder and chaos, but wrong judgment proceeded. When Habakkuk began to pray, God spoke to him and said, "The vision is yet for an appointed time, but at the end it shall speak and not lie, though it tarry, wait for it because it will come!" Looking at the nations today, there is much to be desired. It seems many leaders are doing what is good for them, and not for a nation of people. Oftentimes, the men and women that lead the nations hold the ultimate responsibility to lead righteously. On the other hand, people fight against their leader, not realizing that in any nation the leader and the people are one. Just as a wife is called to stand by her husband, you are called to stand by your leader, and when he is out of order, your next call is to get down on your knees and pray! God will not only respond, but he will direct you to your next move. Like it worked for Nineveh, it will work wonders in the nations of today.

Corruption is the order of the day, as pride and arrogance imprison many human hearts. In many nations of the world, government leaders are twisting their hands as they watch their nations go from one level of decay to another. Almost everywhere there is some level of unrest; most do not know where to turn. The psalmist David as he praised God, declared in psalms 22:27, "For the kingdom is the Lord's, and he is the governor among the nations." No matter whom the elected or self appointed leader may be in any nation, God will always be ultimately in control. Like the woman who is surrendered to her husband, God is calling the nations of the world to completely surrender to him. It is not our right to do as we want. We must and will answer to God as a nation for everything that is done in the land. As we look around at the nations of the world, it is obvious that each and every one is headed for trouble. No matter how it appears on the surface, the truth of the matter is that rebellion in high places is causing many lands to suffer persecution in one way or another, thereby unleashing God's fury as well. But the time will come when the Lord will revive his work.

In the midst of all that our earthly eyes may see, is a nation within nations-God's Nation. A people that have been called out and chosen, whose hearts are committed to fulfilling the divine will of God. "*But ye,*" Peter declared, "*are a chosen generation, a royal priesthood, an holy nation, a peculiar people, that ye should shew forth the praises of him who hath called you out of darkness into his marvelous light. Which in time past were not a people of God: but are now the people of God, which had not obtained mercy, but now have obtained mercy.*" These are men and women who have embraced submission. They will rise up out of the decay to lift up a standard for the people. Even among persecution they will stand. Like the disciples in Acts 14, they will challenge unrighteousness. After Paul and Barnabas healed a cripple man at Lystra, the people wanted to worship them. But they fail to submit to idolatry, and pointed the people back to God. As a result they were cast out of the city and stoned, but even in persecution they stood firm.

God is depending on his people. An entire nation was changed because of Jonah's eventual submission to God. He can do a mighty work with one submitted heart. Even though the people as a nation may not embrace the will of God, you can take up the challenge and stand in the gap. Maybe he has burdened your heart for your nation. It might be that he has chosen you to stand in constant prayer for your leader, or like Jeremiah, it could be that you are spiritually set over your nation by God to pray and pull down strongholds. Let God's will be done! Consider Pharaoh, and be reminded that it is God himself that chooses leaders and dignitaries. No matter how evil or righteous they may seem, they have all been set in place by the Lord himself. He will put them up, and take them down as he pleases; he alone knows their heart and divine purposes in that life. Sin will always be a reproach to any people, but righteousness will forever exalt a nation.

4

Submit, Not Me!

*Pride goeth before destruction, and a haughty spirit
before a fall.*

– PROVERBS 16:18

*Cynthia's caustic remarks tore deeply into the fabric of Eric's already wounded
spirit. "Get out of my face, husband or not, I don't have to listen to you." He
had just suggested to Cynthia that she needed to pay closer attention to the
needs of her family. But she not only resisted his suggestions, she wanted to
let him know that she was in control of her own life, and would not have
him dictating to her what she should do, or when she should go anywhere!
"You just make me sick," she went on. "I'm tired of your complaints." Eric
could feel the vibrating tension as the blood in his veins frantically darted
throughout his body. He could feel the perspiration beginning to peep out
of his pores, seemingly knowing that unless he settled down for 'Peace sake,'
there would be a 'showdown tonight.' Cynthia's eyes mirrored defiance, letting
her husband knows that she meant every word. Her body taut, with the car
keys tightly clasped, she was ready to leave.*

*Fear filled the frightened eyes of the children in the doorway, but this did
not calm her down. An assertive and aggressive, not to mention successful and
educated 21st century women, she would not be subjected, nor submitted to
anyone, and that was that! "Take what I have to offer," she told her husband,*

or you can go. I don't need a man; I can make it by myself." Eric said a silent prayer as his eyes fell to the ground. This was not the first time his wife had challenged him. When it wasn't the finances or the children, it was something else. Standing in the center of the room he wondered how much more of this he would have to put up with. Lately it seemed, every time they had a conflict, things got worse. He thought of just walking away, although what he really felt like doing was slamming her against the wall. But he knew that violence would solve nothing, and besides he didn't want any cops around, then the whole neighborhood would know what was going on. Looking at his children on the sidelines, he knew they had been through enough. Eric wondered to himself, "If I don't do something now, where will this end?" He had not been to church for a while, but he knew he needed God's direction on how to deal with his stubborn wife.

He looked at his wife standing there. "I don't understand how you could spend so much time in God's house and never change, and then you wonder why I won't go with you?" He commented. "Oh shut up, Eric B. Webster, you wouldn't know a godly woman if she lived under your nose! You are no example, so why should I be?" Cynthia replied angrily.

Eric came back even stronger, "I never claimed to be a believer!" Cynthia felt like she had been hit with a bag of ice. She watched as Eric made his way around the table, coming closer to her. She could feel the heat of his body. He was just inches away. In a quick moment he gathered his wits about him. Then with more control than he realized he had, he lifted his chin and lowered his eyes to meet those of his beloved wife. He took a deep breath, and from his lips came the voice of a very frustrated man.

"Cynthia, I love you, and God knows I try to do my best in my home, and provide for my family. All I want is for my wife to be there when I really need her. My home is always a mess. I help you, but the more I help, the less you do. The children obviously need you, but you don't seem to have time for any of us. You expect me to be at your beck and call, but yet you treat me like dirt, you give me no respect. And do you know that, as much as I want to spend the rest of my life with you, I am too much of a man to take this kind of treatment. I can't and I won't settle for this Cynthia. If you mean what you say, there is a choice that you would have to make. I am still the head of this family, and I will not relinquish my place. You can comply, or pack your things and leave! Your next move will declare your decision."

Had she heard him right? Was this the man that she fell in love with nine years before, giving her an ultimatum! Thoughts began to flash before her. She had to think quickly. She heard the voice of the enemy saying, "Pack *your things and leave, take everything. Put him to the test, and see if he can really handle the chores, the cooking, the cleaning and the children. Surely he would not last a day." In her heart she wondered, "Is this worth the fight? She knew physically he could overpower her, yet, how would that affect the children, her marriage, and her life? What would the women in the church say when they heard she had walked out on her family? And those at work; surely they would make her the topic of the lunchroom gossip. Whew! These thoughts played in her mind as Cynthia held her position a moment longer, her eyes locked with her husband's who waited for his wife's next move. The ball was in her court.*

The scene illustrated above is one that is exhibited daily in many homes across the world. It exists not only in the disrespect of wives to husbands, but also in many other relationships. The rebellion of the wife toward her husband is an indication of the level of rebellion that exists in the human heart today. In the world, laborers defy those in authority over them. In some homes, we find parents who are submitting to the will of children. Even on a national basis rebellion has become common ground. Ultimately, mankind has moved to another level of disobedience toward God. We acknowledge him, but we demand to do things our way. "This people draweth nigh unto me with their mouth, and honoureth me with their lips; the scripture states in Matthew 15:8, "but their heart is far from me." Today more women are rebelling against submission as they fight for control, security, and a sense of wholeness. In their attempt, they demand control in the marriage, the family, and anything else they believe they should dominate. The act of standing up to her husband, or usurping authority over him, has become the norm; so much so that women today become uneasy with the concept of submission, and thereby resist it. We have become so comfortable with "wrong" living that we no longer accept what is "right" according to the word of God. Women controlling things is now being regarded as "a women's right." The argument is justified with the following attitudes:

1. *I am just as intelligent and capable as he, so why do I have to submit to him? Why can't he submit to me?*

2. *Because we are equal, no particular gender should have to submit to the other. The more intelligent way would be based on the logic of 50/50.*

3. *And more prevalent, "This is the 21st century and no longer are we held to the laws and rules of yesterday that are now outdated in the times that we live in."*

To today's women this has simply become a way of life. Independence and aggression, is what some mothers and grandmothers told them would bring success. Many have rejected the very thought of submitting, being haunted by past childhood experiences, or poor examples. Others cannot begin to even comprehend what submission really means because of societal influences. Independence has become a goal, instead of being seen as a major form of pride.

Pride

Pride is an ugly, selfish spirit that causes an individual to over exalt him or herself. It comes in many forms and mannerisms. You would find it hiding as religious pride, gender, cultural, or social pride and trailed by his twin brother, arrogance. It is subtle and usually parades itself as harmless. Wherever rebellion is found you will find pride entangled in its root. Proverbs 6:16-19, identifies pride not only as one of seven things that God hate, but also an abominable act. Pride and rebellion has been embedded into the human soul since the entrance of sin into the world. When I discovered it in my life and traced it back I found it nestled deep in religion. I had grown up in the church all my life and never saw the truth about pride until I began to confront that awful spirit in my own heart. I remember the night I began writing this chapter. The things I was writing amazed me and I stopped for a while to pray because I began to see familiar signs within myself. I considered myself a strong Christian but somehow I had never thought that I could be struggling with pride.

My thoughts interrupted my writing and I began to walk the floor in prayer as the Lord began to speak to my heart and unveil the traits of pride. I thought back to messages that I had heard preached and could not remember one about pride. In my heart I felt a dread as I tried to figure out when did this begin? Why was it there? Where did it come from, and how could I get rid of pride? In a moment my eyes became focused on something in the corner of the room. It appeared like a piece of rag that was black, filthy and terrifying, hiding in the shadows. It was like the nastiest piece of trash that one could imagine, but it was alive. At once I began to cry out to God, begging him to cleanse from my life every trace of that hideous attitude and every temperament that was associated with it. Aggression, defiance, stubbornness, a controlling spirit, self conceitedness, and whatever was associated with pride and rebellion. I did not want it living in my life. That's when I felt what seemed like shackles cracking away, and I knew at that moment that by faith I was truly free. When I forced myself to look back in the corner at the frightening thing, there was nothing. I knew immediately that God had given me a glimpse of how detestable pride looked in his sight, and in the lives of his people.

After this experience I became more conscious of prideful acts and attitudes in myself and others. Things I did not take notice of before, was now very obvious to me. I began to realize that pride was more prevalent than I had thought, and walking tall in many lives including Christians. Most people are totally unaware of this very sneaky fault. I'm reminded of a Christian friend of mine who would often say, "I have my pride!" He would also comment, "Everybody needs a little bit of pride." I have even seen bumper stickers that read, "The Power of Pride" on people's cars. The truth of the matter is that there ought to be no place for pride in our lives, because we have done nothing for which we are able to give ourselves a pat on the back.

The accomplishments you have made in the workplace, the material things you have attained, the awards and rewards that you call your own, your beautiful face, the clothing you wear, the talents you or your beautiful children possess were all given to you by God himself. The community or nation you live in is what it is only because of the grace and mercy of God. There is nothing that you have gotten on your own. The very breath you breathe each morning is allowed by the Lord. What do you really have to be proud of! Everything that you have, you ought to give God the glory for. Without him we are nothing! I prayed that God would open our spiritual eyes to see pride as He see it. It is not only there to corrupt our lives, but to put a distance between us and our Lord. Pride works to cause us to be selfish, ungrateful, self-righteous, only focusing on what profits 'me.' God cannot walk with pride or rebellion. When mankind rebelled against God, he was cast out of the garden and his joy was shattered.

When a woman is overtaken by pride it breeds rebellion. Just as a woman models submission, when she walks in disobedience to God it gives us a clear view of how disobedience looks when it has taken root in our hearts. Not only will she destroy herself, but her home will be devastated as well. All over the world women are fighting for, and openly demanding independence, unaware of the dark cause behind their actions.

Jesus drew attention to a man caught up in the spirit of pride. The man, a Pharisee, went before God in prayer, thanking him that he was not like others, but that he was at a standard of right living. A publican nearby also went before the Lord in prayer and repented in humility while asking for mercy to live right. In pride the Pharisee exalted himself over the publican when his self-righteousness blinded him to his own fault. So often among Christians this kind of pride is overlooked. We can identify it as self-righteousness when we esteem our spiritual standing over that of another. Pride asserts, "Why should I submit to you, I am just as good as you?" Pride also masquerades as self-righteousness when saying, "I am a humble person." Often the declaring of humility is a tell tale sign of a lack of humility. The word of God tells us to let another esteem you rather than esteeming yourself. It was because of the spirit of pride that Jesus stood in the temple and cried, "Woe to the Scribes and Pharisees," who made themselves appeared righteous to receive the praise of men but inwardly their hearts were filled with corruption, (Matthew 23).

After God begins changing our lives, perfecting a work in us, or supply us with wisdom and revelation, pride creeps in and we see no reason for continual repentance. We say to ourselves, "It is the others, the liars, drunkards, prostitutes, or sexual perverts that must come to the altar, but not us. We are the born again, the redeemed. We have to help them." This was the level of rebellion that existed in religious arenas during Jesus' time on earth. Not much has changed today. The rich and poor, the educated and the less educated, blacks versus white, denominations against denominations, all are prejudice acts fed by pride. The less humility one possesses, the greater the level of pride. In the above illustration, Cynthia lacked humility but excelled in pride.

As a woman professing Christianity, she was more concerned with what the people around her would think, rather than adhering to what was pleasing in the eyes of God. This is the foot hold of pride, being overly concern about how we appear to others and always fearing that people will not look upon us favorably. The fact that she saw herself as a woman that didn't have to embrace submission was the height of a prideful spirit. What her husband failed to realize was that he was dealing with more than stubbornness in his wife. He had come face to face with the spirit of rebellion.

Rebellion

What is rebellion? How does one commit the sin of rebellion? There are various forms of rebellion with varied results and consequences. However, the root is always willful disregard and defiance. In the book of James in Chapter 4:17, we are given an accurate description; *"Therefore, to him that knoweth to do good, and doeth it not, to him it is sin."* The free will of man, given by God, allows him to choose that which is good and acceptable according to the Word. In order to make a choice, man must have options. In the Garden of Eden, God could have locked Satan out of the tropical forest. He could have secured the garden with righteousness; however he chose to allow man to make decisions for himself and gave him a free will to make choices in life.

> *The stronghold of rebellion is rooted deep within the very being of man*

Man was presented with good and warned of evil. He had a choice, sadly he chose to rebel. A soul that revolts against God rejects His Son Jesus, and turns away from God's Holy word, is rebellious. When one walks away from truth, when one fails to bring oneself into subordination to authority in any form, when one willingly goes against what he know is right to do, and even moving forward without consulting God, all typifies rebellion. When one refuses to submit to, or rejects the fact that they ought to respect authority, this is the beginning of, and manifestation of pride. It will lead to an untouchable, un-teachable, and haughty spirit that refuses to receive. It will result in sin. But God has made a way of escape! Romans 5:20 tell us, "Where sin abounds, grace did much more abound." The mercies of God opens a door that can turn the most rebellious into the most submissive heart for the Lord, all man need to do is simply humble himself and ask for help!

The stronghold of rebellion is rooted so deep within the very being of man that only the blood of Jesus can wash it out. Rebellion came alive before mankind was created. In Isaiah chapter14, we see that before the world was created, Lucifer, now known as Satan, was cast out of heaven because of rebellion. He was once known as the son of the morning when he lived in the presence of God, but he became the prince of darkness when he contested divine authority. His quick journey downward began when he sought to exalt himself above the Most High God. Overtaken by pride, Satan was cast out of heaven, with one third of the angels who chose to follow him.

Rebellion is a spiritual act that affects the very spirit of the human race. This attitude is easy to identify today and we see its manifestations everywhere. It parades itself in children, teenagers, adults, in the workplace, church, and among national leaders. Rebellion never wants to be told what to do, and it gets agitated in the face of instruction. You might hear a rebellious attitude say, "I don't want or need nobody to tell me what to do!" This is because the flesh wants to do as it wishes. It resents authority and is uncomfortable with divine order.

Like a spider it moves slowly, spinning a slippery web that eventually sucks the life out of its victim. If we take a closer look at spiders we will notice that it belong to a class of insects, which include the ticks, mites, scorpions, and the king crabs. These insects are closely related with like identities. Even though they have distinct differences and ancestries the mannerisms are common. The spirit of rebellion is similar in that it fits in well with a class of other spirits like anger, defiance, stubbornness, pride, self righteousness, arrogance, and a haughty attitude. Rebellion is the basis of all sin, and when you see it, other like attitudes are hardly ever far behind.

Many times in the lives of children these spirits lay unsuspected, only to raise its heads on the verge of adulthood years. In many cases, parents are not aware of the deep underlying problem until the onset of the teen years. We are told that rebellion is a natural trait in teenagers, when actually it is the bold manifestation of what is really hidden within the heart. A parent may tell a child not to go a certain place, and the child rebels and will sneak out, because the decision was already made in the heart. Many of us can look back in our own lives and see the spirit of rebellion that existed in our youth. It seems as we grow this spirit grew with us, persisting when we entered the workplace, and into marriage. Except the Lord shake us up and in his mercy correct us, we will be utterly destroyed.

Rebellion will take you where you never dreamt you would go. It places you where you never thought you could be. Ask the man in a prison cell, facing a life sentence. He will tell you that rebellion lead to his incarceration. So will the young woman, who snuck out of her parent's home and later finds herself lonely and lost. The one that was fired from a good job will tell you it was because he refused to listen or take instruction. The road to sin is paved with stones of rebellion. Rebellion against those in authority, especially parents, but ultimately rebellion against the Word of God. Wedged deep within our human nature, the desire to obey God is a daily struggle that every soul will experience. When I began to seek after the truth of submission, and God began to reveal the power that submission brings, then I knew that it was only his grace and power that would enable me to live my life dedicated to him. I was not looking for perfection, but being perfected in time.

Mankind was birthed into the world with a rebellious heart. There is not one of us that can honestly say that we have not experience rebellion. Rebellion grows and is nurtured by various circumstances in our lives, and can only be tamed by obedience to authority. There are a whole lot of people who are totally unaware of the spirit of rebellion and the part it plays in keeping them bound in their sins. When asked, most people would not admit to being prideful or rebellious. But when we see ourselves, and the darkness of our waywardness, it can bring us to a place of conviction, confession, and repentance.

Job himself was not aware of pride in his life, even this just man fell short, until God placed him in a position to take his eyes of his surrounding and focus on the Father. Satan knows well how to hide in subtle sins. One afternoon while entering a gas station, my husband opened the door for a female police officer. The young women refused to walk through the door, and told my husband that it was okay for him to enter first, because she was an independent woman. This, too, is a sneaky spirit of rebellion and pride that hides behind the independent spirit to the point where a woman would reject feminine honor with the perception that it is a sign of weakness.

Pride will make us feel like we must prove ourselves when the fact of the matter is that we can accomplish nothing of ourselves. Independence goes against all that God intended for mankind. From the beginning we as human beings were not created to be independent, but inter-dependent upon each other and ultimately dependent upon God. Many great men and women fell because of this form of pride, and many will continue to fall except they bow down in humility.

To rebel against authority in any form is outright rebellion against God. All authority is set up and taken down by God; therefore there is no excuse for rebellion. The right to govern is a very powerful responsibility. This authority was first given to mankind in the beginning of creation. Genesis 1:28 declares, "And God blessed them, and God said unto them be fruitful and multiply, and replenish the earth, and subdue it, and have *dominion* over the fish of the sea, and over the fowls of the air, and over every living thing that moveth upon the earth."

Mankind, consisting of male and female was given the responsibility to manage and exercise authority over everything that existed including the power of darkness. So how did mankind rebel when he was the authority? He himself was subject to a higher power, the omnipotence of God Almighty. Man lost his authority when he chose to rebel against the authority of God motivated by the power of the enemy. When mankind fell into rebellion, the authority of God took charge to restore order. The command of God declared that the woman be ruled by the man, who was ruled by Jesus Christ. It was at this point that our husbands became our authority. In the day that we as wives refuse to submit to them we continue a steady walk in pride and rebellion, caught in the grasp of that ugly monster that pushes us to reject the order of God.

One of the most frightening displays of rebellion today is the lack of respect seen in children toward their parents and adults. It doesn't stop there, but can be clearly seen as mankind openly rebels against God in spiritual rebellion. When spiritual rebellion takes root, it will evoke judgment. We cannot resist God and get away with it. To this present day rebellion has stripped us of the ultimate peace, joy, and happiness that we were created to eternally enjoy. The planted seed of deception paved a way of destruction throughout time to every race, religion, culture, nation, and kingdom. The tactics of the enemy are not new. They are only intensified as men and women all over the world continue to rebel again their maker, caught in the deception of Satan.

The Deception of Satan

When God brought the man and woman together, they were not only complete, but they were happy. However, as they strolled around the Garden of Eden together, Eve could not ignore the icy stare of the beautiful serpent swinging from the limb of the forbidden tree. All the other animals seemed so happy for them, but not this one. So a few days later when he smiled with her, she decided this was a good chance to question his previous actions. After a few minutes of talking to him, she felt guilty for even accusing him. He spoke so sweetly while referring to her and her husband, even calling them "lovebirds."

After that day it was easy to talk to him. Soon he had gained her trust. She was totally oblivious to a hidden subtle plan of destruction. Finally when he had convinced her of a hidden potential, Eve believed him. His deception caused her to sink her teeth into his well, planned trap. All of a sudden Eve felt invincible, independent, powerful, and she ran to find Adam. At first her husband resisted the persistent pleas of his wife to "try this," but soon after he gave into her enticing entreats, taking a bite himself. When he bit the fruit something transpired in the spirit realm, and they both fell spiritually!

Immediately they realized that things felt different. Something was terribly wrong in their thoughts and relationship. Eve could not ignore the fact that Adam was no longer looking into her eyes. When she tried to talk to him about it, she was not prepared for the searing heated feeling that enveloped her, now identified as anger. Soon she realized that this was not one of her privileges, but a fault. After that day, more and more negative attitudes began to surface. Adam and his wife felt burdened by this ocean of emotions that seem to have swallowed them up. Surely God would notice the animosity between them, but they didn't know what else to do. So Adam and Eve hid themselves. As a result they lied to themselves, and they lied to God. Through this experience they both came to know another manifestation of God's power. It was that of wrath, when they were reprimanded and put out of the garden to suffer the consequences.

Once out of the garden, Eve wondered if she had ever known Adam (doubt). Each day she found herself under condemnation. Her loving husband at times became bitter and withdrawn (fear). He blamed her for everything that had happened. Eve cried every day. Drowning in self-pity she said to herself, "Surely all was not my fault, why can't Adam admit he was responsible too?" But that didn't help. Things grew steadily worse, with a few good days here and there, but never coming close to what they had shared before. They were both laden down with feelings of hopelessness and depression. No longer was food readily available. Many days Adam had to make his way through thorns, weeds, and briers that now sprung up everywhere, to gather a meal at the end of the day (obstacles).

The time came when it was clear to Adam that being disobedient had changed everything. Even though he had his wife, there were times when he still felt so abandoned and alone. As for Eve, she could no longer ignore the fact that, except for the times when she could please Adam, or allow him to manage the home, there was no peace, or satisfaction to be found. He would sometimes go as far as reminding her that she was responsible for them being in this position (accusation). This was the result of man's deception. How Eve wished she had not fallen for the craftiness of Satan.

As we move steadily through the last 21st century nothing much has changed. Men and women alike are still being caught in the web of Satan's deception. Deception causes one to be caught up in half-truth and lies. Amidst the genders it has intensified into what is considered the ultimate power struggle. For the woman it rages on a battlefield that requires the very lifeblood of her soul, her life, and her family. Everything around her challenges submission because it is where her strength lies. She realizes that submission is crucial to everything around her. It enables her to become the powerful creation that God intended her to be. Contra-wise when she rebels, she becomes like the woman who maketh shame in Proverbs 12:4, "rottenness to her husband's bones."

Sometimes we wonder why marriages are failing, but with the level of rebellion that exists in our individual lives, how can a marriage survive? Marriage is about oneness and selflessness. Referring again to the spiritual bride, suppose the church said, "I do not want to be the bride, I want to be the groom," or "Why do I have to submit to Christ, shouldn't he also submit to me?" She will find herself in the same position as Satan, 'on a one way path to the lake of fire'. When he desired control and power, he lost everything, including his life. This level of distrust sown by lies and secrets is a major cause for division in many relationships. It is fertilized on the bed of deception.

The location of today's hottest battleground is not in Iraq and Iran, China, Russia, or the United States of America, but it can be found in homes all over the nation. It rests in the foundational relationship of the family, through the battle between husbands and wives competing for dominance, fighting for control. Men and women in marriages are ignorant of the fact that, when they stand as a united body, they become the strongest dual force that exists. Their stronghold and constant source of power is the word of God, and when submitted to it, this makes them unstoppable, effectual, dynamic, and spiritually explosive However, because so many have turned away from the truth, they have defaulted in gathering ammunition to win the war, oblivious of the power that they possess.

My people are destroyed for lack of knowledge, because
thou hast rejected knowledge, I will also reject thee, that
thou shalt be no priest to me, seeing thou hast forgotten the
law of thy God, I will also forget thy children. Hosea 4:6

When I was very young, around twelve years of age, my mother told me, "What you know can help you, but what you don't know can destroy your life!" Today man is still being swayed by ignorance, because he fails to heed the words of God. When men and women resist submission firstly to God, they jeopardize their relationship with Christ, and destroy the primary foundation of life and relationship, thereby reaping havoc within the family. Knowing this, Satan has waged an all out war to bring division and total destruction to the marital relationship, the family, and indeed the world through a corruption of divine order. In the process we destroy our children and our children's children unless we continually emphasize the value of obedience.

My mind drifts back to something that occurred in my family. It was a beautiful Sunday afternoon; we were all sitting in the kitchen together just having dessert. The kids were laughing together while my husband prepare for a trip out of town. He took a few minutes to go over a few things he needed me to do while he was gone. We went over every little detail, and Lambert pointed out something that he particularly did not want me to get into. At the time I didn't understand his reasoning and began questioning him.

When he insisted that it be done, I reluctantly agreed. As he got up and went into the bedroom, my younger daughter said to me very quietly, "Mom, daddy will be gone tomorrow, so you could do it your way, and he won't know." Even if the thought had crossed my mind, the words from my little girl's mouth shocked me. She was only about 5 or 6 years of age, but even at this young age she was toying with the guile of deceit. When I questioned my husband that afternoon, I realized I had sent the wrong message to my daughter. Immediately I apologize, and exposed the seed of deception.

Today deception holds a common place in our society. Men, women and children are taught to operate under a disguise in order to satisfy oneself, no matter the cost. This was just one of the many evils that invaded mankind through the devil's deception, and it rages on to this day. Man has had to constantly battle for obedience against disobedience. People like Saul, David, Sarah, King Henry, President Clinton, Billy Graham, you and I, must all live in obedience to God in order to experience victory. There are three reasons why one would reject truth.

1. ***Lack of Knowledge*** - *I am totally unaware of this.*

2. **Lack of Wisdom** - *I know I should, but I don't know how.*

3. **Open Defiance** - *I just do not want to do it, I refuse to accept it.*

*When one is ignorant, she can be shown. If she does not realize that true submission exists, when she is presented the truth, she will consciously make the choice between right and wrong.

*When one is immature or lacks understanding he can be taught. Wisdom is to know the truth and how to apply it to any situation. The woman who lacks wisdom need only ask of God.

*When truth is presented and is defiantly rejected this typifies rebellion. It will also cut ones spiritual lifeline.

> *"If any of you lack wisdom, let him ask of God*
> *that giveth to all men liberally, and upbraideth*
> *not, and it shall be given him." (James 1:5).*

The children of Israel did not inherit the promise land because of rebellion and unbelief. The woman that rebels outright may have only a little knowledge of the truth, but refuses to accept it. Rather, she chooses rebellion and insubordination. When a woman fails to bring herself into submission to God, she gives an open invitation for Satan to invade with traits of stubbornness and resistance. This changes her character, spirit, thoughts, purpose and destiny. Women were naturally created to be supportive, creative, of a humble heart, and a meek spirit, but when she allows pride and deception to reign and rule in her life, she becomes intolerant, disrespectful or dominant, destructive, deceptive, and controlling. These are traits most men detest. When her feminine nature is gone, there is hardly anything left to be admired.

In the life of a godly woman or female minister the enemy will use rebellion as a trap to discredit her ministry. Even though the anointing of God is evident in her life, Satan knows that when she fails to respect or submit to the God given authority of her husband, it not only renders her message ineffective, but her disobedience brings reproach to her ministry. Where does her ministry begin? It begins in her heart first, and then in her home. I Timothy chapter two define the attitude of the woman in ministry. She ought to be an example of holiness in her appearance, dress code, character and behavior, in the presence of her husband and other ministers. She is not to be boisterous in presentation, for she has indeed been given a powerful position even in the church.

With the devastating decay in biblical values, we must show ourselves examples to those women that are coming up behind us. Our daughters, nieces, friends, co-workers, or we will all reach a dead end. Every opportunity must be taken to mentor younger women, everywhere. In addition to accepting their created purpose, young women must be encouraged to seek a relationship with the Lord first, before seeking a physical husband. The relationship with the spiritual will prepare and deeply affect that of the physical.

When we as females seek to be masculine, we walk in opposition to our feminine purpose. It could make a man feel as if he is living with another man instead of a woman and go in search of that which is feminine. Submission is not the demand of the husband, but the mandate of God. We must come to the place of accepting and trusting the perfection of His wisdom. Submission is not an act; it's a way of life. Be reminded that of ourselves we can do nothing, whatever good that we accomplish in this flesh is only as a result of the grace of God.

Rebellion Then and Now

Looking back in time, does it seem it was much easier for the women of old to live by the Word of God? Was there really any difference in the hearts of old compared to the hearts of today? Was it easier for them to be righteous, submissive, women of honor? Did they fight the same challenges and circumstances as today's women? They sure did! The problems and situations vary, but the tempter and his tactics remain the same. Sarah, the wife of Abraham, had her times of temptations, but she persevered becoming a model for today's wives because of her obedience. A woman in control of her emotions, Sarah referred to her husband as Lord, a word that signifies nobility, dignity, and greatness. Like her, many women today, after holding faith for their husbands, children, and other desires of their hearts, give up, or give in. When it seemed that God is taking too long, some lose hope, faith is shattered, and in comes old Satan with the power of suggestions.

God promised Sarah and her husband, Abraham, that he would give them the desire of their hearts, a son from her husband's loins. But as the flower of her childbearing age disappeared, she took matters into her own hands. This became the major cause for a lot of heartbreak. There was the woman Vashti, the wife of a powerful king, living in royalty, yet she withheld royalty from him when he called for her so that he may introduce her to his friends. She embarrassed him with an open show of rebellion by refusing his call. As a result she lost her crown.

Let's focus in on Rebecca, a woman known for her self-appeal. The story surrounding her is one of romance and interest (Genesis 24). Her husband made a decision to give the birthright to his eldest son Esau. She didn't think this was the right decision. She believed the younger son, Jacob, deserved it. Unsatisfied with her husband's judgment, she stepped over the line into rebellion when she led Jacob into deceiving his father, and acquiring his brother's birthright. Rebecca was determined to have it her way. As a consequence, she almost destroyed the lives of her children, and lost the son she held closest to her heart.

There is the wife of Lot who resisted the decision to follow her husband. This woman lived in comfort and splendor in a very ungodly city. When God told her husband to walk away, her heart was crushed. She did not want to go. In an act of rebellion, she looked back and lost her soul, turning into a pillar of salt. The urgency of this message is once again brought to light in the New Testament where Jesus warns men of the dangers of living for the moment saying, "Remember Lot's wife." Consider Jezebel, in the book of II Kings, one of the most hostile women in the bible. Jezebel was a woman in an era of political decline with a very evil heart. She was known for her arrogance and desire to control. Let's look a little closer at this woman whose attitude was symbolic of stubbornness, wickedness and defiance.

Jezebel was the daughter of a king, and she married into another royal family that continually rebelled against God for many generations. Her husband was Ahab. When his father died, Ahab became the king, but his rule was evil in the sight of God; more evil than that of his fore fathers. Not only did he serve and worship Baal, but he provoked the God of Israel to anger. This opened his life and home to the spirit of rebellion which is as the sin of witchcraft. Jezebel now became a permanent part of this lifestyle. She along with her husband held no respect for God or his prophets, and desired to destroy them. One of the reasons why the spirit of Jezebel is reigning in many homes is because of open rebellion that exists in the husbands, the head of the home, and the wife who is an extremely important part of that head. This attitude is feeding the spirit of witch craft that subtly works against the order of God.

The spirit of Jezebel strives when there is an Ahab spirit around. Ahab resigned himself to evil driven by his wife. Jezebel did what her husband allowed. Eventually her wickedness ate like a cancer into the critical structure of her family and nation. She defied God, destroyed His Prophets, took matters of authority into her hands, and revolted against spiritual submission in every way possible. The spirit of Jezebel is still alive today, and hidden in the characteristics of those who resist humility.

The spirit of Jezebel has no respect for authority in fact it minimizes authority. In the home, this spirit promotes wrong order as the husband is made to submit to his wife who has now become the head of the home. In a time when men are encouraged to be passive to a strong woman, many stand on the premise that if the woman gets the work done, then she should be the one to take control. Soon the wife ceases to suggest or advise her husband but tells him what to do and how to do it. The husband that resists her will feel her fury as she resorts to manipulation through rationalizing and sexual blackmail. Most husbands will eventually give in for peace.

When the spirit of Jezebel creeps up on a married woman, it causes her to take on the role of mother to her husband instead of wife. You might hear your husband say, "Look, you are not my mother!" It is because he can sense that overbearing feeling of dominance that mothers sometimes exercise with their children. In the early years a little boy might resist this action from his mom, but there is little that he can do. As he grows older he will eventually reject it, but he will not accept it from his wife.

The spirit of Jezebel is strongly laced with intimidation. Its tongue castrates males and make other women feel worthless. It also seeks to hinder the emotional development of children from growing up by making them dependent upon her. This spirit is not only active in women but also in men, especially those with authority. In these cases the spirit works to hinder anyone that it cannot get under its control. It uses it authority to abuse instead of nurture.

The characteristics of men that attract this type of women are easy to spot. Those greatly affected are usually reared under this spiritual bondage. Not only is he passive and fearful, but he allows his wife to make decisions because he is afraid of taking risk. He then blames or belittles her when the results are not favorable. He will refrain from confronting her even when she is wrong for fear of making her angry. The man that is intimidated by the spirit of Jezebel enjoys being treated like mommy's little boy, or being protect, and out of it. He holds back from taking charge, or walking in divine authority. These men are contented in seeking out and hiding behind strong women especially if she will endure his irresponsibility.

The woman that loves him and desires to see him walk in his position of leadership must pray for godly wisdom to help her husband take his place in the home and God's kingdom. She will realize that this is not God's will for him to walk behind her, but is instead a spirit of hindrance entangled in the workings of witchcraft and sorcery.

Sadly this man will become seated in selfishness, feeling that he is hopeless and not able to walk in the headship to which the masculine soul was ordained. When confronted, he often seeks to protect and defend himself. His emotions often leave a string of broken hearts and unhappy relationships, because while he wants love, he is too insecure to give, or receive it.

Even in this late hour we find women being driven with the same evil heart that controlled Jezebel, Sarah, Rebecca, Vashti, and Job's wife. Satan's assignment for the 21st century women is to use them, like he did Eve, to completely destroy the marriage and the family structure. A recent survey indicated that divorce proceedings are motivated by women in 93% of cases. Women of this era cannot continue to embrace the deception of the serpent. Jesus said, "Come unto me all ye that labor and are heavy laden, and I will give you rest."

Maybe you can identify the spirit of control and manipulation that drove Rebecca in your own life. Or like Vashti you have resisted the call of your husband many times. Could it be that when God instructed your husband to make a move forward, like Job's wife you resisted him, and looked back refusing to walk with him? If you have been less than obedient to the order of God in your life, you can be restored through humility. With His power you can defeat spirits of rebellion, defiance, anger, control, or hindrance. Admonish men, children, workers, church and national leaders to flee rebellion. Stand up, resist the enemy and watch him flee. Rise up and submit to being counted a woman of righteousness, in the name of Jesus!

5

When Not Submitting Is Right

*But though we, or an angel from heaven preached
any other gospel unto you than that, which we have
preached unto you, let him be accursed.*

–GALATIANS 1:8

The message of submission is a very powerful and sensitive one therefore it must be well balanced or it will become ineffective. It is easy for those in authority to say, "You must submit!" It feels good to command and be in command, yet when the tide is turned and the time comes for you to submit in return, it becomes a struggle. Many leaders find themselves reprimanding their servants or workers for things that they have done, things that they continue to struggle with, or things that they need to do. We fail to realize that the obedience that we desire from those under our earthly authority is also the same level of submission desired of us by the Almighty God. Authority is balanced by a humble heart. In fact, it takes humility for one to lead or follow. When we reach this place of understanding then we will better understand when we should or should not submit.

The question is asked, "Is there a time when not submitting is right?" Are we ever justified in going against authority? What if that authority is a Parent, the Bishop, President, or King? Is there ever a time when rightfully, I am not expected to submit to my Husband? The answer is, yes! Whenever any position of authority consciously or unconsciously encourages you to go against God, or demand that you go against what God has written in His Word, you are not at liberty to submit. But didn't the Word say to obey those in authority over you, to honor the King, to submit to your husband in everything, one might ask? Yes! This is true, but when those in authority demand that you disobey God, or brings you in disobedience to God's word then not submitting is right. There is no authority above that of God Almighty who sent his Son Jesus Christ to be the mediator between God and man. Psalms 138:8 tell us, "God honors his Word above his Name." Philippians 2:10, states that, "Every knee shall bow to the Name of Jesus." We are to also honor and bow down to His Word.

There was much activity in the courtyard that day. The entire district of Dura was abuzz with excitement as the most influential men of the city entered in. The image in the front of them was breathtakingly beautiful to say the least. As the whole town gathered around, the city chief took his stand in front of the huge crowd of visitors, residents, and friends. Boldly he opened his mouth and declared, "Oh people, nations, and languages, it is commanded that when you hear the sound of the instruments playing, you will fall down and worship the golden image that King Nebuchadnezzar has set up, and if you fail to comply you will be cast into the furnace of fire." Within minutes the instruments began to play and all the people in attendance, both big and small, bowed in submission to the King's request. As the crowd went down on their knees, the guards who were bowing with a watchful eye noticed that three heads were standing erect. Quickly an order was given to snatch up the culprits and take them into custody. How dare they disobey the command of the King?

When this was confirmed in the King's ear, he went into a rage. Who was it that dared not submit to his command? Without hesitation three young men were brought in for questioning. As they stood before the court of Judges, all was astonished at their composure. There was not the slightest hint of timidity or fear. In fact they seemed content and rather peaceful. Placed in front of the King, they gave their full attention and respect to the authorities who were eager to hear the reason for their apparent rebellion, and allow them one last chance to correct their actions.

There was a hush over the courtyard as one of the boys spoke up. "Oh King!" he said, "We have no answer for you. But if you still decide to punish us for not submitting to your request to bow down to a golden image, then our God will have to take over from here and deliver us. He is willing and well able to deliver us from the fiery furnace and from your hand. And even if he decides not to deliver us, we will still remain faithful to him, and not to any other god on earth. This bought another response from the crowd, shocked at the boldness of these young people. Were they intoxicated, or rather insane to stand up to 'The King?' All turned to see the expression of King Nebuchadnezzar. His face was a mass of anger and embarrassment. He had never had such open rebellion in his kingdom. Surely they had to be made a public example!

With these thoughts, the King commanded that the fire in the furnace be made seven times hotter than its original temperature, and demanded that the three young men were punished. Everybody could feel the heat penetrating in the courtyard. The torturing heat immediately fried even the guards whose duty it was to throw the boys in the furnace. Now their bodies lay still at the feet of the furnace. Then, there was a loud cry of alarm. The young men having been thrown into the furnace, had fallen to their feet and were thought to be dead, but now all eyes watched as the three Jewish boys scrambled to a standing position. Unable to believe his eyes, the King jumped to his feet and reached for his glasses. As he lifted them to his eyes, he gasped again. There, before him, he saw not three but four men walking around in the fire. At first he thought one of his men might have fallen in and now their spirit had come alive, but a second look revealed that his men were still dead on the steps of the furnace.

The King grabbed the hand of one of his counselors in fear, hastily asking him to confirm the number of men thrown in. "Why is it," he cried, "that I am seeing four, I'm I going crazy, I'm I seeing things?" "No!" came the officer's reply, "We can all see four men, and one looks like the Son of God." Without another word the King commanded the fire to be turned off, and he ran to the mouth of the furnace. Once there he called out to the boys to come forth. Surrounded by all the great men in the city, Shadrack, Meshack, and Abednego walked out into the crowd. Remarkably, their bodies were not burnt or scarred, neither was their hair singed. In fact, they did not even smell of smoke. The three boys walked out of the fire with their hands lifted high, praising their God. King Nebuchadnezzar, shocked and filled with fear stood and thanked God for sending angels to deliver these righteous men who trusted in their God. In a public declaration, he acknowledged that no other god was like the God of these boys and he promoted Shadrack, Meshack, and Abednego in the province of Babylon.

Even today many look at these biblical events as simply stories when they are testimonies of flesh and blood men who sought the protection of God. God will do what he did back then today, if we would trust him. This is not the only case in the bible where God sent his angels to deliver his people who trusted in him. God raise up Moses in the very house of the enemy then turned around and used him to challenge Pharaoh to let his people go. Moses had to stand up against authority in the name of the Lord, and God mightily backed him up with divine power. Acts chapter 16 relates the experience of Paul and Silas who were bound in jail because they fail to submit to the leaders and magistrates in their city. But God sent an angel to overturn the entire jail that his people might be free. How many battles can be won, even today, if we as a people would dare to trust God like Shadrack and his friends when challenged to go against ungodly authority. It takes a lot of faith and courage to stand up against the influential or powerful, even in defense of the truth, but when we walk in obedience to God, and take Him at His Word, He will not cease to defend His own.

When it comes to boundaries in relationships, there should not be much that those called to submit cannot adhere to. In everyday life, the role of authority and submission work together beautifully. In the normal flow of a family there is not much that a woman should not submit to especially when both people are aware and obedient to their responsibilities. Situations will arise however that may call for discretion or discussion, others, that might require wise resistance as in the case of a woman I studied with a few years ago.

The lady, (I will call Janet) lived a riotous life before she gave her life to Christ. She and her husband partied and drank together many times until dawn. But one afternoon she repented and confessed Jesus Christ as Lord of her life. After her conversion she no longer felt comfortable with her previous lifestyle, and miraculously the desire to drink and party left her. When her husband discovered what had transpired in her life, he became enraged. Her refusal to go partying with him caused a violent commotion. Janet's heart was filled with fear. One night after she refused to attend a drinking party with him, he physically abused her and lifted her into the car. She had never seen him like this before and subsequently, gave in to his demands just to avoid the fury.

There were those who feared for her safety, and counseled her to go with him in the name of 'submission.' However, after going a few times she felt sick. Finally, when it seems she would rather die than go back to the bars, she went on her knees before the Lord, telling him that she only wanted to do what would please Him. After she got up from her knees in prayer, she felt an amazing peace. The next time her husband asked her to go out with him, she again felt that strong feeling of fear to his reaction, but she decided to take a stand. Immediately, she felt the amazing peace replacing the fear again. This gave her courage and boldness and she told her husband that she could not go because God did not approve of her leading that type of life anymore. Her husband responded loudly, "Okay, if that is what you want, watch what I am going to do." With that he left and was not seen for a few days, but Janet knew that the Lord was at work and she was not afraid anymore. While he was gone she prayed constantly for his salvation. She reported that after he returned home, her husband went out once or twice before he stopped drinking and partying completely. Jesus counsels us saying, "If ye abide in me, and my words abide in you, ye shall ask what you will and it shall be done unto you."

We have all been challenged at some point in our lives to go against the flow or to stand up for what is right and it can be awfully difficult every time. No doubt the three Hebrew boys struggled inwardly about how to handle the situation. At some point they were tempted to just bow down and not make a spectacle of themselves. But, when all was weighed, they knew that they were ultimately accountable to God.

When occasions arise where one is expected or demanded to submit to a request that is against their godly convictions; (not will or desire, but conscience,) it produces a platform that demands confrontation. It is often a difficult task to confront issues. It could be a problem with another person or a negative circumstance within your own life. When we come to the point where we realize that the situation can no longer just hang in the balance, but it must be dealt with, then we will find ourselves at a point of confronting. Most people prefer to simply walk away or leave the situation alone. Yet, there comes a time in all our lives when we can run no longer, it's either fight or die. It is at this point where we are challenged to stand for what we know to be truth. Even Jesus while he was on earth found himself confronting the most respected men in the city as they desecrated the house of God. Additionally, he stood up to religious and national leaders and Satan himself. The Christian life is one of confrontation and submission interchangeably, obedience to God and resisting the enemy. There is no way to avoid it in the course of commitment.

When we think of confrontation, we often think of violent behavior, rushing up to someone, or reacting with rage or anger. Contra-wise, confrontation can be passionate, but peaceful. There are three levels of confronting:

The first level is that of humble approach.
The second is that of insistence.
Thirdly is the act of open exposure.

We see the three Hebrew boys responding in a peaceful manner, but this was not always the case as with Moses, who moved with insistence. In the New Testament we found the apostles constantly in a position that required them to openly confront. Let me say here that confrontation must be approached with wisdom and compassion. Disagreement is not bad, especially when it is done decently and in order, and not in haste. Again I say, always seek the guidance of the Holy Spirit.

When Jesus sent his disciples out (Matthew chapter 10), he instructed them and prepared them for conflicting circumstances. If you find yourself in a place where you are not spiritually received, shake the dust of your feet and leave. In verse 34 he cautioned them saying, "Think not that I am come to send peace on earth, I came not to send peace, but a sword." In other words, situations will not always be peaceful, Christians are warned that, the gospel will cause controversy. Simply put, "If you think you are entering la, la, land, forget it! As the end nears, we will be placed in the position where we will have to take a firm stand for the things of God more than ever before. It will escalate to the point where we will be violently confronted for what we believe. Either we will cower in fear, or we will stand up and boldly declare that Jesus Christ is Lord. Present issues as hard as they may be, are only stepping stones leading to the boldness required for the last days. *He that taketh not his cross, and followeth after me, is not worthy of me, Matthew 10:38.* We will have to come to the point where we are willing to die for what we believe.

There are times when boldness and courage can be interpreted as rebellion. Those in leadership must not only walk in wisdom, but in sensitivity to the Holy Spirit or they could very easily mistake a righteous stand for defiance. Guidance and discernment are key utensils for sound leadership. Things are not always as it seems, and this can be applied in cases of both authority and submission. No doubt Daniel was considered to be in rebellion for disobeying the new laws of the land that commanded him not to pray. I can imagine the minds of many around him saying, "And he considers himself a man of right standard, an example to others. He wants to lead another, when he himself cannot walk in obedience." Again, because many were judging from a physical stand, they were totally unaware that not only was Daniel up against a level of wickedness, but he was fighting a spiritual battle. When we trust God and look to him for wisdom, he will always bring us forth to victory, even if we have to sleep at the mouth of lions.

When the question arises, "What should I do when those, or the person over me, is obviously ignorant of truth; should I follow them or confront? Authority must always be approached respectfully, but nothing is wrong with going to them in the spirit of meekness to pursue a peaceful resolution. Doing something that you know is wrong is willful sin. Through confronting the issue you can bring clarity to the situation or help the one in authority to see the error of their ways. It could also be a mistake or misunderstanding on your part in regards to what you considered to be truth. However, bringing everything out of darkness exposes light. In confronting the issue, errors can be exposed.

Like many wives who have found themselves in this position with their husbands, there were times when my husband made decisions that I had misgivings about. After confronting him on the issue, he agreed, other times he didn't. In some cases we were forced to suffer the consequences, others times we won the victory. We cannot force people to do anything. If you have presented truth, and it is refused then as painful as it is sometimes, we must leave the situation alone and patiently trust God to work it out. The important thing is to use wisdom, be open, honest and respectful, and remain humble in similar situations.

There will be times when confronting a situation will backfire on you, or is taken by the leader as a personal attack. I was at the church of a pastor that I happen to know personally when he called a meeting to deal with another minister that he felt was resisting him in the ministry. After confronting the member for refusing to submit to what was termed, 'The set man of the house', the individual's membership was revoked and he was asked to leave. After the minister left without a word, the Pastor turned to his members and told them they were not to have any fellowship with the person. No doubt there were some that were not comfortable with the way the situation was handled, but neither were they prepared to be termed rebellious or not submissive by going against authority or authoritative demands.

I said nothing to the pastor that evening, but I prayed concerning the matter and when we spoke the next day, I shared my concerns with him. He admitted that he felt badly about the way things had worked out and wanted to talk about it, so we did. We spoke about ways of rectifying the problem and bringing the situation to a reconcilable point. In the face of error, humility enables us to give or receive apology. Leaders are humans, no matter what spiritual level they have been called to. They are open to faults and mistakes even though they are in a position of authority. A minister, president, husband, or king is another human being just like you and I. They are first our brother or sister, and we must love them as such, yet they are not above correction. Your pastor or minister is first your brother in Christ, if he or she is in a fault the bible tells us to restore such a one in the spirit of meekness.

Reconciliation is the heart of God. In the book of Matthew we can find instruction on how to conduct ourselves if there is offense in our heart against another, or if another has an offense against us. If a brother or friend is reluctant to seek forgiveness or repent of fault, it is our Christ like duty to continue to love and pray for the person, to look beyond fault to need. This kind of action is not limited to the religious arena. You will find similar action in a family, where one parent may come against the other parent and make commands on their children not to speak to or be associated with the other parent. It also happens in an organization or workplace where people are afraid to have any affiliation with someone that has been classified as an outcast or was fired.

We must come to the place where we allow the wisdom of the Bible to be the ultimate deciding factor in our lives. In the beatitudes, Jesus encouraged His people to be peacemakers, for they shall be called the children of God. Let us pray that God will help us to be peacemakers. Guard against arrogance or pride that comes to bring further damage. God is not a God of confusion. Whether he directs you to wait, move forward cautiously, or confront the issue, if you patiently await his guidance, you will not go wrong. How do we receive direction? We do so through prayer and constant fellowship? Knowing the voice of the Holy Spirit is crucial, and besides, if we can hear God's voice telling us when authority is in error, then we must be equally sensitive to that same voice leading us to submit, to wait, to stop completely, or to go back and apologize when we are wrong. If he ever seemed to be leading you into what appears as a catastrophe, be confident that he is well able to bring you to victory.

Fear is one of the most common obstacles faced when it comes to confronting. Fear of rejection or being isolated becomes a major factor that hinders one from confronting a person or situation. "What will others think of me, will I be left alone if I stand up for the truth, I don't want to hurt anyone's feelings, or suppose they don't like me after that," are fearful concerns that cloud our minds. Two words are immensely important here: love and humility. 'The truth spoken in love and presented in humility will save a soul from sin and destruction. It is not until we confront and conquer the fear of man that we will be able to confront and conquer demons.

I heard a testimony from the lips of a pastor's wife. I will refer to her as Mandy. Mandy and her husband were pastors of a large, prosperous, and very prestigious church. Over the years she watched as her husband grew in pride and arrogance, neglectful of grace and humility, yet she felt resigned to the fact that there was nothing she could do. It wasn't long before Mandy knew in her heart that her successful and respected husband was out of fellowship with God and possessed by the enemy. She could talk to no one. Everybody loved him, and felt he could do no wrong. The individual who dared to oppose him, were ousted from the church. This went on for years, and her husband got worse. In the home, he would rant and rave and sometimes it seemed his eyes would pop out of his head. She thought of divorcing him, but was afraid to damage the ministry with a divorce scandal. Mandy did the only thing left to do; she found the secret place and wailed before God.

She had come to the point where she could no longer live in deceit, or share in the dishonest acts of her husband. The more time she spent on her knees in prayer, the stronger she felt. It came to a point where she was no longer afraid of the evil conquering her husband. Then the situation came to a crashing halt. One evening, as the devil roared within her husband, Mandy prayed silently in her heart for the wisdom of God. She felt no fear, and for the first time neither did she walk away. Her husband's stinging words of insult and humiliation were hurled at her with rage. In her heart she knew it was time to stand up to the demon that had her husband in bondage, and she sought God's direction. As she stood there before him, he demanded that she submit to an earlier request, which she knew was totally against the will of God.

In the swift moments that passed Mandy was tempted to just give in and avoid a scene. In her mind a battle was raging, but the cry in her heart was to 'rebuke that spirit!' All she could think about was how her husband would react when she rebuked that attitude. Would he be offended? What would be the outcome? When she realized that the enemy prompted these thoughts so that she would focus on the flesh instead of the spirit, Mandy took a stand and readjusted her focus. She knew this was not her husband, but the devil himself, over which she had authority. Right then she felt the strength of the Lord, and with more confidence than she had ever experienced before she looked her husband in the eye and commanded him to be loosed in the name of Jesus. The demon retaliated just as forcefully saying, "I rebuke you," but Mandy refused to bend and again commanded the demon to," Loose its hold!" She watched as her husband's continence changed, his body jerked as he bent over and the demon escaped his body. Soon he began to weep and Mandy knew deliverance had begun.

Mandy began to shout praises to God. The time had come for them to be free. Falling to his knees, her husband began calling on the name of Jesus in repentance. A few weeks later as they shared their testimony, it was obvious that something was drastically different. I had not known her before; it was always her husband in the ministry forefront and on the television broadcast. There was a radiance on her husband's face, and peace in Mandy's eyes. They were laughing and crying together, both were aglow. With tears of joy she proclaimed, "I have my husband back, and he is delivered in the name of Jesus!" As I watched them, my heart was filled with joy. I said to myself, therein is the work of a real helpmeet, to not only assists physically, but spiritually as well.

Mandy did not take authority over her husband, but over the demonic spirit that had him in bondage. That which went against the word of God was subject to her because of the power and authority that comes with walking in obedience before the Lord. Many wives lose out because they attempt to attack the person, instead of taking authority over the spirit that hold their husbands in bondage. It could be the result of a lack of knowledge or spiritual strength. A woman should catch a glimpse of the authority given her over the enemy by watching her husband's model of authority in the home.

> *Some women are afraid to even respectfully confront their husbands.*

Some women are afraid to even respectfully confront their husbands. It may be because of his temper, or for fear of hurting his feelings. She may be aware that he is making a wrong decision, but because she feel she has nothing to offer him, or her assistance is not welcomed, she pulls away. It can be as simple as buying an item. Instead of telling her husband honestly that she dislikes it, she gives in, or says what he wants to hear to avoid conflict, anger, or rejection. She fails to see that she is making matters worse. There are cases where instead of being happy that his wife is not opposing him, the husband becomes hurt emotionally, pulls away from her, or develops mistrust of a wife who constantly gives in to his demands be it right or wrong. When her husband realizes the he has made a mistake, he puts the blame on his wife for not being strong enough to tell him the truth. Her spirit is wounded once again.

There is a time when a woman must take an "authoritative" approach, to reach out to her husband. Not in a disruptive manner, but in thoroughness, consideration, and grace. I often look into the book of Acts chapter five, to the situation that existed between a husband and wife team. Ananias, and his wife, Sapphira, lived in a time when the Spirit of God was moving mightily in the church. There was a high level of faith among the people, not to mention miracles and manifestations of God's power. People began to meet the needs of one another. Those who had much gave freely to those who lacked. This man and his wife were members of the church and blessed with an abundance of land. Ananias and Sapphira sold a portion of their possessions, and brought the money to the church. However, before they came, they had decided together to keep back part of the money. Ananias entered the church, and was questioned by the disciples. As a result of refusing to tell the truth, the Holy Spirit struck him dead on the spot. His wife also was called in and question, however in support of her husband, she lied also, and died.

Even if her husband had made the decision to lie about the money, Sapphira had a choice to consent with what they had previously planned, or tell the truth. She chose to cover up the fabrication of her husband and suffered the consequences with him. When a woman is placed in a position to obey God, or submit to her husband, she must in the final analysis bring herself into subjection to the Word. If she needs help, she can look to the Holy Spirit who will lead and guide into all truth. If she rejects Him, and fights her own battle, her victory stands to be lost. Had Sapphira taken a stand for righteousness she could have saved her husband's life and his reputation as well as her own. Had she yielded to the Spirit, he could have spoken through her to her husband to save both of them from this fate. If Ananias had continued to rebel, he alone would have suffered the consequences.

Later on in this same chapter the disciples were also tempted in like manner to submit to man, as oppose to the will of God. When they refuse they were imprisoned for teaching and preaching about the life of Jesus. However, God miraculously delivered them as they openly declared that it was better to obey God than man. As followers of Christ, upon entering into the army of the Lord, we are given weapons for warfare. Our most essential weapons are prayer, praise, worship, and the effectual use of the sword of the Spirit, which is the Word of God. For the weapons of our warfare are not carnal, but are mighty through God to the pulling down of strongholds (2 Corinthians 10:4). Satan, a spiritual enemy, also has weapons with which he fights. His most dependable is fear, supported by doubt and unbelief. Nonetheless with the power of the cross, love, and a sound mind, his weapons are very easily destroyed.

Until we can identify deception, we will not be able to encourage or protect that which is truth. We must understand that Satan can and will use whomever he can to propel us toward rebellion. It could be a husband, or parents, a boss, a pastor, or anyone who may be an influence in our lives. Nonetheless, we must remember that when submitting causes us to rebel against God, we must not submit. Deception will escalate until we bring ourselves into the obedience of Christ, and walk in truth, righteousness and love. When we come to the cross road of doubt there are only two pathways of which to tread. Either will go left to fear, or right to faith!

The Spirit of Fear

The cold, callous, tormenting hands of fear is a form of evil that all men will experience. I came face to face with fear in 1994 after the death of my infant daughter. Doctors could find no reason why my healthy baby girl died suddenly other than Sudden Infant Death Syndrome, a term associated with death in infants who die while asleep for no apparent reason. The tragedy came suddenly and shook our young family. It was the first time that we had experienced this level of grief. As we laid the baby to rest, we went on to accept the fact that this had happen and we must go on with our lives, but a few weeks later I realized that something else had crept into my life. I woke up one night with the dreaded notion that one of my other children was dying in her sleep. Terrified, I sprang out of bed, and ran upstairs to her room only to find her sleeping peacefully. After that I would awake in the nights, unable to get back to sleep until I had checked everyone to make sure they were breathing. The fear of finding another loved one dead was more than I felt I could endure.

This went on for a few weeks, until I went to awake my son from an afternoon nap and seemingly was receiving no response. Just as I began to panic, he rolled over and smiling said, "Don't worry mom, I'm not dead."

I burst into tears, realizing that not only were my children becoming a witness of my fear, but, the devil was making a fool of me, and I vowed to stand up to him. I knew this was not of God. It was the crafty lies of Satan trying to use what I had gone through to destroy me. He had crept up so subtly after the incident that I was not even aware that I was still fighting a spiritual battle. I soon began to pray and come against the spirit of fear that had found its way into my life. I got angry with myself when I felt I was submitting to fear. Finally, feeling overwhelmed, I went on a fast before God. That's when I had a breakthrough. I knew God had given me the authority (Matthew 18:18) to pull down evil spirits in the name of Jesus! The word became my comfort and strength as I sought out scriptures on fear and spiritual victory. I recalled a verse I had learned in Sunday school as a little girl, "For God has not given us the spirit of fear, but of power, and of love, and of a sound mind." When the thoughts of fear came again, I began to repeat the Word to defeat the mind battles.

Before long, I began to talk about what I was going through with my mom, and now I had added support. Soon I was free, and the stronghold of fear was gone. God later allowed my husband and I to use our experiences to encourage other couples that had gone through tragic events in their marriages. Oftentimes when one may experience tragedy or misfortune, the enemy will attempt to use this situation to inject fear. Not fear as in reverence, but apprehension or dread. It could be a divorce, loss of job, death of a loved one, a mistake, bad experience, or failure.

Many victims of divorce are often traumatized by the experience to the point that they find it hard to form relationships with others thereafter. There is always that fear of allowing oneself to be hurt or divorced again. Satan aims to take advantage of our exposed position and produce insecurity. Fear is the premise of insecurity, a manifestation of doubt. It is one of Satan's greatest weapons of attack on the mind. When man sinned, mankind inherited fear. Because none of our lives are perfect, every life will be affected in some way or the other by situations and circumstances that would make us feel fearful. The only way to deal with this tool of the enemy is to rise above it on the waves of faith, with Jesus Christ as our indestructible surfboard.

The paralyzing feeling of dread comes to kill your spirit, steal your joy, and destroy your mind. Adam and Eve experienced it when they picked the forbidden fruit. Fearful of facing the truth of their disobedience they ran for cover and hid themselves, (1 Genesis 3:8-10). Fear caused a servant to lose all that he had because he was afraid to let go and walk out in faith that he might receive an even greater blessing, (Luke 19:21). Fear is a distinct indication that the enemy is at work. It will overwhelm you with feelings of anxiety, insecurity, and torment. If you allow, it will devour your trust and weaken your faith. Fear strips man of confidence in God. When the children of Israel were brought out of bondage, their confidence in God was at risk. They doubted his ability to supply their needs, and make a way out of every situation.

Fear causes one to hide true feelings, faults, beliefs, or the truth from others for various reasons. A child who has stolen a cookie will hide when he hears a parent coming. That child has considered his fate and in order to avoid it, takes cover. Soon Satan enters with guilt, then regret, until the truth is reveal and the situation resolved. At this point the subject is faced with either freedom or insecurity.

Fear rides on the shoulders of insecurity. Satan will have us hiding our testimonies for fear of what others may think, knowing that our experience would help another to receive deliverance. This spirit is no respecter of persons. Fear causes some of the world's greatest men to lie to avoid repercussion, it fact it was fear that caused Peter to deny Jesus. Fear keeps individuals from telling the truth and suffering abuse for years. The word of God tells us that God has not given us fear, therefore if it is present, it can only come from the works of the devil.

My experience gave me a better understanding of fear, and the effect it can have on an individual, a marriage, job, ministry, and upon the human heart. Just as the physical woman who is overtaken with fear is hindered because of her insecurity, likewise the church (the spiritual bride) is hindered by fear. This will cause her to refrain from speaking out on national issues that go against the word of God. This can be dangerous because she in the voice of truth in the earth. If her insecurity keeps her from walking in the authority and dominion that God has placed in her hand, eventually she loses the power to trample underfoot the deception, fiery dart, and tactics of the enemy. As a result, Satan comes in to kill, steal, and destroy. Nevertheless, because of Calvary the church of God will not be defeated. The victory has already been won. Again, when we desire to understand the spiritual we only need to look at the physical.

Countless individuals today are dominated by fear. They are insecure because they cannot trust their husband or wives, they refuse to trust God, and they dare not trust themselves. Fear will build a mental prison that would cause us to become defensive in an attempt to protect ourselves. It will pull us out of the hand of the shepherd and push us into the hand of the deceiver. We eventually fall for the lies of the devil when we refuse to take God at his Word and simply trust him.

Man's only weapon against fear is the security that comes with the perfect love of God. 1 John 4:18 tells us that "Perfect love cast out fear." Except we come to the point where we face our fear, we will remain in bondage. The thing that we fear most often brings us our greatest freedom. The enemy will torment us until we take a stand and say, "enough is enough"! When Queen Esther (Book of Esther) came face to face with her fears she said, "If I perish, let me perish!" Sarah the wife of Abraham, when she came face to face with her fears said to her husband, "You must get rid of the other woman and her child." When I began to face my fears I said, "Jesus if you go with me, I will go anywhere." The time will come for you as well. What will your cry be? It may be in your marriage, your ministry, situations with your children, or on the job, but unless you allow God to move your giant, that giant will move you. To move forward in victory you must take up the shield of faith wherewith you will quench all the fiery darts of the wicked.

The Shield of Faith

The entire Bible has been given us to strengthen our faith in the God whom we serve, and to weaken fear planted by the enemy. The only way that David was able to go up against a giant was because of faith in God. The same is true of Daniel in the lion's den. Paul and his deliverance of soul stirring messages, and Peter, who walked on the water, were all victorious because of their dependence upon God. It is only when we take our eyes of Jesus and focus on the negative situation, that we are overtaken with fear and insecurity.

Be it fear, obstacles, struggles, or disappointments, betrayal, lost, heartaches, or temptations, when you take hold of the shield, and lift it, up you will quench all the fiery darts that the wicked one has sent against you. What will we do without the shield of faith? How far can we go? What wars can we win? In fact we cannot even begin to please God if we do not take hold of it. When Jesus walked on the earth he constantly spoke of two things, repentance and faith. Faith is demonstrating our belief in the God we serve. We might not see, but because we know who he is, we can rest on him. The reason Jesus spoke so fervently on faith was because he knew the enemy that we would be up against. Except we were able to keep a steady eye on Jesus and believe all that he taught us, we would be devoured.

The centurion in the book of Matthew chapter 8 could not stand by and watch a faithful servant die, not when he knew that Jesus was able to change the situation. He heard that Jesus was coming into Capernaum and he made it a point to meet him there. When his eyes spotted the man, he ran to him pleading, "Lord my servant lieth home sick of the palsy, he is grievously tormented." Jesus saw his desperation and answered, "I will come and heal him." The Centurion knew that his house was not in order, but he needed Jesus to respond quickly if his beloved servant was going to survive.

Again he turned to Jesus and said, "I am not worthy that you should come under my roof, but I believe that if you would just speak the word, deliverance will come. My servant will be healed". He went on to say, "I am a man who understands authority, with soldiers under me, and when I say to one go, he goes, and to another come, he comes. When I say do this, it is done." He was telling Jesus if these men listen to me, I know that heaven and earth will respond to you. If I have this kind of authority as a sinful man how much more you have as the son of God. You are so powerful, all you have to do is speak and it will be done. Jesus marveled and remarked to his followers that this was the greatest display of faith that he had seen in Israel.

You will come up against Goliaths. You will be thrown into furnaces of fire. You will be forced to rest amid hungry lions, but you will be able to stand. Will you be able to confront those that deny the Word of God, or trust God when men are hungry for the destruction of your soul? You will, if you can hold up the shield of faith and openly declare your faith in the Lord God. He cannot fail!

Our fight is never against flesh and blood beings. It is a struggle with principalities, powers, rulers of the darkness of this world, and spiritual wickedness in high places that wages war in the spirit realm. To fight and stand in the spirit realm, you need the Spirit of God. It is he that will dress you from head to toe for battle. It will require that you be equip with the helmet of salvation, truth to girt your loins, the breastplate of righteousness, and the gospel of peace upon your feet. Then he will give you His word, which is your sword, and the shield of faith, that banner of steel that will block the darts of despair that Satan may hurl at you. Now you are ready for battle! Not only will it give you protection, but it will give you the assurance that you need to stand strong in the army of the Lord.

6

The Search for Security

*For we are more than conquerors, through him that
loved us.*

– ROMANS 8:37

The garden paradise of Eden was the most secure world that man would ever experience. It was the atmosphere that he was created to dwell in. The earth with all its beauty and serenity was a symbol of our security. Is it any wonder that among mankind there is such a frantic search for this kind of safety? From the day he was put out of the garden, his heart has longed and searched for this paradise lost. For some people security is a true love relationship, money in the bank, fame, fortune, or power. For others it is great health, or a world without pain, violence, and war. But what is real security? Where does it come from? How do we obtain it? Security comes when we are able to put our trust in God.

When a little farm boy by the name of David stood before a great big man called Goliath, he had only a small stone in his hand while the manly giant stood strong with a sword and a shield. But even though the fight didn't seem fair, David's confidence in his God gave him a deep settled peace. Long before this event, he had been placed in many similar situations. One day a lion tried to attack him, another time a bear came across his path, but he had learnt to stand behind the wisdom of a God that communed with him day and night. He had come to know Him well, and found out that his God could not be defeated. With His help, he had killed both the bear and the lion. This was the base of his confidence. He knew it came as a result of their relationship through the years.

Every challenge brought assurance, that no matter how difficult the occurrences in his life, he was protected by a force greater than his father, his brothers, or himself. Even though he told those around him that godliness with contentment was his greatest asset, and that it was theirs only for the asking, no one really believed him. It wasn't until that day, when he marched forth with God at his side and the host of heaven at his heel. When he faced an enemy much greater than anything he had faced before. When his flesh said "Turn and run," but his heart said "Do not budge." It was on that day that history was written and everyone around him realize that little David had found a definite place of safety. He had come to know the peace that comes when nestled in the arms of God.

As humans being we will all experiences insecurity, that overbearing sense of uncertainty. It manifests itself as a lack of trust, and will jump upon you like a lion upon a prey. Our search for security intensifies as we move farther away from God. When sin entered the heart of man, security was forced to share its dwelling place with insecurity. No longer was Adam sure that what he was doing was right. He constantly questioned his work and his mind was bombarded with the suggestions of Satan. No longer was Eve relaxed in his care, she always seemed irritated and disgusted by the way he groomed the garden. The confidence that she once enjoyed would now come, and go. Adam looked around him; he noticed that their actions were mirrored in the animals. They were all affected by the ultimate betrayal of sin.

> *And the Lord God said, "Behold the man is become*
> *as one of us, To know good and evil, and now lest*
> *he put forth his hand and Take also of the tree of*
> *life, and eat and live for ever (Genesis 3:22).*

Since that day, mankind has never seen a day when life was as perfect as before. From birth to his day of demise, life would be filled with questions that could not be answered and situations for which there were no solutions. As a result mankind would be flooded with moments of insecurity. The word of God from cover to cover constantly reaches out to restore the level of security that was lost, if only we would receive it. From the moment of providing physical covering for his nakedness to the shedding of his blood for a spiritual covering, the security of God was made available to man. Until we accept both coverings, we will forever grope about in our desperate search for the peace of God.

Hardly do we feel the rush of insecurity until that which we believe to be our guaranteed place of safety is shaken or removed. Insecurity comes as a result of uncertainty. Uncertainty presents itself when the future or circumstances before us are not clear or distinct. One might walk into an office for a job interview, the uncertainty of not knowing the outcome breeds doubt and fear, which leads to insecurity. The level of insecurity can determine the outcome. A young man in Central Florida became insecure in his marital relationship when he dreaded his wife was having an affair with his friend. Believing that he would lose her, he bought a gun and ended up killing his wife, his friend, and himself. Insecurity causes mankind to take situations into his own hands. When it seems God is not moving fast enough, or not at all, we move to take control of the situation, usually putting ourselves in a worst position. In the face of uncertainty, our greatest defense is total dependence on the word of God.

The children of Israel whom God delivered from the brutal hands of Pharaoh gives us a clear account of what happens when mankind fail to find security in God. In come doubt, fear, and unbelief. They were on their way to a land of milk and honey, but because of insecurity their journey was stifled. One would think that after the ocean was miraculously parted before their eyes, food sent directly from heaven and the sun and moon divinely guiding their way, the faith of the people would be enormous. But not so!

The Israelites murmured and complained that it was not enough. They criticize their leader and cried to go back to the place where they came from, where the things they needed was readily available. Yes there was abuse and discomfort, but they felt for the most part their lives were sheltered. Yet they became fearful of lack all because their heart was flooded with unbelief. Today, many look at them and say, "How dare they do such an ungrateful thing!" But the truth is their actions model the human heart. I think back to the first year that my husband and I went into the ministry full time. We didn't have the income that we had come to rely on in the previous years and things got really tight financially. It appeared my very sheltered life was placed on hold.

There were times I felt I just wanted to go back to the tranquility of the island life and everything else that came with being at home. I told my husband, "Let's go home, I am not use to this." I murmured and I complained. "This does not feel right," I said, "If God called us into full time ministry, and he is rich in houses and land, why is the Lord taking us this route" I had forgotten my words of warning to others, "What you expect is not often what you get." At that time it seemed as though everyone was experiencing growth and success, except us. Everywhere in ministries, there was the shout of 'blessing and abundance,' no one seemed to be carrying crosses.

One evening sitting in my living room reading my bible, I turned to the account of Moses and the deliverance. As I read, I began to cry because I saw myself right there among the children of Israel. I thought about how we didn't have the abundance of our pass, but God provided for us to the point that neighbors and friends faith was moved. But I didn't feel comfortable having it as I needed it; I wanted it stocked up so I could see it. Bills had to be paid as they came, there was no money to pay in advance and this brought out my insecurities.

The children of Israel were not contented that manna was coming down each morning proportioned for each day. They wanted it stocked up because they were insecure, just like so many of us today. There had been times before when I too had marveled at the hearts of the Israelites, but the truth is, it is easy to walk by sight, however, if we want to get closer to God we must walk in faith. Like the Israelites, I questioned whether we had made a wrong move? Had we heard God correctly, or was it flesh? Nevertheless, the Lord would confirm to me over and over again that he had everything covered, and I was confident until the next tidal wave of trials came. But in time, faith grew and the insecurities began to cease, Praise God! At the end of the day, I had to walk this road that I might be certain of this one thing, God is always in control. Another thing I realized was that spiritual standing and God's approval must never be measured by abundance. I knew then that if I was going to walk with the Lord and go where he wanted to take me, it required that I trust him. Step by step, minute by minute, each and every day!

Have we as a people changed, No! Even though God have mightily delivered us from the bondage of sin, made daily provisions, and performed miracles in our lives, we still complain. We murmur when it seem things are not going the way we want it. We become angry when our flesh is not being satisfied. We worry when faced with uncertainty. Every one of us, just like the children of Israel! Our spirit and flesh continue to play tug-of-war when it comes to trusting the Father, depending on him, and taking him at his Word. It is this insecurity that hinders submission. In order to embrace submission we have to believe that He is who He say He is, and He will do what He said He will do. He has not changed. It doesn't matter what is happening in your family, work place, life, or ministry, God is totally aware of it, and he wants to show you how to get through the situation. However, in order to do so, you must submit your mind, heart, and desires, into his hand.

The more we murmur and complain we slow the process down. The more we resist submission, the further behind we fall. This is why Satan feeds us insecurity, to slow us down, to the point that we eventually stop all together and even turn back, like job's wife. Job's wife could not see how, what was ahead of her was more satisfying than what she was leaving behind, she became insecure, slowed down, and finally turned back and died.

When God gives or confirms a direction, in come doubt, fear, and unbelief. We are soon tempted to take our eyes off God and focus on the obstacles and issues ahead. As simple as submitting to your husband or loving your wife, and even submitting to those that are in divine authority over you, this becomes an issue, because by the time Satan is finish showing you, or pointing out their human frailties and short comings, you have compiled a mental list as to why you don't or shouldn't have to love unconditionally, or submit. Before you know it, you find your self under severe spiritual attacks.

The Attack on Women

It appears that we as women sometimes struggle harder than our male counterparts with insecurity. As very emotional beings, security is very important and sought after by the feminine creation. It is in a secure surrounding that she blooms and blossoms. When God brought her out of the side of the man, the earth was ready and prepared for the arrival of the female. She felt safe, loved, honored, and protected as she walked in the care of her Creator and her husband. Adam was also prepared for all that was given him, including the woman who was designed to compliment him. She was at home in his arm, protected in his care, and found warmth in his affection. Everything that God had created from the plants, to the animals, bloomed in the care of Adam before his spiritual attack.

Women sometimes believe that men are not plagued with issues of insecurity, but that is not so. Insecurity is a human fault, a fruit plucked from the tree of sin. Insecurity has nothing to do with gender, in fact, even animals' experience insecurity. With men, it usually hides in the male ego. When his headship or authority is questioned, this often brings on a wave of insecurity. Our greatest level of insecurity is present when we take our eyes from God and proceed to do what seem right in our own eyes. Security prevails when our eyes are focused on Christ. It is when we focus on ourselves, our human resources, and limitations that we are consumed with fear.

The woman as a divine model can cause major damage in her surrounding when she is controlled by her insecurities. Insecurity in a woman can manifest in multiple ways. There could be a lack of self worth, or fear of not being accepted for who she is. It can extend to the point that she allows herself to accept abuse and mistreatment if she believes the lie that she has no significance.

It all started in the garden with the fall, moving through times and seasons. When Eve got attacked with insecurity, she bit the fruit and gave it to her husband, who did likewise. When Peter got attacked by insecurity he found himself sinking after walking on water. Most President and leaders are bitten with insecurity when the political polls do not sway in their favor, or when they feel they are losing favor with the people. What do you do when insecurity comes your way? Most women struggle with insecurity in their relationships. The level of insecurity increases when she believes that she is not accepted as an equal part of her husband. The male man becomes insecure when the woman in his life belittles and criticizes him because she no longer trusts his leadership. Children become insecure when they lack protection and covering. It is at this point that we begin the search for a replacement, or temporary things to fill the void. This opens wide the door of attack.

With the door of attack now open, the assailant boldly walks in. His hands clutching his many missiles, yet there are some that are more detrimental when used against the feminine nature. They are rejection, idolatry, and selfishness.

Rejection: No one wants to be rejected. The word rejection can be defined as being turned down, denied, snubbed or putting away. These negative responses can hurt emotionally. Yet, even more damaging is when that rejection eats to the very core of one's soul and spirit. In the bible book of Malachi chapter 2 verse 16, we are warned, **For the Lord, the God of**

Israel, saith that he hateth putting away: for one covereth violence with his garment, saith the Lord of Host: therefore take heed to your spirit, that ye deal not treacherously.

Rejection is a very terrorizing act of putting one away. This putting away matures into the act of cutting someone off completely if it is not dealt with. In the marriage and other relationship we see this attitude manifesting as divorce and division. Rejection strips an individual of confidence leaving them feeling alone, deserted, and confused. A woman in the bible that experience grave rejection was Leah, the wife of Jacob (Genesis 29). He was married to her, but in love with another woman. Scripture said that Leah was hated because her husband did not find favor with her.

As a result this woman sulked and walked in the shadow of her sister. She was angry and unsure of herself even though God opened her womb and she bared one child after another, something the other wife was unable to do. Still she failed to win the choice seat in the heart of her husband. Some women become very timid, self doubting, and unstable in their ways because they are in a vulnerable position and feel undefended, especially when the rejection is done by a man she loves. It is at this point that the adversary becomes satisfy because now with her spirit downcast and hopeless he is able to further deceive her. She becomes less of a threat to his kingdom and might stop believing that she is God's woman, the helpmeet for her husband, the caregiver for her children, and a woman of dignity and purpose.

Idolatry: Idolatry is the act of worshipping something other than God. But there is also a flip side that is equally as damaging. It lies in the desire to be worshipped. This is how Satan trapped Eve, and today women worldwide continue to fall in the same spiritual trap. It is natural for a woman to desire the love of her husband, but when she comes to the point where she becomes anxious for his love and attention she is headed for trouble. The desire to be esteemed highly can become her death trap. When she fights to be esteemed on her job, in the church, by her children, among other women, and most profoundly in her home, it could be that she is being pursued by the spirit of idolatry.

I walked into the meeting place of a small church that my husband was pasturing one evening, dressed in a beautiful African outfit. I was greeted by a few of the ladies from the church. "Oh, Sister Kim, you look beautiful," one of the ladies said. Another spoke up, "You look like our first lady." In a wink I heard in my spirit, "Don't digest that!" The warning was direct, but I knew the voice of the Holy Spirit. Right away I said to the ladies, "Thanks, but I am not your first lady, in this church we are all first ladies! But when

I walked away from them, my attention went to what had just happened in the moment. I soon came to understand why this popular title of 'First Lady' that has crept into western churches is so dangerous. Not only does the word of God denounce it, but our worship seeking human hearts can not tolerate it. Because deception is so sneaky, many women of God are oblivious to the craftiness of the enemy, and unaware that it's a setup! It is not as innocent as it seems. First come flattery, then a bucket of pride. For by accepting the acclaim, they are encouraging others to worship them. Jesus told Satan on the mountain, "Thou shalt worship the Lord thy God, and him only shalt thou serve!" The apostles in the book of Acts rebuked the people when they attempted to worship them. Worship belongs only to God. Needless to say, I was never comfortable with the title ever since.

Many times women come together, and because of insecurity in their lives they would find themselves in conflict as one strive to be esteemed over the other. In many cases a woman will race to esteem one friend over the other because one may seem richer, more attractive, or simply more talented than the other. Good friendships have been broken because a woman chose to become a respecter of persons - (Philippians 2:3, Acts 10:54, James 2). In most cases it is not because she really wants to extol another, but she desires to gain attention for herself. Worship of self is idolatry.

Selfishness: A woman goes into the supermarket. As she shops she finds herself having to make a decision. Should she gather what she would like to have for dinner, or what everyone else desires for dinner? The woman who is struggling with selfishness finally decides to settle with the things she desires and hope the others will enjoy it. One of the reasons selfishness is so destructive in a woman is because she is the heart of the home. And if this heart center on itself, it can literally scatter those that it was intended to draw together. Women are givers by nature. She is also a nurturer, supporter, supplier, all of which come under the umbrella that assists her in being woman. When any of these areas are under attack she is spiritually hindered. She cannot truly love her husband and children because all of her attention is toward loving herself. Selfishness is a strong mixture of pride and greed, and allowed to grow it will strangle everything around it.

When an individual is overtaken by a selfish heart, that one can be liken to a pump that has no water. A woman who is overtaken by a selfish spirit will have no regard for the need of her husband. She will not seek to nurture and nourish her children. On the job or in the community, she will use others to get where she want to go, but have no regard or concern for helping others. Life as she knows it is centered on her.

While each and every one of us will experience these attacks in our lives to some degree or another, it is when we allow the little spark to grow into a blazing fire that we find ourselves burdened by the subtle attacks of the enemy. The adversary knows the makeup of the woman, and her need to always feel secure. Therefore, he entices her into rejection, idolatry, and selfishness, hoping to trap her with insecurity. Just like he planted thoughts of selfishness in Eve's heart, then offered her the opportunity to be worshipped, knowing that it would lead to her being rejected by Adam.

When the woman's security is threatened, she will either move away from spiritual safety and allows her emotions to drive her to take control of the situation. This causes her to become unsteady, rebellious, rigid, and hard, fighting in her own strength to protect that which belongs to her. She can also choose to grasp a desperate hold to faith, and it will give her a peace that will open the door for wisdom.

Without faith and wisdom, she may begin to move in the position that her husband neglects, and out of the position the she blooms in, or she may run away to an affair, to mama's house, or the divorce court. All are hiding places from unresolved situations in an effort to cover the loss of her security.

The same is true of men who are driven by fear. Their wives and families are weakened by their insecurity. They may experience fear when they feel they can't fulfill their responsibilities for some reason or the other, or when their ability or position is under scrutiny they run for cover. Hiding places such as dominance and control, passivity or neglect are sought as a result of pride and rebellion. They then unconsciously put up walls between their wives and themselves in an attempt to disguise their instability for fear of rejection.

In a marriage, insecurity presents an invisible wall that neither spouse can see. Pride becomes a dividing factor between husband and wife. She reaches for control, forgetting that she is a helpmeet for him. They cannot see that now they need each other more than ever before. Soon they begin to hide in each other's position for comfort. This is visible in the working wife / house husband scenario, or an extreme case as the homosexual/ lesbian relationship. Not only is it totally against the position of the male, but against the very purpose of God. It covers fear, and presents a false sense of security. Many conflicts that couples experience are as a result of fear. II Corinthians 7:5 tells us, "Our flesh had no rest, but we were troubled on every side, without were fighting, within were fears." Unresolved issues and concerns present anxiety that would cause one to act irrationally. It will contaminate the spirit and feed the flesh. A woman with insecurity, await the day when her husband will destroy her trust, but the woman whose security rest in her faith in God, looks to the hour when she can trust in her husband.

The search for security over the past few decades has driven women to drastic measures. When circumstances arose and it seems her back is against the wall, a woman will often times become very self reliant. She becomes very territorial in an effort to protect that which has become her source of security. She will fight against that which threatens to dislodge her safety net. While defending herself may bring temporary relief in many situations, it can result in her immutable downfall. The stronger her grasp, the greater her insecurity as she strives to hold on to what she has gained through her own promotion or influence. She has been given a divine channel that is set in place for her advantage, and sidetracking this channel will ultimately result in a backlash.

Many women never realize that there is safety in fulfilling their divine mission, but there will be major hindrances and obstacles. It is when we commit to what God has called us to, that we hinder the enemy's penetration into our lives and families. When we choose to remain in submission to what God requires of us, the chances of us falling for the deception of Satan will be minimal. God himself provided an avenue through which women would find ultimate protection through the covering of male headship even before she existed. Unfortunately, today's women reject this because they fail to look beyond the physical man.

Looking inward to self, instead of upward to God is the depth of our insecurity. Before the fall, life was for her enjoyment. Every need was supplied. After the fall, fallen spirits of unbelief attacked her and she needed protection. She failed to look and listen beyond the serpent to the creator. And even to this day, we still find ourselves basing our security on what we can see. For happiness, we look merely at the things around us, and not to the grandeur provisions of God. When our relationships are in trouble, we look to the individual and not to the Savior. Because of this we fall.

I can recall many times when I sought security in what I saw instead of looking to the Lord. I grew up in a very sheltered home where I was well provided for. When I got married I looked for things to continue as they were, and they did. But when I started having my children, I wanted the best of both worlds. I wanted to stay home with my babies, and have all the things that I previously had. I needed to make the choice of remaining at work or trusting God to provide for us through my husband. Because I could not see how we would make it comfortably, I fell for the obvious and I went back to work for a few more years to secure the things I considered would make our lives easier at that time. Like so many others, I based my security in what I had, or what I could see. When I began to understand submission and how it related to trusting God by faith, it moved me to pray. Even though I knew that faith moves God, It was still a struggle to think of leaving security, for insecurity. I finally chose to embrace submission and trust God. It was then that we began to watch God move as He blessed us with even more than we had before.

Insecurity Birthed

Some may ask, "Where did all this insecurity come from". The original birth place of insecurity was the tree of good and evil (Genesis 2). Since the introduction of sin in the Garden of Eden, women were stigmatized as the reason for the fall, and this reproach grew thicker with time. Throughout the centuries, womanhood had been condemned to a place of scorn and abuse. Fathers and mothers celebrated and dance over the birth of a male child, because he was seen as strength, one who would prolong a generation. On the other hand, they cried and comforted each other when the baby was a girl, "What could she do, she couldn't even till the farm, or worst, she might bring shame on the family." As time went on their perception of the female child changed, but this mindset has helped in creating a partition between the male and female genders.

Amidst the genders, they looked at each other; he suspects manipulation and control, she suspects pride and domination, and this breeds mistrust. They often go on fighting without realizing that the problem is not flesh and blood, but that they are constantly under the attack of satanic devices. Satan sought to portray femininity as a shackle or an ineffective expression so that it would be rejected. For a long time he has tried to portray her as merely a possession, a slave, or objects of men. In many parts of the world, and to this very day, women are being abused and stripped of dignity and destiny, as the enemy wages war to destroy their intend, determined to tarnish that most beautiful ornament of her being. She is not accepted as an important and crucial element of the male existence, but rather has been blamed for his fall from grace.

When Jesus walked the earth, he went out of his way to minister to women, aware of the unjust treatment of the feminine gender, which contradicted his purpose for her being. Many times he opposed the cultural attitudes of that day which saw women as merely societal rejects. When the woman, neglected and refused, emptied the perfume bottle on his feet, Jesus defended her. He was fully aware of her vulnerability. Time and practices were different back then. For example, it was the place of women to wash the feet of their men.

Most roads and streets were dusty or dirty, so when the men came home their women were expected to wash their feet, just as today she might wash his clothing. It was a domestic duty. When a woman washed Jesus feet with her hair, what she did was not out of the ordinary, but it was her boldness that the men around him questioned. The fact that she, a loose woman or prostitute, casually got too close to a man of influence was unacceptable. But Jesus was looking beyond mere action, it was the love and humility of her heart that caused her to give everything she owned just to bless him.

When he arose from death to herald the glory of his return to life, he chose a woman to take a very important message to his disciples. "Mary, go tell my disciples, to meet me over in Galilee!" When he stood beside the woman at the well, he knew that barriers would be broken in her life that day. And when he had dealt with the core issues that resulted from her insecurities, she ran with desire, freedom, and passion to alert those around her that her life would never be the same. This was the genuine spirit that he had created to flourish within her, the desire to give sacrificially, and he recognized it. To him she was not just a woman, but like his beloved disciples, she stood as one of his own true servants. She was no less valuable than all the men around her. The fact that she was able to make it to her destiny through restraints and difficulty, was prophetic of the truth, that she would eventually reach and fulfill her divine call and embrace the power given her through submission. Nevertheless before this fulfillment there was much that the Woman would accept. In time she will rise to model the feminine nature of God in beauty, strength, glory, and purpose. She will be totally restored.

He must understand that he will never reach the mountaintop if he refuses to accept her as a part of himself.

This deliverance was not only for the woman, but through her redemption her husband too will find salvation. He must understand that he will never reach the mountaintop if he refuses to accept her as a part of himself – one flesh, one team, one union, one force! When she was brought to the man, God intended that Adam accept her for who she was; a powerful part of the man that would give strength. She was never to be treated unjustly, no matter the circumstances. Nowhere in the Word does it say that the woman was second-hand creation. That ideology was the suggestion of Satan. We see the action of a just God in the lives of a family that lived in the days of Moses.

A man by the name of Zelophehad had five daughters and no sons. At that time culture stated that when a man died his possessions would go to his brother if he had no sons. When Zelophehad died, his daughters, considering the law an unjust act against them, declared the remains of their father. They appealed to Moses. Moses felt in his heart the injustice being done, but because of the law, he was reluctant to appease the daughters. He went to God for direction. God instructed him to give to the daughters of the deceased what was due them and also to change the law, thereby blotting out this unfair practice.

With the rise of the feminist movement many women convince themselves that in order to eradicate injustice they must demand control. But according to the Word, just the opposite is true. We fail to realize that God, who is Almighty, will fight our battles, if, like the daughters of Zelophehad, the right paths are tread, with respect and dignity. Your unsaved husband or son will not be changed through your dominance, but through your unconditional love and humility. The daughters could have fought for their rights in many other ways and either lost the battle or won without the pleasure of self respect. Instead, they went to the man of God and allowed God to work through divine authority. They could have lost the battle and the opportunity to change the law.

This is the reason the enemy is strategically fighting to destroy submission. He knows that in the day that women come to the complete understanding of submission and willingly accept it, the fight of the flesh will be over and the battle will be won. They will emerge with more power and dignity than they can hope for. There are women who are so wearied with belittlement that they reject the male gender of God the Father. I say this after meeting a young, attractive woman, 33 years of age. I will call her Irene. I attempted to present God to her one morning and she flatly resisted it. "I am through with men," she said. She shared the awful experience of her youth in the care of her dad, and her step-dad.

From a very young age she was molested, rejected and physically bruised. In conclusion she accepted the lie that she was unworthy of anyone's love. When Christ was presented to her, she rejected the thought of God the Father, who loved her so much that he gave his Son. She concluded in her mind that God the Father and Son were two males genders that would disappoint her like all the other men in her life. Being unable to relate to this type of love and acceptance, she refused salvation. What Irene was not aware of is that God is not considered Father because of his gender, but because he is our source of life, our originator. His desire is never to control us, but to love us and to give us joy.

There are women under the bondage of control and manipulation whose spirits are tarnished by the selfish acts of those who do not understand true leadership. Irene had been abused and manipulated. As long as she pleased her abusers she was given treats and praises, but when she resisted she was belittled and mistreated. It is only the blood of Jesus and the power of restoration that will one day break through the walls of hurt, pain, and resentment to bring a victory and deliverance in the lives of countless women. This healing process will allow many to go forth without passing on the bondage of defeat and bitterness to others.

Even in this age of advancement, our femininity is challenged, and we are forced to fight in a world that makes us uncomfortable, because it goes against the delicate purpose of God for our makeup. It was never intended that the women struggle by the sweat of her brow for food to feed, and protect her family. The very make-up of the male body, soul, and spirit is designed to provide for his family. When the women are forced to carry this load, many times she is destroyed and becomes a victim to failure emotionally, spiritually and physically. Immediately, arrows of attack are aimed at her fragility, her nature, her flesh, her emotion, her value, her strength, to shatter her spirit and rob her of feminine honor. Satan feeds her with lies that she is useless, worthless and never created equal to the man.

If we are going to save our children from this error, we must first teach them the importance of having a relationship with Christ. When we present God's order and respect of authority, they will come to a better understanding of the context of submission. The safest way of protecting our children as they grow is to make it clear to them that when authority demands that they do something that they believe is wrong, or they know is not what Jesus would do, they must resist. Little girls must be taught that they are not expected to submit to mistreatment, or anything that may cause them to feel disgraceful. They are vessels of honor and their bodies are temples of the living God. The same must be taught to our boys.

In times past and even today, when mothers submit to abuse in the name of submission, they send a silent message to their children that this is what submission yields. Some children eventually fall into this same pattern, while others fight against it, so that they too will not fall in the trap. Abuse is not fueled by women being in subjection to their husbands, but women who do not understand the beauty and purpose of submission. When we eradicate submission we destroy authority. When authority rebels against uprightness, it will result in all forms of abuse.

Her Defense

One of the greatest battle axe's available to the woman is the spirit of meekness. Jesus declared on the mount that the meek shall inherit the earth, (Matthew 5:5). A meek woman will move the heart of God. She will be able to speak to her husband's spirit. She will be to him a face of accountability, not afraid to offer him protection even when it seems she is going against him.

I remember one morning as I was serving my husband his breakfast, I forgot to give him the silverware. When he noticed this, he said in an irritated manner, "Kim, how am I supposed to eat without a fork?" I thought to myself, "I know that should be the first thing on the table, but why is he responding in this manner?" However, the Lord had already begun dealing with me about the spirit of meekness, and now I had an opportunity to put it into practice. In a pleasant tone I said, "You didn't ask for one, honey." I wanted to make light of the situation instead of shooting back with some smart remark, it worked. His temperament changed as he said, "May I have a fork please?" "Certainly," I replied, giving him and the children their utensils. "Thank you," he said with a smile.

In my heart I smiled also because I knew he was not just thanking me for getting the fork, but for bringing his attention to his reaction and not becoming defensive. I thought of times before when I would quickly put my guard up, resenting his implication. And other times when I was trying to be submissive but didn't quite understand it, I had responded with a timid apology, in a manner that resembled false humility. By speaking the truth in love and responding in meekness this simple exchange did not become an issue, but an experience that both of us benefited from.

There is a difference between meekness and weakness. A submissive woman should never be mistaken for a weak woman. A weak woman does not see herself as an essential part of her husband's life and will not assist him. She is afraid to face a challenge even though it will aid in his deliverance. In rejecting meekness - God's perfect adornment for her spirit, she will perceive her husband as a predator and not a protector. The power of submission in her hand then becomes a burning ointment instead of a soothing balm. She is unaware that when submission is weakness and not meekness, it will bring depression. Men need, and desire a meek woman. A meek woman is a woman of a gentle spirit who knows her purpose in God and walks in it with humble authority. In the midst of insecurity this is of great importance.

There are situations that may not be as drastic as abuse, but are just as important and require one to wait specifically on the leading of the Spirit for direction. A husband may require that you do not attend a service, or that you accompany him to a place you would rather not be found. Except we depend on God and lean not on our own understanding we stand to be defeated. Who knows whether by not attending a particular service or conference, you may save the soul of your husband?

When Moses was approaching the Red Sea, he knew that Pharaoh's army was gaining ground, however there he was on the riverbank with nowhere to go. He had to wait on God for the next move. The people complained and became angry that he was doing nothing, but Moses still waited for direction. His survival and the survival of the people depended on it. Just when it seemed they would be devoured, the sea opened up and he was able to lead the people across safely. Waiting does not necessarily mean that you should stand still and do nothing but it may require that you wait on the green light of the Holy Spirit before making the next move. He has promised to lead us into all truth, (John 16:13).

There are many who in choosing to obey God have suffered greatly in the flesh. Likewise, those at work and in other positions have suffered persecution for taking a stand. For some, it was an opportunity to minister righteousness to others, even their husbands. 1 Peter 2:19 from the NKJV says, "For this is worthy of thanks, if a man for conscience toward God endures grief, suffering wrongfully. For what glory is it if when ye be buffeted for your faults, ye shall take it patiently? But if when ye do well and suffer for it ye take it patiently, this is acceptable with God." The only time that one should submit to abuse is for the glory of God. In Acts chapter 7, Stephen, a devoted follower of Christ, was stoned to death for the word of God. As the life left his body he cried for the forgiveness of his accusers. There comes a time, when in order to win some, we must sacrifice our very lives, because all that live godly in Christ, shall suffer persecution (1 Timothy 3:12).

The importance of having a relationship with Jesus Christ cannot be over emphasized. Hearing his voice and being led by him can not be overstressed. Our entire lives depend upon Him. Even the smallest decisions must be preceded by prayer. Every sheep must know the voice of his shepherd, or its life will be in much danger. Many times we are bombarded with a multitude of voices. Everyone has a suggestion. That is why it is crucial that we wait for the direction or confirmation of God so as not submit to the enemy. In John 10:4-5 Jesus speaks of the importance of the sheep knowing the voice of the shepherd, but resisting the voice of a stranger. I think of Mandy, she was sensitive enough to hear the voice of God over the voice of Satan. This played a pivotal role in her deliverance. It made the difference between defeat and victory.

The Spirit of God will never lead us to do anything that is against His word. Neither will it question the word of God. This is the maneuver of the evil one when he attempts to spur error or confusion. In order to stand on the word, we must know the word. We must be able to detect error from accuracy. Therefore, study to show thyself approved unto God, a workman that needed not to be ashamed, rightly dividing the word of truth (2 Timothy 2:15). In time, the Word of God will prove to be our safest place for security.

Your greatest place of security is in the arms of God first! If you cannot trust God to provide for you, you dare not trust the arms of the flesh for it will fail you. "Abide in me, and I in you. As the branch cannot bear fruit of itself, except it abide in the vine, no more can you except ye abide in me," Jesus spoke to his people, his church, his bride in John chapter 15. Without him we can do nothing. If he is not working through us, our labor is in vain. We cannot change ourselves; we can only humble ourselves before him and allow him to change us. This is how a woman will then change her husband, her marriage, her children or surroundings, only through total submission to the Lord? Luke 12:32 states "Fear not, little flock, for it is your Father's good pleasure to give you the kingdom." It is the heart of God that we walk in his fullness and our divine purpose, never in fear or uncertainty. This is the ultimate arm of safety, the greatest manifestation of our search for security. I have come to know that when a woman has a husband whose heart is after God, submission is safety. As we become obedient to the word of God, the veil of truth opens wider for us.

God said submit, but when we look at our leaders in their imperfect state, we say, "Surely God doesn't really expect me to submit to this," because our eyes and our trust is on what we see before us. Submission must be our personal decision no matter the situation. Our husbands, supervisors, pastors, or city leaders are not perfect, but Christ is. When your husband is not the leader that you feel he should be in the home, your taking control of the home and everything else will not help him.

Pride, born of fear, will push him in the opposite direction. The only way to combat this kind of response is with the confidence of the Holy Spirit. The assurance and strength that he will give you will provoke your husband to faith, instead of feeding him doubt and insecurity. I have spoken to many women who would prefer to be homemakers, but become uneasy about how the bills will be paid. In fear the women rush out to get things in order. While this may seem logical, it is a deception of the enemy to deceive the women into trusting their worthy actions and not the Lord's.

Just as we desire our children to have confidence in us, Jesus desires that our security and confidence lie not in those that have been given authority over us, but in Him. We would do well to put our men into the hands of the Lord so that God, Himself, can direct, and show them how to run the household, while we take care of things within. They, too, must learn to trust God to take care of their families, and not use their wives as a crutch. In 99% of cases our shortage is spurred by a lack of trust, not in each other, but in God. It is not until we come to a place of resting in Christ that we will be able to experience divine security.

We must rest from striving to get things done our way, and in our time, and submit to God's will and plans. Similarly, those of us who have accepted Christ as our Savior and Lord must release everything to Him completely. We must trust our spiritual husband and walk in faith that all things might be accomplished through him no matter what we see with our natural eyes. Except we come to that place of rest we will not see the kingdom of God. Our uncertainty becomes security when we put our trust in Jesus. We cannot go wrong when we do things God's way, remember the admonition of Hebrews 11:6 **"But without faith it is impossible to please him, for he that cometh to God must believe that he is, and that he is a rewarder of them that diligently seek him."**

7

Expressions of Womanhood

*Favor is deceitful, and beauty is vain, but a woman
that feareth the Lord, she shall be praised.*

– PROVERBS 31:30

There is something about the divine makeup of a woman that is awesomely therapeutic. It begins with the gentle touch of her hand soothing her hurting child, to the tender touch of her fingers caressing the tiny nerves that race back and forth through her husband's body. We can also see it in the creativity of her hands as it beautifies her home. Birthed in the very depth of her heart and spirit, these qualities reveal just a few of the many natural expressions that make her woman.

This nurturing side of the woman is an essential part of her divine makeup and provides an avenue for her to soothe the hearts and souls of those around her. From the physical love of her husband to the emotional needs of her children, she has been divinely empowered to help her family to their next level of maturity. Indeed, she is the iron that sharpens iron.

I often think about how Satan used the feminine nature to snatch away dominion from mankind. His use of the feminine nature was to fulfill his devious plan of domination and control. However, this need not be a reason for shame or disgrace. God has already empowered the woman to snatch dominion back from him. By his grace we will walk in our divine purposes, we will be obedient to his word, and we will overcome the struggles of the flesh. It will happen as we walk in the power of submission.

Welcome to Motherland

I have always felt that there was something very special about the role of a mother. It is no exaggeration that her presence changes the atmosphere in the home and lives of her family. When I was a little girl, I would watch my mom around our home, and she just seemed to make everything come to life. When we came home from school and she was not there, the house seemed dark and empty. But I remember many times spotting her car in the drive way as we approach our house and knowing that mom was home early today. We would not walk, but run the rest of the way. When we got home, the house would be clean, the windows were open and every room was bright. Most of all food could be smelt cooking in the kitchen and there was always some kind of pastry awaiting us. Her presence changed the atmosphere in our home. Indeed, the duty of the mother is one of the greatest responsibilities given to women.

In 1995 after the death of my infant daughter Kymille, I made the decision to become a homemaker. I released my full time housekeeper, walked away from the workplace, and went home. I had toiled with the idea for a few years, but when this tragedy occurred, I realized at that time that at this stage of my children's life it was the best decision for our family. It was a struggle at first, and there were moments when I thought of maybe going back part time, but after a few weeks my husband and children convinced me that mommy's place was at home.

I believe that a lot of women would prefer to stay at home with their children, but are unable to because of financial or other constraints. When the move is one that both husband and wife agree on, this too makes the transition more pleasant. Nonetheless, I believe that God will make a way if this is the desire of our hearts, because it is also his will according to his Word. He will give us the wisdom to properly manage and stretch our finances like the woman in Proverbs 31.

Our children have been given to us as arrows through which to pierce the world. How we handle or value those arrows makes the difference in our life and the lives of those around us. To neglect this responsibility is to walk away from the authority that governs your children. When you fall out of this position, those that are dependent upon you are easily attacked by the enemy and often destroyed. In the spiritual realm the same is true.

The physical gives us an unveiled view of that which is spiritual. In the body of Christ, mothering is much like shepherding. It is very important that believers, especially young ones, are loved and nurtured in the early years of conversion. Even in the work place, young employees who are properly trained in office procedures good work ethics display these qualities for years to come.

In the first chapter of the book of Genesis, God gave a charge to the man and woman to be fruitful and multiply. This means more than bringing forth children physically, but empowering them spiritually as well. In the spiritual aspect the mature women of the church are some of the most treasured members. They are the women that assist in the spiritual growth and development of souls. Their commitment goes a long way in the building of any ministry. Some spiritual mothers are like Martha the sister of Lazarus, busy about other matters that they consider more important. We see this same pattern among natural mothers who chose to have as few children as possible, if any. In the midst of their busy lives children are considered a distraction, having a pet has become more convenient. She is too busy to bring forth babies, to give the time necessary to bring forth young babes to maturity. Mothers who give birth, but find it too much of a challenge to nurse and nurture them to the place of independence can cause these young ones to suffer when cast aside to strive by itself.

To those who want to embrace motherhood, your greatest asset is your godly seed. These godly seeds are sent to make a difference in an ungodly world. It is through their lives that godly teaching and sound doctrine will continue to exist. A mother is one of the greatest forces of influence in the lives of her children. When we think of the way she carries her babies within her body, and pushes them through the birth canal, she is positioned as the gateway to the world. She has the opportunity to pour into her children all the wisdom that she has within herself. Her life becomes an example of grace and humility from which her children can receive and learn. These little arrows, though weak at first, will be strengthened through her devotion. They will then move forth to birth and empowering other arrows as they mature. It is for this reason that we as mothers must make every effort to do all that we can to take full advantage of the role and responsibilities of motherhood.

As with any commitment, there will be distraction. How you handle it determines the outcome. Satan, as a deceiver is aware of the potential of the seed, and he fights tooth and nail for the lives of children. One of his schemes is distracting the young mother during the most impressionable years of her child's life. So many mothers painfully look back over their youthful days, and realize that when their children needed them most, Satan had them caught up in things that were of less importance. Nothing moves a mother's heart like seeing how much her young children desire and need her. Their greatest desire is her loving attention and the security it brings. They trust her to properly cover and equip them until they are able to walk alone. Without proper covering, children are left open to attacks of every kind. By the time many of these children are young adults, weeds of insecurity have taken root in their vulnerable hearts. Seeds of bitterness and resentment rushed to secure its place.

We look back at the many times we walked away, leaving someone else to take responsibility for loving, teaching, and covering these little buds, unaware of the damage being done. Years later when the damage becomes evident, we are overwhelmed with guilt and secretly wish for a second chance to do it all again. We watch the mistake of one generation as it passes down to another, and it hurts, because now we see and understand that the issues at hand are deeply rooted. Oftentimes, a mother can look back and identify when and how the hurt was actually sown. At this point, there is still hope because the seeds of God's word can take what was intended to bring defeat and bring victory for generations to come. That is why it is so important to nurture and train up a child, for when they are old they will not depart from the instructions of their youth.

Young women must be admonished to treasure the calling of motherhood. Married, widowed, or single mothers today must understand the awesome responsibility that they have to God for the rearing of children and training of the young. Too often careers and dreams are placed in the forefront and highlighted as the most important accomplishments in a young woman's life. While these things are good in its place, most women find that the temporal things of life can never bring fulfillment. Neither can it replace the joys gained through embracing motherhood. Motherhood is not only a blessing, but a divine calling.

I first recognized the face of motherhood at the age of four, when my mom gave birth to my little sister. It was beautiful. She cared for her so tenderly, and with obvious joy. To make me a part of the celebration, and to keep me occupied, Mom bought me a baby doll so that I could play 'mommy' at her side. When she washed her baby's clothing, I washed mine too. When she fed her baby, I would feed mine. Soon her baby grew, but mine became worn out and replaced. Very early in our lives, my mother often told my sisters and I that a wedding comes before the baby. Without any brothers, there was no one to play the part of the dedicated husband, so when I played with my dolls as time went on, I remembered these words and would imagine that my husband was at work, while I stayed home to care for the baby.

Over the next eight years my dolls were my pride and joy. As long as I had them, I needed nothing else. It was a wonderful childhood experience that I treasure to this very day, but it didn't come near the joy that enveloped me when I got married and gave birth to my first child. I had always longed for the day when I would have a child of my own, and as the doctor placed him in my arms, there was a sense of joy and fear. Fear of the reality and immense responsibility of having this little life dependent upon me, but joy in knowing that God had given us this little miracle. I remembered, later that night after the nurses had left us alone, I lifted him up to the Lord, asking for wisdom and direction in meeting the needs of this child, the first of four angels. I needed the help of God to train him up so that he could become a vessel, meet for the master's use. As the days turned to months, and the months turned into years, I came to understand that being a mother is more than a heart's desire, it's a place of immense responsibility.

I was in the city of Jacksonville, Florida for a speaking engagement when I spotted the headline in the morning paper. The faces of two men and two women were lined across the page under the sub-topic "Do you know who is watching your children? The newspaper article exposed the arrest of the four, accused of physically and sexually abusing local children in a daycare center. This shocking discovery alone shows the urgent need for mothers to return to full time care of their children. More and more mothers are coming to the realization that they are indeed the most important example in the lives of their children. It is a fact that in order to sufficiently affect their lives, parents must be there, and become totally dependent on God and his Word for guidance.

In these days in which we live, evil is on the rampage to snuffout the innocence of our children. Never before has it been more urgent for parents to make an investment into the training and nurturing of their offspring. There is no amount of material gain that can ever be compared to the visible presence of a mother. Like everything else in life, motherhood requires time. I look at each of my children and understand that each one is different, and requires something different from me. I must find time for all of them both collectively and individually. It never ceases to amaze me how much they desire their own private moments with me, and how it affects them. My youngest daughter values personal time to cook or make crafts together. My older daughter prefers outings, and my son, just want to be loved on and relax with quiet talks. As they mature, their needs changes and so must I.

Armed with submission and intercession the woman of God is unstoppable.

A woman needs time, not only for nurturing, but for preparing herself to care for her family as a whole. The ministry of motherhood was intended to be a full-time position which demands tenacity, submission, and profound faith in God. Personal time is needed to prepare her spirit, quiet moments in which to meditate on keeping her spirit pure. This is done through devotion and prayer also known as intercession. Intercession comes from the root word "inter" which means to exchange, and "cession" which means to surrender, to resign to. Together the word becomes a powerful expression of getting into a deeper place with God. Armed with submission and intercession the woman of God is unstoppable. As she go before God in prayer, she will lift up her children, their plans, schools, friends, and everything else that is associated with their lives. This gives her a peace that she can rest in, knowing her children are secured in the hands of the Lord. Then there is the time needed to bond with her babies. Motherhood is a lifelong commitment. Whether they are in the cradle, in college, or living independently, a child is always in need of motherly attention. Just being confident that she can help her children when they need her, is a request fulfilled.

When a mother loves her children with a kind and committed heart, they become as beautiful as she is. Somehow, I always felt motherhood came naturally to women until I met Joanne (not her real name). I received her call late one evening. "I just need someone to talk to," she said, "before I take my life." She went on to say how situations in her life and home were getting worse, and she felt as if she couldn't take anymore. I could hear the voices of her children in the background, and we talked a while about how her decision would affect them. She replied, "It's for the best, I have nothing to offer them, and besides they will get over it, after all I did." At that moment I realize that she was dealing with deep, agonizing wounds that would only be expelled through the divine healing of the Holy Spirit. As I prayed silently for the leading of the Lord to minister to her conscience, her life story came pouring out. She grew up never knowing her father, in a home that was cold and unloving. Rejection and neglect had become permanent fixtures that she knew well. As she matured she was forced by her mom to give her body to various men who passed through her home in exchange for money, but to her it appeared as love. She was afraid to resist for fear she would upset her mother. Her mother's word rang constantly in her ear, "I hate you! "You've messed up my life!" Soon Joanne came to believe these words.

As the middle of three children she craved attention, careful of every opportunity to do anything or go anywhere just to be accepted. She said to me, "All I wanted was for my mother to love me like she loved those men." Soon, like her mother, she began searching for love in the arms of men. Finally, after much frustration, fighting, marital unfaithfulness, and regrets, her husband took the children and walked out. Joanne was devastated, and her every moment was spent trying to win him back. But even after they returned, Joanne was not happy and would often abuse them verbally. Soon she realized that the abuse of her mother was being repeated with her children. This troubled her, and she tried to understand why she never felt the motherly feelings other mothers spoke about. There was never that bonding with her children. She didn't know how to love them, or anyone else for that matter, and now she just wanted to die. That night Joanne received a breakthrough. Over a period of time, tears, and ministering of the word she was able to stand on her feet again. To date she is reunited with her husband, and the Holy Spirit is renewing the joys of motherhood.

Many women find themselves in this predicament, in a world of confusion, they stumble without a foundation. No one showed them how to love, and because of this they don't know how to love in return. It is the ministry of womanhood that teaches the younger women how to commit to expressing herself as a mother. When God created Eve she was create to mother the earth. As she helped her husband to care for and nourish the things that God had created, she saw firsthand how loving care brought forth growth and maturity. She basked in the way her husband cared for her, and how the Father cared for them.

Although Satan tried to distort it all, God had made a way for Eve to continue to care for her own, just by submitting herself to his will, and allowing him to show her how to be everything he designed her to be. The same is true today. Although we live in a totally different time, where it is seemingly more and more difficult to rear up godly children, God is still the same. If we as women will allow the word and Spirit of God to direct us, and become humble to his will, God himself will equip us with what we need to be the mothers that are needed for today's generation.

Like Joanne, many young women have not been afforded the parental example that they needed. We live in a time when it is seemingly not important for a woman to just stay home, or spend the time that is needed to foster and prepare children for the times before them. I believe that situations have not changed, but people have. We are still faced today with all the good and evil that existed from the beginning of time, but the faith and submission in many lives is not the same. Children still need care. Homes must still be provided for, and fathers must still till the ground as wives continue to be a helpmeet for their husbands. All of these facets need to be in place for the systems to flow in the home. A lack of any one of these could cause a disaster.

God is aware of this, and the spirit of God continues to strive with mankind, desiring to show us how to live amidst the deception of the enemy. However, in a fallen state, we continue to resist and fail. Our lives are at stake and so are the lives of our children. When we reject God's plan, we cause his word to be blasphemed. A former schoolmate of mine, after having her first child desired to be a full time mom. At the time both, she and her husband held good jobs, and didn't see how they could live on one salary, but they prayed for guidance. Amidst criticism, they decided to make the sacrifice and stepped out in faith.

As the child grew older, she started a small home business to assist her husband with the financial needs of the family. Things were really difficult, and many encouraged her to go back to work, but she refused to place her child into someone else care. Within a few years God blessed the business so much that the profits fully supported the family. Today, she is happy and financially stable. When we are obedient to God, blessings will flow. Many look at the obstacles and challenges, and become fearful, but when we trust in the Lord, and allow him to direct our path, we will eventually reap the harvest.

As women desirous of the will of the Lord in our lives, we must take a stand to do all that God has called us to do, and be. I know that this is a very controversial time and topic, but it is crucial to our families that we be faithful to the word of God. There are many women who desire to raise their children themselves, but because of numerous situations beyond their control the decision becomes a very difficult one. There are single and widowed women with children, or a woman whose husband may be disabled, and she may have to support the home temporarily. Yet, even in these cases God is able to grant the desire of the heart. God is able to remove that which can hinder, to enable us to walk according to His Divine Will.

There are also women who want to be home with their children and also fulfill dreams of acquiring assets through business and investments. This doesn't mean that she cannot seek to realize these dreams. God has blessed women with creative talents and abilities and he intends for her to use every one. With the level of technology that exists today, it is becoming more convenient for individuals to establish home businesses and work from within the home. It can become very beneficial for a mother with school aged children, in that she is able to be at home with her children and at the same time assist her husband financially while working. Having the opportunity to also fulfill her dreams can be emotionally rewarding. Women like Martha Stewart capitalized on God given talents that has greatly aided many women in expressing themselves at home. What is important in the midst of our pursuits is taking steps to ensure that we are not distracted from the central or ultimate focus, which is our family. She must be careful not to allow exteriors to consume too much of her time and attention. Let every move be preceded by prayer and the request for wisdom. I would encourage young women to further their education, and enter into the job market at will. However, when we chose to be married and bear children, we must be prepared to sacrifice our needs and wants for the betterment of our family. Upon accepting the responsibility of marriage and then motherhood, everything must take second place behind what is most important for her husband and children.

Some wives face the challenge of a husband who will not hear of his wife being a homemaker. This situation can be frustrating and disappointing. It will, like all other disagreements, bring division in the marriage relationship. Even though it is the will of God for the woman to stay at home, this woman must respect the position of her husband, and entrust the situation to God, allowing him to work it out for her. There are times when victory may be immediate, other times we will be placed in the position to patiently wait on God. I encourage mothers to train your sons for the responsibility of headship that lies before them. Impress upon them the responsibility of the husband to care for his family and home.

There may be areas in both your lives that God is working out. Our prayer must be, "Lord, give me the wisdom in making decisions according to your will for my life." This position cannot be taken lightly if we will reap godly results. Just as important as the physical mother, is the spiritual mother or shepherd. Many young women may not have a mother who can minister to them, but God has place in the body women who are called to minister to their blood children as well as others. As with adoption or foster care, children are at times placed into the hands of guardians who will love and instruct them in the ways of the Lord. In our spiritual lives there is also a need for guidance from those that are mature in the things of God. Shepherding or spiritually mothering holds the weaker one steady until he or she is able to walk on his or her own. God has placed into our hands vessels to be molded into lives that will change generations. When you offer a child your hand it may last but for a moment, but when you offer your heart, it will last a lifetime.

Making Your Home a Haven

Walking into a home that is beautiful physically and spiritually is like a therapeutic healing session. A dwelling place that is fresh, clean, and nicely decorated, and where you can sense peace and tranquility is extremely welcoming. This idea is expressed by many new home developments who open the doors to a model homes in order to give home buyers of taste of what can become their own. These houses that are put together by manufactured homemakers, present a sanctuary that tugs on the emotional heart strings of shoppers. But every home can look like a model; all that is needed is a homemaker.

A home will tell you a whole lot about the people who live there and each room will give you insight into the life they lead. Home is the place we long for, the place we feel most relaxed, where the family runs to, and the mother feels assured. Her loving heart in the home nurtures the spirit of those who enter, dispersing warmth and happiness that covers like a blanket of peace. The obvious special touches not only create a mood of acceptance, but a feeling of welcome. This brings true appreciation for a homemaker.

Many homes today are in shambles because they lack a homemaker. Being the one who maintains the home, and keep things in order, it is a major hazard to run any home without her. Even model homes, though empty of occupants, must be cared for on a regular basis. The position of a homemaker is more than a career; it is a means of survival for every home. Like other career choices, the woman who chooses to be a homemaker must give both time and commitment to ensure daily success. The more time and devotion you put into it, the better the results.

What does it mean to be a keeper at home? This very vital position is demonstrated by many women of the bible. The woman in Proverbs 31 focuses on a model wife and mother. There was a time I envied the Proverb 31, because she apparently got everything done until I realized that she is a standard for women to follow. She was a woman of great patience, emanating virtue and faith. She was dedicated to the upkeep of her home, the rearing of her children, while under girding her husband and supervising her workers.

The average woman today spends less than 1/3 of each day attending to the needs of her family and home.

Traditionally, women in that day and time were deeply committed to maintaining and establishing their homes. The normal duties of these women were drawing water, grinding grain, spinning wool, weaving fabric, sewing clothing, laundering garments, preparing meals, and taking care of the needs of their husband and children. Social responsibilities included hosting travelers, and guests with food and rest. Spiritual responsibilities found mothers shaping spiritual values in their children, preparing their families for worship, and taking them to the temple. These routine tasks were a woman's top priority. We can see these things witnessed in the lives of women like Dorcas, Lydia, and the sisters of Lazarus. The virtuous woman did all this and more. She went beyond the call of duty. Her industrious and creative heart was centered on her family and household. So blessed was her family that they rose up with grateful appreciation, because of her commitment. The principles practiced with her home also aided her economically. It began within her heart, to her home, and finally to the outside world.

There is an urgent call for committed homemakers today. The home is like a manufacturing plant that sets a course for every member of the family. Sadly, the average woman today spends less than 1/3 of each day attending to the needs of her home. Most of her time is filled with other commitments. This makes it very difficult for her to meet the vital needs of her family.

On an average most women get about 6-8 hours of sleep. Another 8 hours is allotted to work or career, not to mention the hour that spent commuting to and from work. When she finally arrives back in her home it is now early evening, however her real work has just begun. She has to cook, clean up, and do laundry or other household chores. In most cases, tidying up her house has to wait because she is tired or something else has taken priority over that chore. She might have an hour to help kids with homework or sort through mail, before retiring to a bed that she did not have time to make up that morning. On the daily clock it is now late in the evening and she begins to prepare for the next day, put the kids to bed, or maybe entertain an occasional friend or neighbor. If she has extra commitments such as church activities, study classes, or civil organizations, PTA etc, this is taken from the hours in the evening or sleep time. When she finally falls next to her husband, intimacy is the last wish on her list. If this pattern continues, her marriage or the relationship with her husband will pay the greatest price.

Even when it appears everything is well, the working woman knows her life can very easily spin out of control. Having a full time career may be modern and self satisfying but it carries a very cancerous price tag. The weight of this price tag can be seen in statistical reports that are reflective of home life. The book of proverbs tells us that, "The rod and reproof give wisdom, but a child left to himself bringeth his mother to shame, (Proverb 29:15). How many children suffer miserably when a marriage fails? It doesn't end there, how many marriages are destroyed by the added stress in the home, caused by individual loses, external pressure, and dilemma of a home neglected. Indeed, the very fabric of our nation is shaken because of neglect and rejection in so many vital areas of our lives, especially the family. I would like to share a letter that I received from a young woman whose personal experience is indicative of this conclusion.

Dear Kim,

I grew up in a very sheltered home. We were not millionaires, but we never seemed to lack anything. My mom and dad worked in very influential positions and so as a very little girl, I was always used to having a housekeeper around our home. When I got up in the morning, I left my room a mess, but when I got home it was always clean, and food was cooked, I never got involved. As most young women do, I desired to get married and I did. My husband and I went on a beautiful honeymoon, given to us by my parents as a wedding gift. It seemed everything was perfect until we came back home to live as husband and wife.

I will never forget our first meal. I wanted to cook something simple but even though the menu was simple, the dinner was a disaster. My new husband said to me "That's alright honey, let's go to my mom's for something, or we can eat out. Things will get better." The trouble is it never got better. The truth was that I didn't know how to cook. In my home, I had never learned to cook, clean, iron, or anything else, like most young girls did. My mom never told me it was important for me to learn these things. I responded to my husband pretty much the way my mom responded to hers, and it drove a wedge between us.

I had graduated from college with honors and got a well paying job that I was good at. I moved up the ladder of success quickly, but when I got married I found that none of these things prepared me for marriage. My husband soon began to go by his mom's house quite often to get our dinner and to relax. He said it was hard to relax in a dirty house. Eventually, I did what I thought was best, I got a housekeeper. Then things really began to fall apart when I felt the young housekeeper was becoming attacked to my husband. I had to act quickly, fearing I'd lose my marriage, so I fired her. For a while, I really tried to commit to keeping things in order, but I couldn't.

After a few weeks I decided to hire another housekeeper, but one that was much older. The lady that came into our life was not just a helper, she was an angel. She not only kept my house, but she taught me how to cook, clean, bake, care for my husband, and fight for my marriage. This Christian woman poured herself into me, and showed me what it was to be a godly woman. My good looks didn't do it, or an active sex life. It was the power of God working through this woman to teach me what I desperately needed to know.

Your recent article that stressed the importance of training our children in the right way really hit home. It brought tears to my eyes as I thought of how close I came to losing my marriage. Mothers today must be encouraged to teach their children the ways of the word. Too many young girls are going down the aisle with one thing on their mind-sex. Like me, they don't know how to cook, clean, keep house, or keep a husband. In many homes, parents are pre-occupied with building careers, going to school, working overtime, or rediscovering their youth to teach their children how to be responsible adults. We say the divorce rate is climbing. Here lies the major problem. We are running after the wrong things and we are not giving our children the right examples to follow. Daddy is never home, and fails to take care of the family so the sons grow up to do the same thing. Mom comes home too late to cook or clean, the house is filthy and food is ordered out. When our daughters get married, they continue what they have learned.

My parents were good moral people, but they were not Christians, so they were unable to impart God's word to their children. As a result, I was never interested in Christianity in my youth, but it is amazing how God reaches us through the dark times in our lives, when things take a turn for the worst. I thank God I acted quickly, or I too might have been another statistic. Today I have two sons and a daughter, whom my husband and I are teaching responsibility, accountability, honesty, and godliness. I will not allow my children to grow up as I did. As a homemaker I have made some major sacrifices, but it is worth it. My husband is now a Christian and our marriage continues to grow from strength to strength. To God Be the GLORY!

The price of neglect and absence
Is but a down payment,
There's no way of knowing the cost,
For money can't conquer the hearts that are broken,
Nor buy back the souls that are lost.

There was a time in my life when I felt I could do it all - the duties of a wife and mother, the homemaking, and balance a career at the same time. Finally, I realized that the world of 'super woman' was a fantasy. I found myself struggling to get it all done properly, and as a result my family suffered, as well as myself. Many evenings I came home so exhausted that I was too tired to enjoy my children when they came running to mommy just to get a hug or some attention. Having a housekeeper helped, but this is not what I envisioned as a committed wife and mother. I would tell my housekeeper, just entertain them for a few minutes so I can settle myself and then I will romp with them awhile. I wanted to manage my home, care for my children, and make them my top priority. Finally I made the decision to commit to my family full time. The minute I made the decision, I knew I had done the right thing. I refused to let my mind reflect on my very comfortable salary, or all the other thoughts that clouded my mind. Believing that this was God's will for my life, and having made up my mind that there was no other choice, I moved forward in faith and obedience. What a relief it brought!

The change in my home and family as a result of this decision was amazing. There was a change in my husband, my children, and myself. We were all more relaxed; we became even closer, and really began to enjoy life as a family. We ate dinner together most evenings, before running down to the beach or just having some fun. To my amazement, our financial situation also improved. Many husbands have to stop at the donut shop in the morning to have a cup of coffee, but when his wife is a homemaker he can get a better meal at home or spend a little time with his family at breakfast, and save the $400.00 that he would spend over the 365 days of the year on the beverage and a donut. A year later when we had settled into this new lifestyle God began using us to minister to other marriages in our nation. This is something I knew could not have been possible if I was still on the job.

Even though many may not admit it, balancing a home, motherhood, a marriage life, and full time job is almost impossible. It is difficult for a woman to fill all of these positions simultaneously, and be successful. Something or someone will have to suffer and in the majority of cases, it is the home. The home, which encompasses her marriage, her family, and her soul, bears the brunt of this loss. Managing a home is a full time business venture, and a woman needs time to prepare herself for this task like any other. A good night's rest, a strong body, and a relaxed mind are all required for the job.

As a homemaker, her day should always begin with time in prayer. It may be in the wee hours of the morning, or after the children are off to school and her husband off to work. This puts her in a frame of mind that will set the pace for the rest of the day. It is during this time of prayer and devotion that she brings everything that concerns her before the Lord, including her husband and his job, her children, their friends, school, and teachers. She would also pray for strength and wisdom and other needs in her family, church, community, and nation. When this is done she can move about her home with a happy heart, putting things in order. She may want to share an encouraging word or prayer with a neighbor in need. She has time to take a baked good or bowl of soup to someone that may be ill or shut in. Spending time with a good friend is now possible. She might even decide to have lunch with her husband.

By mid afternoon when the children come home from school, she is there to hug, and hold them, enjoy a game, favorite book, or share time together in the back yard. Time is available to teach her daughter to cook, or share a valuable lesson with her son. The average wife and mother is not afforded this luxury today. She finds herself running home after a day at work to cook, clean, and attend the needs of her husband and children. In this fast paced century, fast-food chains are fast becoming the family kitchens.

Oftentimes she finds her moments hindered by much anxiety, overwhelmed by added commitments that are hard to handle, causing her to become agitated and disgruntled. Her husband and children come home to a dirty house, because she doesn't have the time to properly clean her home. There is no time to relax as she strives to fill the few hours left in the day with overdue chores. If she wants extra time to enjoy a favorite magazine, a relaxing bath, a quiet moment, a minute with her family, it would not be possible without leaving so many other things undone. Her family has to eat out more often or settle for simple meals thrown together because that is all the time her day would allow. She needs time, but she cannot afford it on this schedule.

We must get back to the place that God has design us to bloom in. Over the past decade, women have proven to themselves and men that they have the potential to be anything they want to be, from clerk or plumber to corporate leaders. We have taken over nations, churches, and more, however it has robbed us of many more meaningful things that have been entrusted to our care. Women want to begin outside the home and work their way in, but the cost is more detrimental. They figure that when they have obtained their dreams and accomplished goals they would then retire to their homes. However, for most women by this time the children are gone, and there remain hardly any relations in the marriage, if any. When we begin within our homes, we can build firm foundations for our children, and our marriages. Before we know it our children are grown up and beginning families of their own. The nest is not empty, but open to love and laughter. When we begin from without, we attempt to create a forest with mature trees that may soon die from lack of strong roots or firm foundation. In the end we lose both the tree and the potential seed.

Our future and that of our family and nation depends upon it. One may ask, "If women begin to go back to the homes, how will we fill the jobs and positions that they have created?" Not only can our men move into these positions, but so will our sons. We need not pray for the help of our husbands in the home, but that they will go forth and fulfill the role that God has assigned to them, to support their families by the sweat of their brow. Additionally, unmarried women, single or widowed mothers who must work, can fill positions in the job market. For this reason it is good that young women be encouraged to equip themselves educationally, while being trained to accept the position of a wife and mother. Upon completing their education, they may enter into the workforce. Here, they have an opportunity to pay debts and even prepare themselves for the time when they will move on to becoming supervisors of their own homes and helpmates to their husbands. In the course of reality however, husbands die, walk away, become sick, afflicted or more. Therefore it is good that a woman prepares herself in life, that should it become necessary, she will be able to support herself and her family.

Many wonder if this will push us back, causing us to forfeit all that women have struggled to achieve. The answer is definitely not. We have tried it both ways, now we can look back and make a genuine assessment. We can look at the mistakes of our mothers and grandmothers, as well as our own and see where we have gone wrong. Then we can look to God's divine plan and the world around us and reach for the better. This time it will not be by force or obligation, but willingly and by choice. Choosing that which is best for ourselves, and the ones we love.

The woman will be returning with a renewed vision to make her home a haven. Her motivation will stem from the sheer satisfaction on the faces of her husband and children, as they come home to a clean home, well prepared meal, and a companion void of the pressure and demands of the boss man. How beautiful, says Paul the apostle, are the feet of them that preach the gospel of peace, and bring glad tidings of good things. From the position of the homemaker, the woman of God calls her family to a place where they can dine at the banqueting table.

When Jesus came to earth he was known for his miracles. His love for his people resulted in his turning what was ordinary into something of splendor. In like manner, the woman that will allow God to minister through her existence to her family, can spread a table for her loved ones through devotion, commitment and obedience, and turn simple homemaking into the manufacturing of lives that will change a generation. Hats off to you homemakers and future domestic engineers for God has much in store for you! If you would humble yourselves before God, and obey his word you will find out that indeed this is just the beginning of great things for you. The choice of the homemaker is no longer a luxury, but a necessity!

Hints for the Homemaker

The homemaker has the ball in her court; her biggest challenge will be discipline and time management. Her position is one where she basically works without supervision, therefore her ability to be self motivated is extremely important. This calls for organization, planning, strategy, creativity, and commitment.

- It's a good idea to organize a timetable according to your commitments. Every homemaker's schedule is different, every minute is crucial.

- Morning time can be allocated for simple lessons in cleanliness, for example: teaching your child to make his/her bed, brushing teeth, dressing properly, putting together an outfit, and putting away their clothes.

- Devotions can be done as early as you want. It could be in the wee hours of the morning, just before the family awakes, or maybe after everyone leaves for work or school. However it is essential to begin your day committing everything to the Lord in prayer.

- Mid mornings hours are generally set for tiding up and making the house feel clean and bright. During the middle of the day, you might have a free hour or break. This is a good time to take a leisurely bath, and freshen up after your housework is done, so that you can be refreshed when everybody gets home.

- Free hours can be used for lunch with a friend, getting a beauty treatment, hosting your hubby to an unusual lunch break, or just a special time of relaxation. Participation in school activities, e.g. field trips, class visitations, shopping, crafts etc. can also be a pleasant treat.

- Avoid getting caught up in television and unnecessary phone calls, that tend to rob you of valuable time. Consider yourself at work for the Lord, your family, and yourself.

- It would be good to get cooking done during the early afternoon before the smaller children come home so that you can spend time with them or take them to extra-curricular activities. Upon returning, dinner is ready for all. Mothers of teenage daughters might opt to prepare dinner during late afternoons to teach her daughter or son to help with cooking, or share a few family secrets.

- For homemakers who work outside of the home, the name of the game is preparation. It helps to plan your family meals on weekends. You can also use off days like Sunday to cook enough for two days meal. Before freezing meats, wash and season them first to save time during the week. (There will be evenings when I worked outside my home that I would prepare two meals at one time. The next morning while I prepare for work, I would partially cook the extra dish, and then refrigerate it for later. This would allow me additional time that evening.)

- After dinner is a quiet time for relaxation, homework, or if you have a community, church, or social meetings you are free. It is a good practice in any relationship to come into agreement whenever possible about the things that are important in everyday life. For example daily church services are good, but consult your spouse to make certain that this schedule is good for all. An occasional evening out for the homemaker can give hubby an opportunity to spend time with the kids.

- Assign chores for your children that will increase with age and maturity. It is good that children of school age be given a bedtime between 8:00-9:30 p.m. to receive the required rest, and to allow parents a few extra hours alone before their bedtime.

- Homemakers are Homemakers are often not weary at night. Chores are done during the day therefore evenings are often less hectic. She is ready and prepared to spend quality time with her husband. Remember he was not home all day, so in the early evening allow him some winding down time to relax alone if he desires, and later he is all yours.

Her Natural Essence

I awoke one Saturday morning to the ringing of my bedside telephone. When I answered, the caller pleasantly offered me a product, but I bowed out gracefully. He went on to apologize for calling so early in the morning. I assured him that it was no problem because I had intended to get up early to pray. Then I asked him what time it was. "It's seven o'clock", he said. Then I realized that the voice became very gentle saying "That's right my child, get up and pray." I jumped out of bed, but not before realizing that my phone was disconnected, and it was all a dream. I looked at the clock and realized it was indeed 7:00 a.m., the exact time I wanted to get up and pray. I got up and thanked the Holy Spirit for awaking me. Nonetheless, the dream left an impression upon me because the voice was so gentle, so delicate. All that day I thought about what had happened, but more than that I could not get pass the voice in my dream. It left an impression in my spirit. It was so tender, so peaceful, I thought to myself, "How beautiful is the softer side of God, that is also secured within us as women."

One of the most alluring essences of a lady is her sweet and gentle nature. This is what accentuates the real beauty of a female. The characteristic of her gracefulness, a meek spirit, her soft laughter, all mirrors the part of God that makes the female so wonderfully attractive. Peter speaks of this hidden person of the heart, that meek and quiet spirit that makes a woman so precious. It begins from within and emanates to her outward appearance. It makes a difference in the way she walks, and in the way she talks. Many times women believe that they have to be course or hard to get results. They watch the masculine nature operates and attempt to model him. But the nature of the man is out of place in the natural essences of a woman.

Every woman wants to be beautiful, yet so many neglect the feminine nature that makes her attractive. Physical beauty is fleeting, and can be marred at any moment, but the true beauty that comes from within will last forever. The negative force of feminism has stripped many women of their most precious assets without even realizing it. The spirit of masculinity in the body of a woman breeds confusion.

When we look at the coming fashions, it seems women are being drawn away from the look of femininity. In action, adornment, and speech a lot of women are becoming more masculine. I remember meeting a young woman working on a construction site. She was dressed in overalls and covered with cement and dirt, struggling to lift a load of cement blocks. In time past men would never simply pass a woman by and not help her, because they honored her femininity, but today things are different. We have disregarded our femininity and others are quickly following suit.

There are women who are offended if one implies that they are doing a man's job. Some women even struggle to prove that they can do just what a man can do. While it is possible that she might make the accomplishment, it is not always profitable to her. A woman is built differently from a man. Her womanliness is like a crown, accentuated by her gentle strength which stems from the lower middle part of her body. She will carry her baby for miles on her hip or back. The male strength stems from his chest or upper body. He can carry his wife over the threshold, or lift her one mile up the road. God designed them this way to fulfill their divine purpose; therefore, the two cannot be compared.

It is important that we as women preserve the natural qualities that make us female. A female should never appear boisterous or hard. Her demeanor should make other women desire to be feminine. When I was growing up there was a female evangelist in our church that I considered the epitome of a godly woman. She was graceful and womanly in the way she spoke, dressed, and conducted herself. The only time she exhibited a stronger side was during her messages when God would use her to minister to the church. She was like a lamb, but also a lion. As a young girl I was impressed by this. I thought it was beautiful. She would preach the word with authority, and it would make you wonder how a woman who appeared so soft could expound the word so powerfully.

There exists a side of God that is likened to the lamb, that tender, nonthreatening attitude that exhibits grace and humility. Then there is the nature of the lion that exhibits strength, dominion, and authority. These are both attributes of God. The nature of the lion comes forth with power and authority, the nature of the lamb is exhibits grace and humility. When the woman moves in the nature of the lamb she is teachable, reachable, and forgiving. This too affects her outward adorning.

A part of the outward adorning of a woman is the way she dresses herself. Her dress code should not bring attention to the flesh, but accentuate her spirit. Today's fashions are changing rapidly, however the woman of God must remain focused on what is best for her. While in the mall recently, I questioned a sales lady about nice feminine dresses for my daughter. It seemed all that was being offered were pants, short skirts and other apparel that I didn't particularly want my daughter wearing. The lady said to me, "well, we have to buy what sells." The world is not concern with modesty, but as women of God we must be.

In the church the customary dress code has also changed drastically. A few years ago a woman ministering the word of God would not be caught in pants in the pulpit, whether she was singing, praying, or exhorting. Many say pants are comfortable. While the wearing of pants is not a sin, it is not the most feminine attire for a woman, we as women must be very careful in the way we adorn our body. Our standard for dressing must be set by our godly conscience and not by Hollywood designers. One woman admitted that when she wore slacks she sometimes felt manly, and there is much truth behind this. There is an attitude that presents itself with the wearing of various clothing. Dressed in a mini or short skirt a woman may feel very sexy or flirtatious. In an evening gown she tends to feel queenly, elegant and beautiful. Adorned in an expensive outfit there is a sense of affluence. In shorts she may feel active or playful, and in pants she may feel mannish and brave. A woman would not likely sit with her legs ajar in a dress, but in a pant, it's accepted.

The word of God admonishes the godly woman how to appropriately adorn her self (1 Peter 3). She should take steps to be well covered, discreet, and presentable, in a manner suitable for the feminine look of a woman. Her adornment is a representation of what and who she is. A Policeman is respected because of who he is, especially when he is dressed in his uniform. If he wore plain clothing he could easily be mistaken for just about anyone. In fact he may wear plain clothing to hoodwink the rebels, a very dangerous position, that could cause his life. The uniformed police can demand a level of respect because of his attire. Likewise, the woman adorned as a woman is able to demand the respect that is rightfully hers because of your feminine rights. When we act or portray masculinity, this brings detriment to who we are as a feminine creation. The bulk of this is seen in the lesbian, a woman who has abandoned the adornment of her soul and spirit to defend that which she is not. The result will eventually be seen through her inward and outward adornment when she rejects and rebel against who she was created to be.

When the Spirit of God began dealing with me on this issue, I began sharing it with other women and found that what he was saying to me was indeed being said to others. Beware! While the inward adornment is extremely important, the outward appearance of a woman is essential to her being, and her testimony. Many young girls today reject the feminine look, because it is not esteemed. Mothers today must insist on teaching their daughters to adorn themselves femininely. Beginning from a very young age, we become accustomed to dressing them in cute sports wear, and not enough pretty dresses, ribbons etc. My two school age daughters wore uniforms all of their lives until we moved to Florida. They gladly wore dresses for the first few weeks of school, and then getting dressed each morning became an issue. To me the way the little girls dressed looked so immodest, but to them it was "cool." I began to tell them the importance of being an example, even in the way they dressed.

Within weeks my daughter came home and said, "Mom you know a lot of my friends are beginning to wear dresses like me, so I guess it is alright." Whew! Sometimes it can be a fight, but as parents we must take authority especially when we stand as the most impressive role model our children have. Young people are crying out for hope, for direction, for someone not only to tell, but to show them an alternative to what they see around them. In most situations we must convince them that what is right is best; because of the power of suggestion in the era that we live in adamantly influencing them to embrace what is wrong.

It is up to the older women to protect the younger one by being godly examples. The older woman is not necessarily older in years only, but a woman that is mature in the faith, strong in the word, disciplined by God. She can set a standard for those weaker in the faith to follow. It should never be a challenge to identify the woman of God and the woman of the world, there has to be some difference. When we have become so identical that there is no difference, our relationship with God is bought into question. James 4:4 tells us that our friendship with the world makes us an enemy of God.

The Call

The call to motherhood, homemaking, and femininity are powerful tools placed in the lives of women. These are as important to the married woman as they are to the single woman and the spiritual bride. In the life of the single woman, ability to reach out and touch the lives of other women through her singleness is extremely important. She might not have children of her own but her ability to shelter, protect, and love others in need is a ministry within itself. The same is true of her ability to perfect her surrounding and keep her home. She too must treasure the natural essence of her being.

The life of the spiritual bride or the body of Christ is in her mothering. Keeping her temple clean is a daily responsibility for it is where her Lord resides. Her natural essences are the fruits of her spirit that makes her so attractive that she stands out as an individual, in the home, on the job, and in communities, churches, and nations. Together they remain the expressions of the feminine creation.

If any of these are diminished in any way it hinders our message and purpose. But God is able to repair, restore, and retain that which might be damaged or lost. If we ever seem to fall short, we need only to say, "Lord show me how to become what you have ordained me to be." My mind goes to the story of Cain and Abel. God required of them both to offer up a sacrifice. One pleased God, the other did not. Looking at our lives, how would God respond to our sacrifices for him through our children, our husbands, and our faith? Would he be pleased with our obedience or daily offerings? Would he be pleased with our desire to build his kingdom?

If we embrace the Word of God, the Word will return to uphold us. The book of John 15:7 affirms, "If you abide in me, and my word abides in you, then ye shall ask what you will and it shall be given to you." All that is required of us is an act of faith. God has made a way of escape for all of us. His Holy Spirit is with us to show us how to fulfill the destiny of our lives. He is unique, and so are we. We need not compare ourselves with anyone else, or try to live up to what God is doing in another individual, because the spirit of God that lives in each of us will make us what we ought to be. If allowed he will make our calling, ministry, heart and lives as unique and beautiful as he is.

8

Submission In the Midst of Adversity

*Now no chastening for the present seemeth to be
joyous, but grievous: nevertheless afterward it yieldeth
the peaceable fruit of righteousness unto them which
are exercised thereby.*

– HEBREWS 12:11

It is with little or no difficulty that we will submit in favorable situations or circumstances. But what about when there is adversity, for instance, in a marriage where a spouse is unsaved, on a job where you dislike the supervisor, or to parents that you feel are controlling. Can we still find the inner strength to keep our peace when the waves of turmoil roll?

To submit in the face of adversity is not giving up or resigning to hopelessness and despair, but coming to the place of resting in the divine control of the Savior, knowing that He has everything, our life, our family, our future, in His hand. We are assured that He cannot fail, He cannot lie, or be defeated, and nothing ever takes Him by surprise. Why? Because He knows all things! We can safely submit to His direction, His guide, His care, His will. When we do, we will never be led astray, but move forth believing that if we are faced with a struggle, He will help us to carry the load. If we trust Him to have His way, He will enable us to make it through.

There is a time in every life when one will face adversity, for life is never sunshine all the time, or everything will die for lack of rain. Adversity enters our lives in the form of financial burdens, broken relationships, health problems, death, struggles, and disappointments. Our responses vary from bitterness, fear and anger, to guilt or total surrender. Oftentimes, the way in which we respond determines the outcome. So many times in adverse situations, God desires to show us a way out of our dilemma, but in our rejection of him, fear of man, or lack of faith, we resist His hand and suffer needlessly, instead of rising to the challenge, weathering the storm, and gaining spiritual strength.

Every circumstance that we experience serves to prepare us for a greater battle ahead. However, no matter how often they come, or how many battles we win, when we come to another mountain or challenge in our life, few of us will readily submit. Submission in the face of adversity takes time and spiritual maturing, but eventually we move toward a place of perfected trust and faith in a mighty God. I found this out when I had to face one of the most challenging circumstances in my life and stood face to face with adversity.

Your mess becomes your message,
Your test becomes your testimony

It was a warm but beautiful day in mid January 1999. We were finish with our appointments early that afternoon, and I sat down with my husband Lambert, to relax together before the children got home from school. As we sat together near the window, his hand wondered over my left breast and I felt his body stiffen. The next words out of his mouth were, "Kim this thing is getting bigger. You have to check this out!" My mind went back to a dream I had exactly one year before. In the dream I felt lumps up my armpit. When I awoke the following morning I was frightened, realizing that lumps were a sign of cancer. Very quickly I saw my husband off to work, and the children to school, before getting dressed and going to see my physician. I was assured that it was probably fibrous tissues and nothing more. Ten months later when I felt a small lump, I assume that it was nothing to worry about. But my husband's word reawoke the fear that afternoon, and I quickly made an appointment to settle my concerns.

When I entered the doctor's office two days later, the nurses kidded with me that I was young and had nothing to worry about. However, after the examination I saw the concerned expressions on their faces, and I knew something was wrong. I walked out of the doctor's office with a heavy heart. "The lump in your breast is almost the size of a quarter," the doctor had said, "And even if it is nothing, it shouldn't be there, and must be removed!" I couldn't wait to get to my car, and once inside the tears flowed unhindered. The first few days were terrifying as I wrestled with fear and the tormenting thoughts of cancer. At first, I tried to understand why this was happening to me. Religion had convinced me that somehow as a Christian I was exempt from this kind of suffering. That God would not put more on me than I could bear, but as far as I was concern at the moment, this was more than I was able to bear. Demonic thoughts from hell shouted that God had deserted me. When my husband tried to console me, I turned from him. "Kim, let's pray", he said. "It will make you feel better. It's not like we don't have any one to go to, the Holy Spirit is still our refuge." But I couldn't, I was afraid, confused and angry, and I did not feel like praying. During the day I would try my best to keep my composure in front of the children, but at night I would have to turn my pillow over to avoid the dampness from the tears as I wallowed in self pity. Even though I had committed my life to the Lord Jesus Christ a long time ago, all of a sudden I found myself questioning my relationship with Him.

The next afternoon I was sitting quietly when I heard the Lord speak into my spirit, "Kim, haven't I always been there for you!" In response I said quietly, "But Lord, why would you bring me all this way for me to die here?" My husband and I had just entered the ministry full time, and had moved away from family and friends to a large city where we knew hardly anyone personally. Again I heard in my spirit, "This is not unto death, but would assist you in ministering more effectively." I had no idea what that meant, but when I thought back over my life, and how the Lord had always been a part of my life, I began to cry again, only this time it was in humbleness of heart. It was not as if I was going to a stranger for a favor, this was my Savior, my Lord, the God that had been a part of my life for as long as I could remember. I knew I had to find a moment to be alone with Him. That night I waited until the house was quiet and my family was asleep. I crept out of my bed, went into the living room, and fell on my face before God. I repented and submitted everything to him. When I got up from my knees, I felt like a bird that was released from a cage. My faith was uplifted, hope was restored, those lying voices had been chased away and the fear that had me bound for days was replaced by His peace...*Glory to God!*

After that, things began to move quickly. I determined in my heart that if God allowed me to be in this situation, that He would take me through. When I went for the mammography exams, the surroundings in the medical office seemed cold and impersonal, but I refuse to be affected by the atmosphere. I knew what the ladies in that room was going through and passed the time talking to and encouraging those around me. Within two weeks I was before the surgeon. "Mrs. Sands, I recommend that you undergo a radical mastectomy (total removal of breast), followed by radiation and chemotherapy, and we need to do this immediately because of the size of the mass." At that moment I was willing to do anything to end this nightmare, but my husband's quick rejection to the breast removal stopped me, "We have to pray about this first!" The surgeon seemed startled, but agreed to give us some time to agree on a decision.

Later, I was happy that my husband had slowed down the process, because it gave both of us an opportunity to really seek God's wisdom in what He wanted in this situation. I knew no one personally who had gone through this experience, and even less about this dreaded disease, so I began to research the internet for information. I called a friend who was a nurse, and I spoke to another doctor who answered some of my questions. He referred me to various vehicles including the American Cancer Society for additional support. With every step I took I prayed, asking the Holy Spirit to lead and direct me. I needed to know what I was dealing with both physically and spiritually. The Lord began to bring people in my path from all walks of life that had, or were facing cancer. The more I heard, the more I knew that the only way through this drastic situation was totally relying on the Lord Jesus. When I went back to my next visit, the surgeon wanted to know what I had decided to do. "I have decided against a radical mastectomy", I replied, "but I would like to have the lumpectomy (removal of lump) performed. I didn't have a freedom in my spirit to go any further than that, so we discussed the possibility of the lump being malignant, and the surgery was scheduled.

Meanwhile, my husband, and immediate family continued to pray and encourage me. I wanted a miracle and prayed that before the surgery date I would wake up and the lump would be gone. But the day of the operation the lump was still there. When I was prepared for the surgery, my husband came into the room and the doctor joined us in prayed for God's guidance. When the operation was completed the physician uttered the dreaded word - Cancer. Nonetheless, I was not afraid anymore, I had made up my mind that whatever the Lord allowed *in accordance to His Will* was all right. I could feel the presence of God all around me and I knew at that moment that I was not in this alone. I vowed to use this situation to encourage others and began volunteering with the American Cancer Society where I was assigned to meet with and befriend other women whose lives were being shaken by this diagnosis.

The surgery was successful and I healed quickly. When I sat down with the doctor during the follow-up visit, her recommendation was further treatment of radiation and chemotherapy if you are going to survive and beat this, but I felt strongly that I should not go through with either and expressed this to her. Not long after I answered a knock at my front door and was greeted by a postal representative. My first thoughts were, "Why is he coming to the door?" He was there to hand deliver a letter from the doctor. Quickly I opened the envelope and read that I was being released as a patient because of my refusal of medical advice. It also stated that the doctor was not to be held responsible if anything happened to me, and that I should seek another physician. I was already under tremendous pressure and this made it more difficult, but I signed choosing rather to do what I felt the Lord was leading me to do. Instantly the question came into my thoughts, "Whose report will you believe?" At that moment I lifted my hands to heaven and declared, "I will believe the report of the Lord!

It was here that I realized more than before that this was a spiritual fight. As the mind battles continued to rage, I found myself in constant prayer. *"Lord, please help me to do the right thing. You alone know what is best for me. Do not allow me to be led by my flesh, but by your Spirit. Let me know that I am doing what you would have me to do."* I had been scheduled to meet with the oncologist and as my appointment date drew closer that old familiar feeling of fear came lurking in the shadows of my mind again, but it was not alone this time, doubt was there as well. I didn't want to be pressured anymore. That Friday afternoon, I was introduced to a pleasant young doctor. We talked a while about the different treatment and I told him that I had decided to not have chemotherapy. My heart lifted when he said that the type cancer that was present was a rare type and did not demand chemical treatment. After advising me to keep up with regular mammograms and check ups, I was dismissed. When I left the office building I breathed a sigh of relief.

I continued volunteering with the American Cancer Society. There I met individual who had experience much of what I had. Some of them had chosen to have mastectomy, others had taken or refused chemical treatment, some had been healed and deliver, and there were also those individuals who had died in fight. A lady I will call Jeanette shared with me how she now walked with a cane because as she put it, the chemo had destroyed the bones not only in her leg, but also some of her memory was delayed. One of the individuals whose home I was sent to was a young woman in my area who had been diagnosed with breast cancer. When I walked into her home that afternoon, she wanted to talk, so I listened. She was discouraged because two years earlier she had gone through a radical mastectomy, radiation, and rounds of chemical treatment, and after all of this the cancer had now returned. When I walked out of her home that day it was apparent that no particular treatment was guaranteed, our greatest hope in any situation, whether good or bad, is to have faith in God. One songwriter penned,

> "We dare not trust the sweetest frame, but only lean on
> Jesus name, on Christ the solid rock I stand, all other
> ground is sinking sand, all other ground is sinking sand."

I accepted this and moved on, then four years later I felt another lump. I couldn't believe I was facing this battle again as my mind reflected on the situation a few years earlier. Lord, I cried, why am I back here again? I felt my faith growing weak, but I had to keep my mind focus, so I surrounded myself daily with praise and worship music, and Christian voices that were strong in faith.

Within days I was recommended to a surgeon. He had read my medical files and told me right away that he would strongly recommend a radical mastectomy. I saw, and understood his concern, but previous experience had taught me not to rush into anything. I told him I needed time to consider my options. He stated emphatically that *these* were the options! However, I had had the opportunity to find out a little more about cancer and the various treatments and I did not want to move ahead on assumptions. When I told him about the young woman that I had met whose cancer recurred even after treatment, he seemed agitated. Mrs. Sands, this is all we have. At that moment I knew that as a doctor he was really giving me all that he had, all that he knew or had learnt, and I appreciated that. I knew how harsh chemical treatment was on the entire body and shared this with him as well. I needed time to pray, and hear from the Lord so I asked the doctor to go ahead with the basic procedures and then we will make the decisions. When I walked out of the office I felt what seemed like a grieving in my spirit again and I knew I would not go through with the radical mastectomy, still I questioned the Lord. "Lord Jesus" I said, "I am confused, because I know that you put the doctors here, but how do I tell them again that I cannot take their advice." Again the words from Proverbs 3:3 came to me, "Lean not unto your own understanding but in all your ways acknowledge Him; He shall direct your path." I decided to just keep moving, and see how the Lord would direct me this time. I knew I had to continue to believe that God was in control, still there was a fierce inner fight.

I was feeling sorry for myself one afternoon; "Lord," I whispered in the stillness of the moment, "Say something to me! Let me know that you are right here with me." Instantly these words came to me, "My grace is sufficient for you, and my strength is made perfect in weakness." Recognizing this was a scripture; I turned and reached for my bible to look for it. I opened my bible to the exact place, and there it was before me, highlighted in red. The Lord is so *awesome!* These words again brought the peace of the Lord to my heart, and lifted my spirit. I was again scheduled for a mammogram.

When the results came the x-ray showed not one, but two lumps. Again, my faith began to stagger, and with it came the questions. Was I being directed by the Lord, or is it self? I began to think that since there were two lumps, then maybe I should take the recommended treatments this time" On the platform of the mind, my flesh and spirit were in an all out war. But I began to think of the words the Lord had spoken to me through the years. Every biblical account of healing came back to me. I had read God's Word, now the time had come to believe it, to live it! I opened my bible, and there was my confirmation, "Without faith, it is impossible to please God!" I knew what I had to do, there was no time for tears or fears; it was time to war!

I went on a fast and came out with a determination to fight the fight of faith. I recalled a testimony that I had heard back in 1986 of an evangelist who had made a call to prayer around the pulpit. As a lady stood before him, he saw what looked like a small monkey-like beast clutching one of her breast. He called the lady forth and asked her if there was any pain or problem in that area. It was then that the lady admitted that she had been diagnosed with breast cancer. The minister began to pray, rebuking the demon of cancer. Instantly the monkey-like creature loosed itself and flew over her shoulder. The woman was re-examined by a doctor, but the cancer was gone. I said to myself, if God can deliver her, he can do the same for me.

My perception of my situation changed. I began to see cancer as a demon that was sent to pester me, and I began to war in the spirit. The Lord began to reveal to me root spirits to take authority over and bind up spiritually. If God said, "It is finish," I said to myself, "Then I will believe that it is finish!" I believed that no weapon formed against me would prosper, and I declared it. I took my bible and looked up the word 'breast' because this time my doctor was determined that they should be removed but, I didn't feel this was what I needed to do at this time. I anointed my body with oil, and served Satan and his demons eviction notice to vacate the premises. I knew I was in an all out war, but I also knew that greater was the power of the Holy Spirit in me! I was not standing alone, neither was I alone as a child of God.

A week later I laid in the hospital room as the medical team prepared me for a surgical biopsy/lumpectomy. The nurse attending me was attempting to mark the spots and soon called another doctor. "Call her doctor" someone said. "What's going on," I wanted to know. "It looks like you might be going home," she said, "We can't find one of the lumps, and the other is clearly filled with fluid." When my doctor came in he reconfirmed the good news, but decided to continue with a lumpectomy of the fluid filled lump for precaution and further evaluation, nevertheless, the results was enough for me to know that God was indeed working in my favor. All I had to do was trust him, Halleluiah! Later that afternoon my physician discharged me. "That's my God" I walked out rejoicing.

A few days later, I went for a follow-up visit. The result of the fluidfilled lump was back, and showed a thin lining that was suspicious of cancer. I refuse to believe anything other than the fact that God had it all in control. The suspicious tissue and margins were completely removed. When that was done my physician said to me, "I have scheduled you for chemotherapy first, followed by radiation and gave me the names of the two doctors that I was scheduled to see. I went to the oncologist who again informed me of the required procedure, and arranged to have me prepared to begin treatment within a few days. He share with me that this cancer was quite different from the one four years ago, therefore he was recommending systemic treatment. But when I got home that afternoon, I felt restless. I tried to dismiss the feeling, but it only got stronger. As I paced the floor, I again began to pray. "Lord," I only want to do what you would have me do, please order my steps." "I come against the spirit of confusion and every spirit of hindrance. I only ask divine guidance in this situation, accordingly let Your Will be done!" The day before I was to return for treatment, I called and cancelled all appointment, and the feelings of hesitation vanished.

My physician released me with the advice to continue periodic checkup. I had proven the Lord yet again in a battle against Satan's choice weapons, doubt, fear and unbelief. I realize that this was not so much about cancer, because cancer and its cells must bow to the name of Jesus, but more about my submission to the Lord, even in adversity. As a result of my experience I have learnt to trust God even more than I did before. A few years later during a periodic checkup, the enemy again tried to attack my body. Shoot, these demons don't give up! I said to myself, "Well, neither will I!" The left breast that was affected previously was fine, all tissues were normal with no sign of suspicion. In my right breast there was cause for concern. I began looking for a new surgeon because again the surgeon I was dealing with chose to release my situation. With each day the lump in my right breast was growing bigger and becoming uncomfortable. "Lord, give me wisdom in this situation and a strategy to overcome." I prayed. God answered my prayer quickly. Before the week was over, the lump had reduced in size and I was no longer in pain.

When I sat down to talk with the doctor he said to me, "I can look at this and see that it has spread, we have to move quickly". I knew enough that if the cancer spread then advance precautionary measures were mandatory. "Well Father, I trusted you before, and I won't give up on you now, so here we go again!" I said. I sat down to talk with the physician, that's when it became clearer to me how God was working on my behalf. When I asked if he was going to recommend a mastectomy he shared with me that more and more doctors were moving away from that practice. Many of the earlier ways of treating cancer were now becoming obsolete. I thought back to how the Holy Spirit stopped me a few years earlier, I lifted my hands in praise to thank him. I knew it would have been difficult to accept this if I had submitted to such drastic procedures a few years earlier only to learn this new information. With this, I understood why more than ever that I had to trust Jesus Christ completely to order my steps and decisions.

One morning as I was taking my daughter to school, I was listening to a CD that I always kept in my car, but this morning as the song played it seemed as if God was speaking directly to my heart to stand and not be swayed by the enemy! In the moment I began to worship him and laying my hand on my affliction, I rebuked the powers of hell and declare that cancer will not run freely in my body! A week later, God through the surgeon, pulled that lump out of my body again. Upon returning for the results, I heard the doctor's puzzled response, "It has not spread, and I was so sure that it had!" I left the office with another praise report. I continued to see and be monitored by both the oncologist and surgeon, both of whom I deeply respect and thank God for. Indeed, my life is in the hands of the Lord to do His will and have His good pleasure.

God responded to David, He responded to me, and He will respond to any one that will ask in accordance with his will. My desire was to be healed once and for all and never go through the experience again. But, I realize that every time I was faced with adversity, and climbed that mountain, it brought me closer and closer to the Lord Jesus and stronger in faith. In humility our prayer must always be, *"Thy will be done, in earth as it is in heaven."*

Our physicians are set in place by God, and family and friends are tremendous sources of encouragement. Personally, as individuals we too have a choice to make, but let us never forget who is ultimately in control. In the book of II Chronicles I read of Asa, a man that was sick with a disease. The scripture said, ***"And Asa in the thirty ninth year of his reign was diseased in his feet, until his disease was exceeding great. Yet in his disease he sought not to the Lord, but to the physicians." II Chronicles 16:13.*** Asa died.

Each year millions are faced with cancers of every kind. The diagnoses may be different, but the fear is often the same. My word to all is, do not leave the Lord out of your decisions, trust him and allow him to direct you. I look back today at my experience, and I thank God for it. Through it all my relationship with Jesus was strengthened. I can truly say that he is indeed my healer and a God of His word, but he is also my friend. Lack of faith or fear is a direct attack against the peace of God. At one point in my experience when a particular procedure was recommended to me, I refused it. Unable to understand my reasoning the doctor refused to treat me until I had spoken with a psychiatrist on his team. After the first visit the therapist dismissed me with a report to my doctor that I was making decisions soundly, was not fearful or threaten by anyone, and needed no further visits. Thank you Jesus, I said as I walked to my car.

It is often a fight to walk in faith when faced with trials of any kind, when doubt and unbelief is all around us. But no matter the situation, God can give us victory, faith in Him is victory! The miraculous accounts in the bible somehow have become even more real to me, because like many others I have proven God when all seemed hopeless. Had I not allowed the

Lord to direct me in my situation, I could have made many unnecessary decisions? The enemy tried to convince me that God was not powerful enough to rid my body of cancer and that was why it returned, but I soon learnt that each attack was different. Satan tried, but he failed. I also realize that many illnesses including cancer are not just physical but satanic attacks. It is only through the power of God that we are able to not only fight, but win the battle. God said in His word, "My peace I give to you!"

Another thing the Lord impressed upon my spirit was discipline in the way I maintained my body, which is His temple. I became more conscious of what I put into it. I realize that disobedience in any form had its consequences. As I minister to God's people today, this experience has given me a confidence in God that is not easily shaken. It has also strengthened other areas of my life and ministry. I know that weapons may form, but they will not prosper. I declare that, "I am healed by the blood of Jesus, and faith in His Name!" No matter what storm arises in our lives, whether in your marriage, children, health, or home, there is no storm that God cannot calm. Like the psalmist David, (Psalms 30:2) I cried out to the Lord and he healed me!

Many times in our trials we may feel as if we have wronged God, thus the reason for our distress, until we come to the knowledge that all men will suffer persecution of some kind, whether saint or sinner. Still He is there for all of us. There are many times when God chooses to conceal the reason for our suffering, so as to preserve its purpose. We must know, however, that he is acquainted with our grief. He said, "I will never leave you or forsake you," and I believe him! When we are at our weakest point, the power of his strength is waiting and ready to sustain us. Because he knows us so well, nothing that comes our way is ever more than we can bear. In many cases his aim is to destroy carnality and strengthen the spiritual man. He didn't say that we will not meet adversities, but he did promise to give us a way of escape!

Wherefore let him that thinketh he standeth take heed lest he fall. There hath no temptation taken you but such as is common to man; But God is faithful, who will not suffer you to be tempted above that ye are able, but will with the temptation also make a way to escape, that ye may be able to bear. I Corinthians 10:12-13

At times we cry out declaring our innocence, wondering about the justice of God and why we have to face such misery. It is truth that if we do not accept the supremacy of the Lord in every situation, the enemy will use our problems and afflictions to destroy us. In times of adversity we must see Christ as our advocate, and not our opponent. It makes for strength in times of trouble and a doorway to submissiveness. In the book of II Corinthians chapter 4:8-10, we can find encouragement through the word. "We are troubled on every side, yet not distressed. We are perplexed but not in despair, persecuted but not forsaken cast down but not destroyed, always bearing about in the body the dying of the Lord Jesus; that the life also of Jesus might be made manifest in the body." The life of Jesus was not a simple one. There was hurt and pain, joy and sorrow. So often people ask, "Why so much suffering? Why war, famines, violence, death, and sickness. Why is God allowing it to happen?" But God is not our adversary. He receives no pleasure from broken homes and marriages, killing, and natural disasters.

When God created man he desired that man live in a world of beauty and serenity. He created the best for us (Genesis chapter 1). However, evil was present and God showed man how to avoid evil, offering a way of escape. He also gave man a will of his own so that he would be able to make choices for himself. It was man, not God, that allowed his flesh to be seduced, thereby opening up the door to all of the evils that we face today including marital unfaithfulness, abuse, sexual immorality, deceit, death and sorrow. Man made a bad choice, but the God that we serve, the God of a second chance, made yet another door whereby man could escape. Through the doorway of repentance and forgiveness, man was given the gift of salvation.

Christ gave his life that we may find freedom once again. In the midst of sorrow we can find peace. In many instances the effects of these discomforts on our lives tend to make us more conscious of the greatness of God. When God *allows* suffering, it is never for bad, but that we may be propelled toward his way of escape, justification through the blood of Jesus.

Adversity also brings us to a place of accountability. In the same manner that we are to bring our lives into subjection to the will of God in the midst of turmoil and disaster, wives too must bring themselves into subjection to their husbands whether he is loving and kind, or aloof and uncaring. 1 Peter 3:1 says, "Likewise ye wives, be in subjection to your own husbands, that if any obey not the word they also may without the word be won by the conversation of the wives, while they behold your chase conversation coupled with fear."

Some of our most devastating moments of adversity occur in relationships. When we are wronged, betrayed, hurt, or rejected by someone we have come to love and trust. Many times the adversities in marriages could be heartrending. Equally, as hard is watching a child go to prison, or suffer a debilitating disease, which cause you to question your faith. Emotional, financial, or mental devastation, either place us in a corner of defeat, or chase us to the cross. In whatever situation you find yourself, know that if you cannot trust God almighty, you dare not trust yourself, anything, or anyone else. The hardship may stem from un-forgiveness to desertion. We go through the cycle, but when we trust God we soon find out that he makes all things beautiful in time. It is our obedience to the Word of God that eventually brings victory in our situation.

I was privileged to hear the testimony of a woman faced with the bitter and unforgiving heart of her husband. I will call her Madeline. After 26 years of marriage, their relationship was falling apart. The children were gone and it was just the two of them. The wife of a prominent, wealthy businessman, she had spent most of her marriage helping to build a life that both of them were proud of. Now, they hardly spent any time together, and when they did come together, there were multiple conflicts. So it was no surprise when Roy, her husband, wanted a divorce. Although Madeline did not want a divorce, she did not hinder her husband in his proceedings, but she went to God asking him to intervene. It was then that she heard the Lord speak to her spirit saying, "Show him love!"

Ever since Roy had approached her about his decision, she had shown resentment. She promised God that she would try her best to show him love. Very quickly the day came for the Hearing; however, because of his displeasure with the distribution of assets, Roy somehow got the judge to put the case on hold. He felt as if he was losing too much to his wife. The very thing he wanted, the family home, had been awarded to his wife. Reluctant to give up his home, he agreed to remain in the residence, and they began to live as roommates. As time went by Madeline saw very little of her husband. They hardly spoke to each other, except when necessary. It hurt her heart to see what their union had been reduced to. Family members and friends told her to move out for fear that he might be tempted to hurt her, but she decided against it.

One morning a few weeks later her husband woke up late and scrambled to make it on time to a morning meeting. As he got dressed Madeline noticed that his shirt was wrinkled. Her first reaction was to let him go and humiliate himself, but again the spirit spoke in her heart, "Show him love." She quickly asked him to allow her to iron the shirt. Without answering he threw it on the chair. As she picked up the shirt tears filled her eyes, but there was joy in her heart. She pressed the outfit and hung it up for him to see. Without a kind word, or thank you, he dressed and left. That day she did something that she hadn't done for months. She made sure his clothes were washed and prepared.

Things remained the same as Roy continued to avoid her. About a month later she was fixing breakfast for herself when he came down the stairs. "That smells good," he said. Shocked by the compliment, Madeline searched for an unkind word to say that would hurt him as much as he was hurting her, but she knew that would not help the situation, so she simply offered a meal, but he refused. A few mornings later, he came down early enough, and allowed her to fix his breakfast. Soon she was feeding him every other morning, but the bitterness was still there.

During her prayer time, Madeline would often pray for her husband, but as the days went by, it seemed nothing changed. Then one morning he walked into the kitchen, but he was not alone. With him was an attractive young woman. When she walked by, Madeline felt as if she would pass out, but she offered both of them breakfast and watched them leave. All day her heart ached and the tears flowed as she asked God "Why?" What had she done to deserve such belittlement and disrespect from this man? "Every day I show him love, Lord, and what do I get in return?" she screamed. She had gone out of her way to make peace, but now she felt she could not go on. The day was spent in prayer and spiritual song. It was the only way she felt she could gain strength to go on. That evening when she heard the door unlock, she knew he was home. She went to her room, because she did not trust herself to see him without bursting into tears.

A few hours later when she thought he would be in bed she went downstairs to the kitchen. Upon turning on the light, she was startled to find him sitting in the dark. As she turned to leave, he called her name. Her body came to a halt. There, standing in the doorway, she began to weep. Her husband got out of the chair, and came nearer. That's when she noticed that he too, was crying. "What a hateful man I have become," he said, "I never meant to hurt you." He confessed that his own inner hurt and pain caused him to want to destroy the joy that was so visible in her everyday life. Madeline did not pull away, but she began to minister words of comfort to her husband. She was amazed that there were words of hope left in her heart for her him. That night Roy gave his life to the Lord, and the healing in their marriage began. Today, they are both retired and active in their local church. Whenever she shares her testimony, Madeline often says that what remained with her though it all was the words her husband said to her that night; "If this God you know is responsible for the person that you are, then I must meet your God." He was not a religious man, but he saw the word alive in his wife through "unconditional love." The apostle Paul said even in the ugliest of circumstances that God has called us to peace. 1 Corinthians 7:16 states, *"For what knowest thou O wife, whether thou shalt save thy husband, or how knowest O man whether thou shalt save thy wife?"*

So often we look for physical attributes to repair a marriage, but because marriage is spiritual it must be repaired with spiritual tools; tools that flow from the heart, nurtured by the power of God. It was indeed a very humbling experience when this woman realized that all along God was using her to minister to her husband. When she "Showed him love," she was actually presenting Jesus. How thankful she is today that she was obedient even when she did not understand.

After the change in her husband's life another struggle presented itself, that of seeking to dominate and control. Because God had used her in winning her husband, the enemy constantly tried to convince her that as the more spiritual of the two, her place was to control spiritually. When she realized that with his born again experience was the capacity for spiritual development, and all he needed was her prayer and encouragement, she witnessed as he became more confident in Christ. In order for the sweet smelling savor to come forth, the box had to be broken. It was hard many times for her to (as many would say) condescend to that level, but it brought forth the victory. Thanks Be To God! *The flower that blooms in adversity is the most beautiful of them all.*

It's amazing what a little love will do, not sexual love, but loving your imperfect spouse as a soul in need of a Savior, thus offering the unconditional love of God. It is true that every situation may not result in reconciliation; however the word of God says that "He can do exceedingly, abundantly above and beyond what we can ever ask or even think, *according to the power that worketh in us."* (Ephesians 3:20).

Submission pays, all God needs is a vessel through which he can channel his glory. Divorcing a spouse or walking away from a relationship that was intended to last a lifetime is not easy. Neither is remaining unmarried (1 Corinthians 7:10-11)) when one is not willing to return to a spouse. It truly takes the power of God, and only the power of God to make it through any adverse situation. We cannot do it without Him, especially when the obstacles fight again us like a raging wind. Except our relationship with him is a strong and personal one, we will succumb to doubt, fear, and unbelief instead of trusting him for victory.

Pressures and problems will arise, especially when we rebel against the word of God, and refuse to bring our lives into subjection. Sometimes, God speaks to our spirits and we refuse to listen, opening ourselves to much unnecessary hardship and pain.

When the Holy Spirit says keep trusting, have faith, and praise me for the victory, we are often tempted to give in to what we feel. We allow the flesh to control us, we stand up to our husbands, neck to neck, word for word, knowing most of the time that our attitude is wrong and that we are displeasing God. We say to ourselves, "I don't care, nobody is perfect." But a greater part of submission is bringing that selfish, self centered attitude under control that we may continue to walk toward perfection with God. (Romans 8:6-10).

As obedient children, not fashioning yourselves according to the former lusts in ignorance but as he which hath called you is holy, so be ye holy in all manner of conversation. 1Peter 1:14

In the course of life, no matter how much we desire it, things will not always be perfect.

In the course of life, no matter how much we desire it, things will not always be perfect. Every problem, obstacle, or adverse situation will not end in harmony. We are encouraged to press forward no matter the outcome. Even when the situation seems to go from bad to worst, we must come to a place of perfect peace in the midst of the storm. When that husband or wife refuses to come back home, when that disease or illness keeps recurring, when the children seem heartless and uncaring, or when the letter arrives after you have fasted and prayed to inform you that you have been terminated. When the members walk out of the church or the bank repossesses the house and the car, when the bills are due, and you come home to find the electricity disconnected. When it seem every devil from hell has been sent to hurl mental darts your way, you can climb to the top of the mountain, lift your hands up high and say, **Lord, I praise you, I give you glory, I give you honor anyhow!** This is the true test of submission.

Be patient and in your patience possess ye your soul." (Luke 21:19) Don't allow an unsaved husband or a failing marriage, rebellious children or Satan himself rob you of your fellowship with God. Keep your eyes focused on him and he will work for you, and bring you through. There are angels that have been given charge over your situation, and it is your faith that puts them in action. God knew from the day you were born that you would go through what you are facing now. He could have stopped it if he wanted to, but he knew that this situation would bring you closer to him. It would give him the opportunity to purify your life that you may shine. It would bring you to trust him, prove him, and know for yourself that indeed he is God and he is real. He knew that like the woman at the well, it would become a testimony by which others would be encouraged. That woman didn't dream that a walk to the well would entail all that happened that day. When she spoke to the stranger and realized that he knew everything about her, she dared to trust him.

So much peace is forfeited, and such needless pain is bared, when we do not trust the Lord. There are times when things may appear hopeless, but Jesus said, "In the world ye shall have tribulation: but be of good cheer; I have overcome the world." (John 16:33). Like him, you too will overcome life's circumstances, and when we are at our weakest point, his strength will empower us to go on.

When the enemy tried to afflict my body, and the doctors told me that the lump in my breast was cancerous, I knew that it was out of my hands and in the hands of Jesus. I was his child, and there was no way that Satan could afflict me without His permission. There was nothing I could do, or needed to do, except be courageous and keep the faith. The world had no cure and the doctors were left baffled. All over the world souls were dying from this demonic force, but God has the answers. When we, in our weakness, go to God for help and understanding, he will be there for us.

The book of Hebrews 11:6 tells us: "But without *FAITH* it is *IMPOSSIBLE* to please him, for he that cometh to God, must believe that he is, and that he is a rewarder of them that diligently seek him."

Faith moves God and brings victory. Looking into His Word daily for strength to continue on, brings comfort. He never shows us the big picture right away, because if we knew how things would unfold there would be no need for faith. All he requires is that we put it all in his hands. Our situations are not always easy to understand, but clarity will come. Understanding will come. Revelation will surely come to strengthen our hearts that we might faithfully trust the Lord. Then we can move forward with power to influence others.

9

The Power to Influence

And I will give unto thee the keys of the kingdom of heaven, and whatsoever thou shalt bind on earth shall be bound in heaven, and whatsoever thou shalt loose on earth shall be loosed in heaven.

– MATTHEW 16:19

Melony kicked the door closed with her foot as she quickly made her way into her bedroom. Hardly was she inside when the packages began to fall. On to the bed they tumble as Melony tumbled with them. She didn't intend to do so much shopping, and when she got to the cash register, the total almost cost her legs to wobble. What would she tell Phillip? She knew he would go into a fit of rage that she had spent so much of his yearly bonus at the mall. She quickly looked around for a place to hide them, but there was no place in the room where he would not notice the packages. As if on cue she heard the sound of the garage door opening. Panic struck her heart as she realized her husband was home. She had to think quickly. Something had to be done right now, or else!

In a flash, Melony reached for the gold package with the decorated white ribbon. Dashing into the bathroom she changed hastily from the burgundy business suit into the tiger print sleepwear she had just purchase.

She knew one glimpse of her in this designer lingerie would wash all of Phillips cares away. Not only that, but it would also distract him until she could hide some of her shopping bags or tell him about the purchase. With a quick spray of his favorite perfume behind her ear, she was out the room and at the door to greet him. Just as she expected, the afternoon was awesome, but it was the evening that changed her marriage forever. She had almost forgotten about the purchases until she heard Phillips irate voice calling her into their bedroom. He had put two and two together. How dare you, he said, his face a mask of disappointment, and confusion, "How dare you stoop so low, to manipulate and betray me like that. Don't you have any respect for me at all Mel, and you want me to trust you, huh, forget it! He looked as if he was on the verge of tears as he slammed out of the house. Moments later the car engine started and he was gone.

Manipulation and control are telltale signs that a relationship lacks trust. When a woman desires to influence a man, she must realize that unlike the feminine creation, who feels respected when shown love and attention, the male man associates respect with reverence and honor, this is the pathway to obtaining his trust. Respect goes a long way when gaining influence in any relationship. There will be no power of influence except a man senses that the heart of the recipient is trustworthy. Many wives fail to influence the lives of their husbands because they fail to realize that humility, and the grace of God, are the mechanisms that inspire, and cause change. We are unaware of the insecurity we cause when we chose to influence him through fleshly methods of manipulation. Our greatest tool is a submissive spirit. If we refuse to submit, forget the rest. Other things may work for a while, but never bring forth the results that true humility unveils. If there is going to be influence, there must be trust.

> *It is a fact that he will continue to trust his mother, until he could truly trust his wife.*

Trust plays an important part in building any strong, healthy relationship. It is also an essential tool when one wants to walk in the power of influence. Any woman who desires to reach and win the heart of her husband must seek to win his trust. The element of trust is not easily obtained. A man might give his body or money much consideration, but his heart he reserves for the one he has proven can be trusted. It is a fact that he will continue to trust his mother, until he could truly trust his wife. Many people are married for years before real trust is manifested in the union. Trust develops over time and on different levels. A mother may trust her daughter to walk to the store and purchase an item, but be more reluctant about having her travel over distance by herself to do the same. When you go to a job interview, the interviewer may not know you, but along with the credentials he will hire the person he is confident will do a good job. In deeply committed relationships, trust is even more important, because it will often become the foundation on which the relationship will thrive. Our spiritual relationships will be reduced to just a religious practice if we cannot trust God.

Manipulation on the other hand causes one to obtain trust in a way that is selfish, and deceptive. I was at the checkout counter with a girlfriend of mine when she reached for one of the displayed magazines. "Oh Kim look here." I peeped over to see what she was showing me. It was an article under the heading, "How to Influence a Man." The picture that accompanied the article showed a woman lying back on a white bed with a sexy red dress and a rose. "Oh please," I remarked, as she burst into laughter. Smiling I said to my friend, "Seduction may work, but for how long?" It's better to stick with Deborah." "Deborah?" she asked. "Yes," was my replied! Deborah influenced with her heart, not her body. Through her spirit, and not through her flesh, and guess what? She got what she desired and she didn't even have a rose." As we walked out of the store laughing, my friend said to me, "Well girl, I guess it's time you introduce me to Deborah!"

Deborah was a wise woman with a spiritual heart; she was a judge in her city and also a known prophetess. Few women in history have attained her place of public dignity and supreme authority. Like Joan of Arc, who rode in front of the French leading them to victory, Deborah led a leader by the name of Barak and an entire nation into war and won. She was married to a man by the name of Lapidoth, not much is spoken of him in the bible. When lethargy overtook the people, this woman rose up in the power and strength that true faith brings to encourage her people to move forward in victory. With a humble heart, her faith in God became the strength and spiritual vision that would light Israel.

She lived in a time when the children of Israel were still in bondage. There was much sorrow in the land because of the evil that they had done in the sight of the Lord. The people were desperate for a change that would bring deliverance. For centuries women in the bible have inspired the lives of women the world over, but none on the level of Deborah. In a day and time when God is calling forth his people like never before, Deborah becomes a prime example of a woman being powerful, and yet humble. In her role as counselor in her nation, judge in their disputes, and deliver in time of war, she exhibits the traits of a woman of excellence, all because she trusted God explicitly, teaching others to do the same.

God was about to bring deliverance to the children of Israel and called forth a man by the name of Barak to stand up and conquer the enemy. He was commanded to take ten thousand men and go forth to battle against Sisera, but he was afraid. He feared that the Jews were not a match for Sisera and his men. Barak faltered in leadership when he cowered in defeat. He refused to move forth, protect the women and children, and secure their land. When Deborah saw this she burned with displeasure. How could these men cease to stand in their calling and refuse to take the reins of responsibility? With much zeal, a patriotic enthusiasm, and the power of God, she went in search of Barak, the man at the helm. In the spirit and attitude of a godly woman, with a feminine, unpretentious, and earnest nature, she began to offer power packed words from God that birthed encouragement, strength and courage. This kindled a fire in the men, and they rose up with vigor and confidence to devise a plan of action against their foe. They saw and accepted her spiritual faith and wisdom, and she became a vibrant part of the team. Happy was she as she proclaimed, "I will go and God will receive the glory." With that they went forth and won the victory. The road was rough, and sometimes awfully difficult, but armed with godly faith; this woman influenced the men forth to winning the war.

This unusual, yet remarkable story of faith and confidence is the only one of its kind found in the bible, where a woman was given the responsibility to influence the man so strongly, that it resulted in victory for an entire people. Deborah was a woman whom God had highly exalted. She was trusted to lead in humility, and she did so without fear or aggression. Even though the men were walking in idleness, she did not push them to the side or move pass them, but she walked in the feminine grace of submission and assisted them to victory. Our homes, churches, communities, and nations, need women like Deborah, who will walk in the wisdom of God and bring about a change in the atmosphere.

What is the woman to do who is living with a man who is overtaken by lethargy: a kind of spiritual sluggishness or exhaustion? He fails to protect her, cover her, provide for her, or defend her. In many instances she finds herself protecting him as he seemingly hides behind her skirt tail. What should the worker do when his plea for change or support fall on deaf ears or stirs up a defensive attitude? What about that one in ministry? He is troubled because he feels in-effective, and overcome with feelings of displeasure. This is the plight of many today. Unable to see change or hope they either walk away in disgust or simply ignore it all. However, the prophetess Deborah is telling us that there is another way to deal with this dilemma. First of all you will never be able to see pass the problem without the cloak of a humble heart. Insults and unkind words will drive him further away in fear and timidity. Your desire must be to lead him to a place of trusting you and ultimately trusting God. As he begins to move forward, you too must stay focus and encourage him to press forth faithfully. When he falters along the way, your prayer of support will keep him grounded so that he doesn't revert or run in the other direction.

The grace to submit is wrapped up in the wisdom of God. It is wisdom given to the feminine creature that provides her with divine insight to help her husband, to understand and be sensitive to his masculinity, to help raise her children and help govern her home. It is this same wisdom that will assist her husband to walk in authority and dominion. The Lord hath created a new thing in the earth, says Jeremiah 31:22, "A woman shall compass a man." She will divinely assist him, empower him, uplift him, and she will help to bring about a change. She will be that pivotal point in his life where he will find guidance that directs him not to her heart desires, but to the desires of God.

Because of his desire for godly wisdom, King Solomon became known as the wisest man that ever lived. Deborah the Prophetess gained the same experience, knowing that without the wisdom of God, her people would perish. Today, except the woman of God walk in that same power that influences everything around her will eventually fall!

Wives and mothers find themselves in a position where they must balance both roles of the husband and wife in order to preserve the family. Some women out of frustration or rebellion have pushed the men to the side or even out of the home completely, focusing on fault instead of need. Unlike Deborah, who still respected the men, and convinced them that they were needed. She fought the urge to trample over them, confiscating their position as head of the home, and shredding their egos with cutting words of doubt. Instead she used this opportunity to inspire and build them up. This is the result that comes with walking in godly wisdom instead of falling prey to the plans of the enemy.

Women today take submission lightly. If only we will open our hearts and realize what has been placed inside. Housed within each female creation is a part of God that would motivate any man into his rightful position. This is a manifestation of God's power secured within the woman. Wisdom is available to all, simply for the asking. Ask and it shall be given (Matthew 7:7). With wisdom you will be able to better meet the needs and desires of your family. You will access avenue through which your job or ministry can reach that platform of excellence.

Most women have been encouraged to use their appearance, bodies, or worldly knowledge to influence men. There are times women have been known to use deceit in an effort to make her husband include her or confide in her. To succeed she may try tactics like backing him into a corner, or even shedding a few tears in an attempt to break down some of the walls that he has surrounded himself with. When these fleshly endeavors fail, and she still can't get through to him, or he still won't open up to her, her self esteem crumbles and she becomes resentful. The artful motives of manipulation have failed again, resulting in more apprehension and creating a greater challenge. The man begins to feel deceived and he becomes more distrustful of the woman. When he becomes insecure, he will become suspicious and defensive, or reject her altogether.

Looking back to the Garden of Eden, Adam was created complete. Then God took the women out of him and he was still complete because the other part of him was now within the women, and they were one.

Together they housed two very distinctive governing powers. He, had the strength to govern, she had the power to influence. (Genesis 2:19-24). Of all that was created nothing moved Adam, like Eve. Satan realized that he could reach the man if he could weaken the woman. His prime weapon was deception. The ability to influence can be marred by deception. When we are in relationship with the Lord and our spirit focus is adjusted we can better see the trickery of the devil and guard against it.

Deception is used by Satan because he has no real power to work with. He also uses and encourages manipulation when his victims are weakened by insecurity. It is so very important for us to stay in constant fellowship with the Holy Spirit, because by ourselves we will be crushed by the enemy. The word of God admonishes us to "Pray always! " Spiritual survival means keeping your mind and heart focused on receiving direction from the Lord. This will keep us sober, so that we will not become an easy target for the enemy. At times I pray, "Lord, help me to see Satan from afar, so that by the time he gets near, I would be ready and equip to resist him." As we resist him and is able to righteously influence others just as Deborah did, it goes beyond mere purpose to power. Not only to give the men in our lives encouragement, but to inspire him in times of complacency and fear. After the fall, the male man was also affected by the results of sin, therefore he, like his wife, experience fear, doubt, or insecurities. Through redemptive power she is given the ability to help him to overcome the attacks that came as a result of the fall. When Deborah went to Barak, her zeal and confidence in her God reassured the men. They trusted her and invited her to march along in battle.

Not many husbands trust their wives enough to open their hearts to them. What would your response be if your husband came to you and said, "Honey, there's a lady at work that has been playing up to me, and I feel somewhat attracted to her. I need you to help me pray about this." Can he trust you with this level of honesty and know that it will not be held or used against him later. Would you help him to work through the situation, and try not to respond out of hurt and insecurity with resentment and accusations?

In addition to maturity, a wife who desires to win the heart of her husband must be open to a level of honesty and openness as well. It brings to mind the woman of Proverbs 31. Her lifestyle influenced the very reputation of her husband. He was known among the mighty men of the city, and he was confident that his wife was one that would not use her (Proverbs.31:11) persuasion to control, belittle, or embarrass him. As a result "his heart did safely trust her." He knew that in the good times and the bad, this woman would look out for his well being and assist him toward this goal. In biblical terms she would do him good and not evil all the days of her life. Her overall conduct of faithfulness and perfect trust exalted her as a model for all women desiring to walk in virtue.

A woman's capacity to influence her husband depends heavily on the depth of their relationship. When Eve came to Adam with the fruit of deception, one of the reasons he fell into the trap was because he trusted her. A woman who resorts to craftiness will open the door to a level of betrayal that will destroy everything around her. The entrance of sin, which bought insecurity, taught her how to maneuver, and use her good to obtain evil. Eve played up to her husband to get him going her way, because she had contaminated the precious natural power of influence. Her feminine power was corrupted. This is what we are seeing today in women the world over. When we reject submission this opens the door to rebellion and corruption of the power that God placed in the feminine creation. As we come into covenant relationship with God, and walk in obedience before Him, we will obtain grace to walk in his will for our lives. This includes, submitting to our husbands and learning how to righteously affect others. There will be no need for fleshly controls if a woman humbles herself before God, because He will teach her how to influence those around her, whether it be her husband or supervisors on her job.

Manipulation and control are also basic forms of witchcraft. Our greatest destruction comes when we go beyond the plans of God to obtain that which we desire to have 'our way', or when we are drawn away by fleshly lust. When I think of the carnal nature that man inherited, I wonder how far Eve went in order to influence Adam to submit to her, and eat of the fruit. Did she use the same strategy that women of today resort to? Maybe she withheld intimacy, or some other physical pleasure, or refused to gather fruits for dinner, just to have 'her way.' Maybe she kissed up and rubbed up to him like Delilah did with Samson. Whatever the route both Adam and Samson paid the awful price that comes as a result of manipulation.

This type of action is not confined just to marriage. How far will some workers go just to get a promotion, a position in the church, or a political candidate, a seat? How cold, callous, and utterly selfish, to resort to belittling, rejection, lies, and even murder, just to have our way. This is the very nature of Satan. He works tirelessly to shatter our trust in God first, then in each other. In the marriage relationship when a man trusts God, no matter what his wife may do, it will not destroy him because his total dependency is in God, and it is from him that he seeks instruction. A woman can submit to her husband, knowing that by doing so she is submitting to God, who has full control. In the work place, a supervisor may abuse his authority and mistreat you, but we are defeated if our trust is in people and not God, as our source of security. If your life on the job is subject to the word, (Ephesians 6:6) you have won the battle, because your trust in a higher power puts Jesus in the boss's seat. He will not only work through you, but he will honor you with divine favor and open doors that only he can close.

Through the course of my Christian walk, I have discovered how vital trust is to both my physical and spiritual relationships. Success in both areas depends largely on our willingness to trust God. Having confidence to not be moved by what we see, but by what He speaks. If God tells you to move, tells you to close your eyes and move, even though the area may be worse than where you are presently, go! When God leads and you follow, you will have no regrets. In our Christian walk and in every relationship we will have on this earth, trusting God is a means of survival.

The couple who cannot trust God will opt for separation or divorce. The man or woman who is not trusting God will resort to passivity, issues of control, crafty deals, compromising positions, and even adulterous relationship in an attempt to find protection. Many times in the case of marital affairs, Satan cleverly pits one woman against the other. Here we have two females, both with the power to influence. However, the woman of God should never allow herself to be tempted to use anything other than what God has given her to restore a relationship with her husband, or to tear him from the hands of deception. She must also know that her power to influence goes beyond feeling and emotions to faith, with which she will defeat the enemy, and bring him to shame time and time again.

All that is required of her is to seek God for divine instruction and walk in obedience. It takes the total woman, with the physical and spiritual presence, to influence the man in her life. Both women can capture him through their bodies, a facet of their domestic roles and ideals, and the physical qualities consisting of their feminine radiance and charm. But what the woman who is fighting with her physical attributes lacks is the spiritual qualities of purity, a deep rooted sense of joy, peace, long suffering, gentleness, goodness, faith, meekness, and temperance that can only come from a committed relationship with God. That is what will help the spiritual woman to ultimately win the war. When women begin to realize what can be done through the power of submission, they will stand up in the fear of God to rightfully take back what the enemy has stolen from them. A lady once remarked, "If I had known the power of submission a few years ago, I would never have lost my husband."

We have the power in the name of Jesus to combat all of Satan's devices as long as we walk in obedience to God's word. Not understanding the call to submission, many women relinquish a powerful opportunity to change the world through godliness or make a difference.

Like the church at Ephesus who was spiritually rich, yet lived as a beggar, many women occupy the hut when they can own the palace. The devil is fully aware of the power of submission, and he is very much afraid that you and I will embrace it. He knows that as women begin to pray for understanding and look to God for grace, his plans to lead men astray through rebellion will be ruined. Submission, like influence, requires trust, and you will be greatly challenged in both.

Your husband will not always seem to be making the right decision, nor will he always look to God for instruction, in fact he might not regard God at all. Nevertheless, as a woman or wife you can embrace the power that God has reserved for you by willingly accepting submission as God's plan for your spiritual walk. We can understand the importance of trust when we look at how important it is for us to trust the Lord Jesus to direct us through His Spirit. Except he leads us, one day, one moment, and one situation at a time we would be eternally lost and in despair. When we begin to move in the pathway of reliance, not only will order return to the family, but it will turn the world right-side-up. It will influence husbands, sons, fathers, brothers, and uncles to get into place, thus strengthening the power of authority. This will destroy Satan's kingdom and bruise his head. In addition, it will issue forth the ultimate plan of God for His children. Men and women will rise up as mighty nations conquering and not being conquered, but boldly accomplishing the mission of the Lord. His will, will be done upon the earth as it is in heaven.

The examples set for us from the beginning of time are numerous. A good example of a woman who used the influential power was Hannah. Through prayer she released the blessing of God in her life. Her prayer changed things and greatly affected the existence of her son, Samuel. In this day and age God is still looking for women who will embrace the power of submission and model godly influence. Is the man in your life under the attack of the enemy? Is he losing courage, and cowering in fear? Is he faltering in his leadership? God wants to use you to build him up just like he used Deborah, Hannah, and so many others. The power that he has placed in you has been put there for such a time as this. Be courageous, receive God's wisdom, and keep focused. It is time to arise to the standard that God has given us and possess the land, God's way!

You are powerfully and wonderfully made. Rebellion will not open the doors, but the keys of obedience will. Allow the authority of God's word, the power of his name, coupled with faith and forgiveness to lay a foundation of influence in your life. God created the man as the executor of his family. Like Deborah, it is in your best interest to be a helpmeet to him by motivating him to take the lead, not taking the lead from him. In taking the lead from him, whether you put him out or walk away, you will destroy the very foundation of your family. The husbandman was designed physically and spiritually to be the head of the home. Like Barak, this might not be obvious, or it might be dormant and hidden under anger, hurt, arrogance, or fear, but the fact remains, it is there. It is waiting to be stirred up, inspired, and unleashed. It is hidden within his soul, a mighty man of valor, a sober, vigilant, man of faith and promise.

As the woman desiring to do the will of God, you are empowered to bring it to life. Let the words you speak influence him always. Encourage him in everything he does, whether he does it well or not, Support him in his job, pray for him in every aspect of his life. Praise him when he brings you something to drink without being asked. Let him know how much you appreciate it. Tell him what a wonderful father and man of God he is, even if he is a drunkard, outcast, or backslider. Maybe he abandoned his family or neglects his responsibility in his home; do not be discouraged by what you see. Speak life over him and lift him up with words of faith. (Romans 4:17). When you lay beside him at night take the power of influence with you, and instead of just laying there like a piece of brick, get involved, and let him feel your confidence in him. Let your actions confirm that you are proud of him, need him, want him. The spark of trust you awake in him will produce the creativity your marriage cries for. It will put the spice back into your love life. Motivate him in your walk with the Lord, for you may be the most effective epistle that he will ever read.

It's in your hand, natural and powerful. This is what First Peter Chapter 3 speaks of when it states, "It is in this manner in the times of old, the holy women also who trusted in God, adorned themselves. Being in subjection unto their husbands, called him Lord, whose daughters you are as long as you do well, and are not afraid with any amazement." It takes determination, and faith void of emotionalism and fear. Emotion wavers, but standing on the irrefutable word of the living God will bring stability. The Word will never change, but will remain the same for all eternity. Know that when you submit to God in faith, you will influence your husband into the will of God.

10

Aim to Please

*The voice of my beloved! Behold, he cometh leaping
upon the mountains, skipping upon the hills.*

– SONGS OF SOLOMON 2:8

When a man's ways please the Lord, he maketh even his enemies to be at peace with him, (Proverbs 16:7). To please God, man is required only to love the Lord with all his heart, and love others like he loves himself. For too long we have strived to please out of the flesh realm instead of through the spirit realm (Romans 8:8). As a result we have experienced numerous hurts and hindrances. Real pleasure must stem from the spirit to the flesh because there is no root in the flesh or soulish realm to sustain it. To walk in a level of satisfaction that empowers and reassures, there has to be wisdom and obedience. It is displayed in both words and action, two distinct expressions that symbolizes the art of communication. In this chapter we will look at the woman as she models the joy of serving and uplifting others as she aim to please God.

So often we see communication as only verbally speaking to others. Communication is also touching lives with physical attributes. Through communication, God spoke the world into being. Through the physical, he redeemed the world with his life. This resulted in man's ability to live abundantly. Jesus has set a path for us to follow, and when we follow his lead we cannot help but prosper. Our words and deeds can also affect others immensely. When we aim to please out of our flesh it usually yields fruits that are not long lasting. True pleasure will yield satisfaction that reaches into the heart and soul. It is like a meadow brook that will continually supply fresh water.

This must be the aim of the woman of God, like the Shulamite woman in Songs of Solomon who ran to please her lover. Her desire was to give until he was satisfied and had need of nothing else. When we make up our minds to give, let us make a liberal release. No matter what it is that you are giving, be it love, service, material goods, or kindness with a smile, give liberally without reserve. This is the depth of giving that every woman should strive for. The married woman in I Corinthians 7:34, is also a model of one who gives sacrificially. Through caring for the things in her life that are physical and temporal, she will demonstrate the beauty of serving others through submission. Submission to her husband becomes a demonstration of her submission to Christ. Her giving to her children becomes a way to give back to God. The single woman's body and spirit exemplifies our individual service to the things of God. In each scenario your life symbolizes the relationship between Christ and His bride. If then, we as women have been given the grace to faithfully portray such a powerful aspect of the Lord's nature; it should be our ultimate intent to bring pleasure to the ones we love.

One of our biggest obstacles is "self." Self always looks out for the flesh. It will focus on "me, what I need/want" and constantly demand self satisfaction. However, this attitude will never please the Lord. Jesus said, "It is more of a blessing to give, than to receive." This has been the trademark of the ministry of Christ. He gave of himself to others, not asking anything in return. He fed the soul, and when he was finished he fed the body. If we follow Jesus' example, how much more we can do. When you attempt to give, the enemy tries to convince you to hold back by planting thoughts of doubt in your mind, "They're only using you," or "He is taking advantage of you," he might say. However, when you give of yourself, you have chosen the better part. We must not allow ignorance, fear, selfishness, guilt or any other tactic of Satan to cause us to lose our blessings or divert us away from what is righteous.

A supervisor on a job site was responsible for setting out various assignments for the workers. This was one of the duties that came with her promotion. After a while the young woman began to feel as if she had been given too much work, and was being taken advantage of. She began saying to herself, "Why should I have to do this for them when they can do it for themselves?" Soon, she was demanding that they seek out their own work, and they did. In a few months the office was in chaos, because many of the workers were involved in things that they were not responsible for. Office procedures were corrupted, resulting in the young supervisor's demotion. This scene is also played out in many areas of our lives, including marriage and family. As women, we dream of the day when we would be married, we want a husband, children, and a home, but when we get it we refuse the things that come with the package. If we are not careful, many of us, like the young supervisor, will lose out because of selfishness, ignorance, and lack of knowledge.

Because a woman possesses a natural desire to please, it is important in her single life that she remains focused on Christ, keeping herself pure, chaste, and discreet. This is also a spiritual requirement of the married women, but it does not end there. She also has a commitment to God to meet the needs of her husband, and accept his position of authority in the home. By so doing she strengthens the man who carries the power to strengthen the family. When I thought on this concept I understood why a woman is only as strong as her husband is, and why every successful man is often accompanied by a strong woman. By fulfilling her purpose through Christ, she greatly increases her level of effectiveness.

Just as flowers need water, men need the power of God in us to assist them in fulfilling their purpose in the home. One songwriter penned, "God has no hands but our hands, and he has no feet but our feet." Just as the body of Christ will help to accomplish his will upon the earth, most women are unaware that they too have been called to help their husbands accomplish God's will on the earth. This should be done willing, and with pleasure. For it is with the same willingness that we serve and reverence him, that we spiritually serve and give reverence to the Lord. The physical is an indication of what is happening in the spiritual.

In Words

Even so the tongue is a little member, and boasteth great things. Behold, how great a matter a little fire kindleth! James 3:5

The tongue is a very powerful tool. When we open our mouths to speak we can cause destruction, hurt, and even death, therefore we must be careful of the words we utter. Mankind has learnt to communicate to each other, animals, and some people even talk to plants. However, our most rewarding form of communication is to our heavenly father through prayer and worship.

The time we spend together just talking, and being spoken to and even singing is powerful. Consider the same to be of great importance in your relationship. Words are spirit and they are life. Likewise words can bring destruction and death. Words of life spring from the heart and out of the heart the mouth speaks. We are educated in the book of James about the power of the tongue. The man who is able to control his words is a perfect man, in control of mind and heart. Words can be very persuasive and has the potential to bless or to curse, to spread good, or evil.

The woman who desires to please the Lord is first and foremost a life giver by the words she expresses. If we are to build our homes and husbands we must begin ministering the words of God. Our words must first be pleasing to God, before they can edify anyone else. Words can either restore a marriage or bring it to ruin. Words spoken can lead men to eternal life or eternal damnation (Romans 10:13

It is no secret that women naturally enjoy conversing. However, if we are not careful, Satan will use our words to bring destruction. What is meant to inspire can become like a knife that cuts to the core of the heart. I met a young woman in St. Petersburg, Florida. She was a very gracious woman, a wife, a mother, and principal at a local school. When I was finish speaking, this beautiful lady walked up to me and shared this experience. Her husband had lost his job and was forced to take a less paying position. At first she encouraged him, to find a better job, but when his search came up empty and things became tighter financially, she found herself becoming very critical. She knew the words stung, because she could see the expression on his face, yet she continued to beat him down.

One evening she went to bed and had a very disturbing dream. From childhood she had been terribly afraid of roaches. She was flabbergasted when in her dream she realized that as she spoke roaches were racing out of her mouth. The angrier she became the bigger the bugs were and in larger numbers. Frightened out of her wits she awoke in fear. Sitting up she began to pray, asking the Holy Spirit to reveal to her the reason for this ugly dream. That's when He showed her the damage of her ugly words, not only to her husband, but to her children and others around her. In tears she awoke her sleeping husband, asking for forgiveness as she repented before God. She began praying that the Holy Spirit would guard her words and give her wisdom to use her words wisely. Needless to say she watched as her marriage relationship change before her eyes.

Jesus said in Mark 7:20, "It is that which cometh out of a man that defiles him, those things that protruded from the heart." Proverbs advises the wise woman to be careful with her words. Like Sarah, the wife of Abraham who became a model for women of all ages, she reverenced her husband by how she spoke and what she said. We all at times get angry, anxious, or disappointed, but we must guard our words to avoid bitterness and strife. Even in the lives of god-fearing women this can become a challenge in the flesh. The book of Proverbs also tells us that it is better to dwell in isolation, than in fellowship with a woman who cannot control her mouth. Angry words can leave lasting scars in relationships. What we say and how we say it can make a world of difference in the life of our family and friends.

Pleasant words are as an honeycomb, sweet to the soul, and health to the bones. Proverbs 16:24

Words soothes, they comfort, inspire, motivate, relaxes, and they can even change the atmosphere. Oh how sweet the honeycomb. We can't go wrong with kind words that bring peace. To the most selfish or downcast, compliments or soft answers will turn away wrath. Consider your words before you speak them. You can bring hope or despair through the delivery of a spoken word. People around you and even those in authority over you may at times be harsh when they speak or respond. Guard your heart by thinking before you respond. When you do speak chose your words carefully, conscience of the manner in which they are being delivered. Your husband or children may make a decision that you consider unwise. Your response at that time is crucial to both parties. A response that brings condemnation such as, "I told you so, you should have listened to me, or you deserve what you get" breathe guilt and shame. The woman that desires to inspire those around her will refrain from using such language. Threatening words are used to control and belittle. When we find ourselves using such words we ought to stop, and search ourselves. Find out where and why these words or feeling are surfacing. People tend to respond in this manner when they are tense, frustrated, fearful or afraid, or boxed in. A gentle word goes a long way to the restoration of peace.

The woman that feareth the Lord will desire to respond in love and compassion. In wisdom she may refrain from any type of response until the appropriate time, or she will trust God to work out the situation. Needless to say this is easier said than done, because the flesh will reject it. It calls for submission first to God then to your husband, and others in authority over you. Your choice words, your manner of humility and respect, will stir up in your husband a sense of courage, a will to succeed, and a desire to treasure you. Words out of place can destroy a relationship (James 3:6), but a word spoken at the right time can change the world. (James 3:13).

In Action

Words are powerful, but so is action which actually sends a stronger message than mere words. Therefore the desire to bring pleasure through the things that you do can change lives. A woman in Jesus' day reached out in faith to touch the hem of his garment. This simple action changed her life forever. Are you ready to minister with your heart through your hands? This could very well become the secret to your success.

Take the time to look around you. Open your eyes to the place where your husband resides. Is his personal area fit for a king? Many times we tend to think this is not important. Again, let us refer to the spiritual to reinforce the physical. The heart of man is referred to as the temple where the Holy Spirit resides. (1 Corinthians 3:16-17). For this reason it must not be defiled, for it is holy.

The surrounding for your husband should also be sacred. Let him feel your love and dedication when he enters. Make your home a special place. The size doesn't matter, but what is inside that counts. As a little girl my mother taught my sisters and I this poem:

> *The cottage was a little one, the outside old and*
> *mean, but everything within that house was*
> *wondrous neat and clean. Author Unknown*

It accompanied the story of a young woman who owned a little cottage. She was thankful for it and kept it well. Mom would emphasize the importance of keeping our surroundings clean, "Especially when you have a husband," she would say. When things are in place it makes it easier for him to relax after a hard day at work. My older sister would often remark, "So who is to make everything nice for me?" We would laugh and say how we would marry men who knew how to do the housework, but mom would quickly pull out her bible and show us Titus 2:5 explaining that the woman of God should be a good keeper of her home. Today, however, I thank God for His wisdom spoken through my mother, because even though there are times when I fell short, I see the truth of her words.

> *Don't be reluctant to pamper*
> *him, to put up his feet and*
> *massage them, as he relaxes.*

Please him in the way you love him. Don't be reluctant to pamper him, to put up his feet and massage them, as he relaxes. Run his bath for him, and prepare clean scented sheets for him to rest on. Don't hold back on anything but aim to please always. The seeds that you plant will one day come back to you bountifully. At first the tiny seed is not seen for a few days, but slowly the little green stem appear, and with it the joy of harvest. There will come a time when your husband will return the pleasure, that is, if he has not already done so. Make it a joyous occasion in preparing yourself for your most intimate moments together. Guard against having him come home to words or actions that would make him feel rejected or neglected especially if you are a homemaker. Avoid excuses that will push him away from you or kill your moments of bonding. It is true that most women, after a full days work, are wearied by early evening (refer to chapter 7) "Making your home a Haven," however, do not deny yourself or your spouse' the pleasure of an intimate approach.

Couples with young children should make sure that they have a bed of their own. When parents continually share the marriage bed with a child it can cause problems in their intimate relations and the child too can suffer from attachment issues. Find an appropriate time to put them to bed so that you may properly prepare yourself like the Shulamite wife of Solomon. Before the wedding you desired his affection intensely, now that you have him, there are no need for stop signs. This is one of the major reasons many married men or women look elsewhere. If you don't feed him somebody else will.

The woman that has a husband should look forward to the moments when her husband desires her body. This is the time for her to be lively, fresh, creative, stunning, amazing, and captivating. Like most women, I love when my husband caters to me. As we freely receive, we must freely give. When King Solomon wrote his songs he reported that his wife told him constantly how his kisses were to her sweeter than wine, a sweet smelling savor as she invited him to lie betwixt her breasts. She reported that when he placed his hand beneath her head, and with his other arm embraced her, that she chased away the other maidens and demanded that they not disturb her until she had satisfied her man. When the night came she would go after him and if he wasn't nearby, she would go looking for him so that she could satisfy him. In comparison to this, how far have we fallen? One wife spoke of her anger toward her husband who awoke her out of sleep for a moment of pleasure. Apparently she had been up very late with the baby, and after finally getting to bed she was awoken. The aim here is to be considerate of the other. This husband might want to adhere to his wife's desire for rest, or this wife can sacrifice a few moments to passionately and surprisingly please her husband.

We must be considerate of each others needs with mutual respect one to the other. One of the rules of the kingdom in Luke 6:38 say, "Give and it shall be given unto you, good measure, pressed down, and running over." This kind of giving calls for conferring liberally, not because you have to, but because you want to. Oftentimes when our husbands do not line up to what we desire of them, we refuse to give. This scripture does not only refer to money, but it can minister to us even in our marriages. Practice giving in every aspect of our lives. If a neighbor asks you to take him one mile, take him two. Pray that God would give you a profound desire to bestow upon others freely, expecting nothing in return. For with what measure we give it will be measured back to us. How many wives can testify of when they began to love from their heart, they began to see changes in their marriages? It is still true that what we sow is what we will reap. When I fully committed myself to my family, everything changed. Not only was my home cleaner, but the children were happier, and I was no longer so overwhelm and tired in the evening, but was able to wait on my husband.

Nowhere in the bible does it say that lovemaking in the marriage must only take place late at night. In fact the way you dress before coming to bed should shout to the attention of your husband. There is no need for this gift of God, made only for wives and husband to be mundane, routine, or dull. That is the response of sex outside the marriage bed. Within the bond of marriage lovemaking is a menu that is good for any hour of the day. Cherish it for what it is, a chance to refuel your spouse, to fan the fire, to deepen your love, and to glorify the Lord Almighty.

Make it your project to search for every way possible to make it all that it can be. Don't be afraid to ignite the flames, to search out the tender nerve endings in your husband's body, to explore and be creative, and to let that carefree spirit in you come forth. Don't be reluctant to give of yourself freely. Touch, feel and caress as you please. Remember, you made the vow to love and to cherish, to have and to hold; therefore you are only fulfilling your promise to God. His body belongs to you and vice versa. It is ungodly for either the man or wife to withhold themselves from each other.

For so many married women sex can be difficult. The reasons or causes are varied and can stretch back to confusing or very complicated times in their lives. Women who have been raised in very religious home or overly strict environments can encounter numerous problems upon getting married. There she might have been given the impression, that sex is unclean or that she herself is unclean just because of her divine makeup. There are also women who become unresponsive as a result of emotional abuse, physical abuse, or molestation. Here sexual relations can be a constant reminder of hurt, fear, anger, and rejection. When she is married, it becomes difficult to relax in the marriage bed. In the back of her mind this individual might feel uncomfortable, incompetent, or immoral. Herein is a struggle, because before the wedding sex was taboo, but now after the wedding it is declared holy, many are unable to make this adjustment. They are not able to envision sex as a beautiful part of the relation to be shared, but as another opportunity for them to be used, abused, or taken advantage of.

Many wives remain locked in this mindset for some time, going from relationship to relationship and never finding emotional freedom. This will definitely cause major problems in any relationship because they begin to feel like they are being used in other areas of the relationship as well. Men as well as women encounter these problems. It is for this reason that counseling is recommended at the first hint of marriage or just prior to engagement.

There are many individuals likewise who have suffered abuse or bad experiences in churches, ministries, or religious or respected persons. This becomes a stumbling block in their relationship with God. They cannot get pass what happen, by whom it happen, or what was done to them. It affects their ability to love or receive genuine love. With kindness, sincerity, and God-directed ministering these issues can be resolved. Individuals can be freed from many spiritual bondages and strongholds. Hope and fulfillment can be found in lives and relationships. In these situations it takes time to recondition the mind and become knowledgeable to the purpose of God for lovemaking in the relationship. God wants his people to be free in every area of their lives. That is why he gave his life.

The bible spoke of the Israelite women as lively women, the women of God should be lively women as well. When God created sexual intimacy in the marriage, it was to be the height of physical closeness, and the most intense depth of spiritual oneness designed for the man and wife. Without this understanding it is easy to see why many women feel uncomfortable about openly conversing with their husbands about this profound part of their relationship. The world has perverted and exploited sex to the point that many fail to recognize it as a divine gift from God. We must recognize this as the work of the enemy. It is one reason why in so many relationships the mere mention of our sexuality causes ill feelings or damaged pride. While others refrain from discussing the topic altogether, even in the proper context of scripture there are some who still consider it to be indecent or disgusting. There should be no shame in asking your husband how, or what can you do to please him. The marriage bed is often filled with confusion and secrecy. Few find courage to seek or ask for help until it is too late or the marriage is destroyed. When preparing a meal for our children we might ask them if the meal is too hot or cold, because we want it to be just right. Follow this same mindset with your spouse. Give due benevolence. You may ask, "How does this feel? Do you prefer this or that? What is most enjoyable for you? How can I please you! If these are not things that you know, you can always find them out. These are the rights of a husband and wife.

One afternoon I gave my husband a piece of paper, and asked him to write everything he wanted me to do for him that day. He looked up with bright eyes, sensing that I just wanted to please him, and began writing vigorously. I realized once again that aiming to please can be extremely powerful and very rewarding!

How to Help Your Wife to Submit!

*That the man of God may be perfect, thoroughly
furnished unto all good works.*

– II TIMOTHY 3:17

A farmer was on his way home and spotted a shiny rock in the dirt. At first he was excited thinking it might be a cluster of seeds. Already he could see its potential, but alas he realizes that the hard substance was not seeds after all. After securing it carefully, he slipped it into his bag, and continued home believing it was just another extraordinary find for his collection of rocks. He soon got to his crooked little house at the bottom of the hill. There he emptied the contents of his pocket into his treasure chest, and forgot about his find that day. Sometime later he died. His oldest son, upon clearing out his father's belongings came across the dusty rock. He had been taught how to determine the worth of jewelry while working in a pawn shop a few years earlier. Very quickly he brushed the dust away and took it to the goldsmith to be appraised. It turned out that the shiny rock was in fact, an expensive diamond worthy of a large sum of money. All his life he watched as his parents struggled to feed their children and provide a modest living with just the barest of necessities. How different their lives could have been, he thought, if only his father had discovered the true value of a simple find.

Whoso findeth a wife findeth a good thing, and
obtaineth favor of the Lord. Proverbs 18:22

The same can be said of many men who find a wife, yet because he is not aware of her value in his life, he continues to skimp. He has not realized that in his presence is a diamond worth millions. Because he is ignorant of her purpose, he destroys this jewel through physical, emotional, and mental abuse, belittlement, rejection, or withholding appreciation. Like the farmer who under estimated his find, many husbands under estimate the real worth of the woman they married. There is a reason that God, in his infinite wisdom, brought the woman unto the man. In the position of authority in his home, he can determine whether his family lives in shambles or spiritual victory. So often men see submission as a feminine thing, but in order for a home to be governed by the law of God, the man must also accept this feminine response and submit to the headship of Christ. Through submitting to Christ he will allow himself to be shown how to make his wife a true part of himself and how to help her to embrace submission.

Most men, because of pride and insecurity, are afraid to open up and let their wives into their lives. The average man fails to trust his wife because he is still fighting with issues that hinder him from completely trusting God. This is his greatest hindrance to eternal blessings. The wife, as a helper brings about fullness and completion. The man that cannot understand this will reject her physically. One gentleman put it wisely, "He will operate like half a man."

The very fabric of a woman's spirit is ripped when she is constantly rejected or misused. Likewise, when she is dominated to the point where she loses her free will of expression, or is not validated by her husband, her spirit is torn. It is easy for a man to do this when he is overcome by fear or vengeance. His actions will result in more insecurity, a low self esteem, or rejection for the woman. Living under this type of leadership she may begin to doubt her ability to be who she really is, and her ability to help her husband. When she crumbles, the strength that she brings to the marriage goes with her, and eventually all involved are affected by her hurt. The man, who desires his wife to be submissive and amicable, just pushed it a little further out of reach. Many women get even with rebellion. Either way, except the power of God intervenes; the marriage relationship and home can be headed for trouble.

A man can help his wife to fulfill her role by accepting the position of authority that God has given him. This does not mean that he must be bullish or hard. Neither will it require that he become weak and passive. It does mean that his actions toward her should reflect the love of Christ. It is a kind of love that is void of conditions. This is what true love is, "I will love you regardless." A woman must know that no matter what she does, he will always love her. This is the kind of love that Jesus has spent his life on earth demonstrating to us. Why? So that we may be able to demonstrate it to those He has called us to love. God told Hosea, "Even though your wife is a woman of whoredom, go and get her, Hosea 1:2. Every human being knows that loving others unconditionally is almost beyond man's natural ability. The only way he can recapture the art of loving is through allowing the Word of God to take root in his heart. He must not only read it, but he must live it and practice it in his daily relationships. The fact that God called him to this position is assurance that he will help him to fulfill it and be successful.

There will be times when the man will falter, and times when he will utterly fail. These will become learning experiences. None of us can achieve anything without them. When men begin to understand that God intended that he and his wife fight a battle, not as individuals but as a united force with Christ, then he will begin to see Jesus Christ as his stepping stone to becoming the kind of man he was created to be. As a result, loving their wives like God intended them to be loved, completely and without reserve, will not become a task, but a desire. Loving unconditionally is as difficult for men, as submission is difficult for women.

Most men marry without understanding the intricacies of manhood, or the true purpose of women in their lives. Without proper teaching, and the absence of good role models who are willing to open themselves and share both victories and failures, young men, like young women, enter marriage blind to the will of God in the marital relationship. They go into relationship looking for perfection only to find that perfection comes after the struggle, and is only available to those who are willing to go all the way to the finish line. Like Adam, how men respond will determine whether or not their relationship remains like a Garden of Eden experience. Too many women have been hurt by the emotional wrath of mentally or physically absent fathers, bully brothers, insensitive lovers, and selfish sons. It is time for the men of God to come forth with the healing balm that only they can give. The ability to love has been divinely placed within the man, for the woman. As he brings his life into subjection to God, this raises a hedge of protection around his family. Many husbands and fathers open the door to the spirit of rebellion and stubbornness in their families by themselves rebelling again God and his Word.

> *It is time for the men of God to*
> *come forth with the healing balm*
> *that only they can give.*

The authority placed in the hands of a man is a very awesome responsibility. To whom much is given much is required. There are men who fail to reap the blessings of God because they neglect their first responsibility - that of cultivating the garden. No garden, no flowers. They want the dominion, but they reject the responsibility that comes with dominion. One husband exclaimed, "It doesn't matter how I speak to my wife, because I am the head." This man is ignorant of the fact that when you separate the head from the body, both dies. Being the head does not mean that you do as you please, but it does mean that you lead by example. You speak to your wife as you want her to respond to you. You treat your children like you would want them to treat others in their life. Being the head of a home is indeed a priceless position of responsibility. A man's greatest individual responsibility is to remain in his position and trust God to lead him not when he thinks he needs it, but daily. Once out of his position, he pushes his wife out of her position, and his children likewise out of theirs.

It is a fact that one's ability to lead depends largely on his ability to follow. I surveyed a group of men asking their view of wives and submission. One young man in particular who had recently married said, "I don't believe in that, I feel we should both share the load, no one need submit to anyone. My wife and I share the mortgage, food bill, expenses for the children, housework, and anything else." When I asked how he felt

about having her stay at home his response was immediate. "Why should she stay home and lounge while I work my butt off, no way!" Many men run from the responsibility of governing and are at ease to just ride the wave. Few have a genuine understanding of what submission entails. This young man saw it as a burden or injustice. Submission allows a man to submit to the will of God in his role as husband, and the woman to submit to her role as a wife. It should not be a burden or injustice for neither; in fact submission that comes as a result of a burden is not really submission. Societal changes and biblical teachings taken out of context have left many confused as to what God expects of them. Submission to him puts both man and woman back on the pathway for direct impartations and direction from God.

God has said to the male, "By the sweat of your brow you will eat bread." Men were to be responsible for providing protection, provision, and direction for their family. This is where they would find fulfillment. The world suffers for lack of men who will take up the mantle and allow the Lord to show them the way. I urge men everywhere, whether fathers, husbands, brothers, or sons, to enable us as women to follow you as you follow Christ. This will spur the power that will change wives from being weak to strong, from frightened or discouraged hearts to courageous helpers and friends. You will then watch as the women around you that are referred to as hard, rebellious, and mouthy, become respectable, honorable, and submissive lambs.

As men nourish and cherish their wives like a precious ornament, they will build character and resiliency. This is how you help your wife to submit. Submission is a place of rest for the woman that is so often made uncomfortable because of issues of trust, unforgiveness, and a lack of faith. Every woman desires to see her husband be the responsible man, friend, and lover that she needs him to be.

In time your wife will come to resemble a beautiful flower growing by the river. The words men speak will not shatter the woman's self confidence, neither will they feel insecure by his leadership, but their husband's spiritual strength will bring security. The loving husband finds time to talk to her, play with her, hold, encourage, and delight in his wife. This must becomes his way of life, not only at night, but throughout each day. The closer he comes to her, the more he feels what she feels, and sees what she sees. He gives her support and not belittlement in front of the children. In short, husbands would treat their wives as they would treat themselves.

Allow Christ himself to be your role model of how to honor your wife with the kind of honor that disperses kindness, service, preference, devotion and passion. Watch how he values his bride, and do likewise. The fact that God has given her to you to assist in your greatest moments of life, qualifies her for your love and acceptance. Given the proper atmosphere, most women will readily submit and embrace meekness. In an atmosphere of love and honor how can a woman not submit? It is never too late for change, and it can be done through your obedience to the Lord. You will discover that within that house coat and those worn bed shoes is a treasured and priceless diamond!

12

Where Do We Go From Here?

Receive my instruction, and not silver, and knowledge rather than choice gold.

– PROVERBS 8:10

From cover to cover of this book, there is one thing that stands out: total submission requires faith and confidence in God. When I first seriously surrendered to him, I was twelve years old, excited and relieved in my childlike mind that I was on my way to heaven. But more than that, I really felt a difference in my heart. My mind goes back to that evening; it was a quiet ride home. My family was aware that "Kimmy" was now born again. I guess they were thinking that now there would be less trouble in the house, seeing that I was always at the hem of whatever happened. We were home for less than an hour when my older sister began to fuss at me for something I had done earlier. I tried to be patient, but then I got angry with her. She said to me, "I knew nothing changed in your life. You say you got saved, (born again) well, repentance brings change!" My heart sank, and before long I had convinced myself that perhaps nothing happened after all.

This went on for a few more times. It seem every time there was a revival I would confess and repent, but it always seemed as if nothing changed when I got home and was put to the test. Later in my Christian walk, I realized that what my sister said was indeed the truth; but there was more to that truth. When one repents there is a change, but the change is often gradual. We do not become perfect over night, but minute by minute, day by day, we mature in our relationship. My sister expected that I would immediately cease to do things that she thought were unfitting for a Christian. Being a few years older and a young believer like myself, she too had to come to the understanding that as long as we live we would always have cause to repent. Having knowledge of the word is good, but having an understanding is critical to spiritual growth. 1 Peter 2:2 says, *"As newborn babes, desire the sincere milk of the Word that ye may grow thereby."* The most important thing for a newborn baby is its mother's milk which is fortified with what the baby needs for growth and maturity. Just as newborn babies need the sincere or pure milk, we as children of God needs the pure milk of the word to grow and mature spiritually. The pure word of God becomes our most necessary food. The words that caught my eyes in that scripture was "grow thereby."

> *Growth like submission is a process that requires time and development.*

Spiritual growth, like submission is a process that requires time and development. As long as we live we will develop on different levels. When we think we have submission down, and packed tight, we will find that there is always something new to learn. At the age of 16, I truly gave my life to Jesus Christ. At this point in my Christian growth, negative statements no longer sent me hurling. I knew it was forever this time, I was born again, and made up my mind that doubt would not send me backward this time. There were times when my faith was tested, that I felt weakened and wondered if I would be able to continue on. Many times I stumbled, and fell, but each of the struggles brought me into a deeper understanding of who God was and how much he really loved me. This gave me the confidence to hold on no matter what happened. I continued growing and maturing like a fruit in the vineyard. Looking at salvation gave me a better understanding of submission.

Submission is much like salvation. You don't say one day, "I am going to submit," and suddenly you are surrendered and submitted, but day by day, step by step, you learn, you fall, you get up again, and you understand more. It is not emotional or adjustable at your convenience, but it is a commitment fed by a desire to live according to God's word and by his grace. It is not something that can be forced on an individual; it must be willingly sought for. It must never become a burden, but a desire. The scripture says, "For by grace are ye saved through faith; and that not of yourselves: *it is* the gift of God, (Ephesians 2:8). Having this knowledge the question is "where do we go from here?"

The act of submission is an attitude that fosters restoration. Except one is willing to "give in" or submit, resistance will prevail and hinder the flow of things. We have gained the knowledge of good and evil, what will we do with it? Will we rebel or will we submit? "How long halt ye between two opinion, if God be God, serve him, but if Baal then follow him" (1 kings 18:21). The first step to submission is to believe in God's order of divine authority, then confess your rebellion, repent, and turn to righteousness. This will enable the Holy Spirit to direct your every step. There will be times when you may fall short. Your spouse might make you angry, or you may feel you are being taken advantage off. Nonetheless, remember you have a built in helper, who is there when you need him, and even when you do not realize you need him. Before Jesus descended into heaven, he made us a promise that he will be with us always, and that he will send his Holy Spirit to lead and guide us in all truth. His promises are real.

Finally, to bring closure there must be forgiveness. Jesus said, "If you forgive not others, neither will your heavenly Father forgive you." His teaching on forgiveness is strong and powerful as he instructed the multitudes on the mountain that day. Without forgiveness there will be no true growth, peace, or reconciliation. Forgiveness requires humility, and humility is the most assured platform to greatness. II Chronicles 7:14 states: "If my people, which are called by my name, shall **humble themselves and pray,** and seek my face, and turn from their wicked ways, then will I hear from heaven, and will forgive their sins and will heal their land." Before change comes, there must be repentance. Before repentance, there is submission.

Praying is an act of humility. When an individual bows his head to pray, he is acknowledging the existence of God Almighty. A humble heart will recognize and submit to divine authority. No matter where you are in your relationship with him, or if you have no relationship at all, when you humble yourself before the face of God, He is able to transform you into what you ought to be.

I am reminded of a story I heard some time ago of a little teapot. He had been very useful in his early days, but now he was old and worn. Eventually, he was tossed on the dump. A potter was passing by and spotted the little teapot. Immediately he saw beyond the piece of old iron junk. He saw potential! Quickly he picked it up and took it home. He was going to restore it to its original purpose. The little kettle was amazed at the new surrounding. When he heard from the other pieces of iron what the potter had intended to do to him, he laughed, thinking it was indeed a great challenge. He sat on the shelf for a while until one day the potter came in and picked him up. The first part of the process was the cleansing. At first it was soothing as the fingers of the potter rubbed over him, but after a while the little kettle became upset as he was washed again and again. Then the potter took a harsh, hard material, and begins to scratch and scrub him. The little teakettle began to rant and rave on how rough the potter was.

It did not end there. The potter covered him with a sticky, yucky substance, left him for a few more days and then returned to begin the harsh process all over again. Many times he wanted to say, "Don't you know what it means to be gentle? Can't you see what I'm going through? But when he saw the potters smile and the look of admiration in his eyes, he changed his mind. The pain was often unbearable, even though he realized many of the marks and holes that covered him were vanishing, but this did not stop his train of complaints. One day the potter placed him on the shelf, and seemingly forgot about him. The teapot made up his mind that when the potter returned he would scold him. He would say to him, "Do you realize how hot this shelf is? What kind of a heart do you have?" However, when the potter did return, it was evident in his eyes that he was sharing the little teapot's pain, so the teapot said nothing. What happened next was a shock. The potter came in early the next morning, and moved him, but instead of putting him near the cooler end of the table he placed him in the fire. The little kettle thought he would die. The flames were hot, and he cried until he felt all his tears were gone. Finally he came out and was covered for days by what felt like a gruesome potion. It was taken out of a few different cans.

Finally, he was covered by a clear, cool, liquid before finally being left alone. He stood in the corner of the shelf, happy to be in a comfortable spot. After a few days in this position he decided to shift to the other side. As he began to turn he caught a glimpse of a pot in the mirror on the adjacent wall. "Gosh," he said "What I wouldn't give to look like that! That is simply the most beautiful pot I have ever seen." "It sure is!" the cup on the side of him said. "You are a masterpiece!" It was then that the teapot realized that he was looking at himself. He had become a treasure, a classic, a model of perfection. Suddenly he realized what had happened, what the potter was doing all along. He never imagined he could ever look like this. Tears began to flow down his eyes as he though of all that he had endured, it was not easy, but it sure was worth it. How happy he was that he had submitted to everything. He shuddered to think what could have happened had the potter just discarded him, and left him unfinished as a result of his insubordination. Truly this transformation was worth the price he had to pay.

How many of our lives can be compared to this little teapot? We were found wounded and worn, filled with holes, and looking rather depressing, but then comes Jesus, our potter, making us into a whole new creature. At times there were aches and pain, disappointment, shame, and so much to endure. We even cry out to the potter that we are not able to accomplish a task. "I can't be submissive, I can't sing, I can't break this habit, I don't want to forgive, I hate speaking in the front of people, yet you want me to preach?" What we do not realize is that the potter is fully aware of what you can or cannot do and he will never put more on us than we are able to bear. There is always a way of escape when we allow him to show us how to not only overcome our struggle, but defeat it. If you can't, he can, for there is nothing impossible with God! When it is all over, when we submit and allow the potter to bring us through, we will look back and marvel at the work of His hands.

I can think of many situations in my life when I did not want to submit, but when I did, I found growth, beauty, and maturity that I had not known before. Like the little teapot, I look back, thankful that through Christ I can begin to embrace submission. Submission is not simple. Fighting the flesh is war. The good thing is that the battle has already been won. *Jesus said, "Be of good cheer, I have overcome the world!"*

When I began writing this book, my focus was on submission of the wife to her husband. Today I know that more importantly it is the desired response from mankind to God. Submission is what God needs from us. When we submit to God, husbands will submit to Christ, wives will submit to their husbands, and children will submit to parents. On the job, in the church, community, and nation, submission will be the response to authority, and we will do it not by force or with resistance, but willingly from the heart. When you invited Jesus Christ into your heart, you opened the door to allow the sixty six books of the bible to come in and take residence. Let these books come alive in your human flesh. Everything that he did, he can do through you. This would enable you to fulfill that divine plan that God carved for you even before you were in your mother's womb. You do not know the plan, but God owns it. In order to get it, you must submit to his will for your life.

By faith you will conquered the flesh and win, however you must go through the process. This is the only way it can be completed. You can never love anyone enough or vice versa to motivate you to submit, for it is a work of the heart, of which only God knows the intent. We must cleave to him, and seek his face, forsaking our way, yet hungering after the ways of Christ. Then, and only then, will we be able to reap abundant joy and life.

God has given the final decision to you. Whatever the choice you will receive your just reward. He is saying to women today, I have called you, chosen you, anointed you, and appointed you, but I am a God of order and not confusion. Not only women, but men, children, leaders, workers and indeed the Church, His spiritual bride, we are all called to embrace obedience and humility and allow the Lord to rearrange our lives. He that hath an ear let him hear what the Spirit says to the churches. As the world prepares for the wedding of a lifetime, the bride maketh herself ready; the groom is even at the door. Will he find his bride, the church, you and me watching, without spot or wrinkle, waiting for our groom to come? Stand up and reveal him through *The Power of Submission!*

A Prayer for those Desiring a Submissive Heart.

Lord Jesus,
I believe that you are the son of God, who gave his life that I may
live. I also believe that you are a God of truth and order.
I now confess my rebellion against your word and your divine
authority in my life.
(Husbands) I accept you as the head of my home, marriage, and
Lord of my life.
(Wives) I accept you as Lord of my life and marriage, and, my
husband as the head of our home.
(Singles) I accept you as head of my home and Lord of my life. I
claim forgiveness and deliverance from the works of the flesh and
the dictates of the world.

I know that your blood cleanses from all unrighteousness,
I repent of my actions before you, in my heart, and in my home. I

now ask you to empower me that I may be submissive.
Cleanse and make me the individual that you created me to be.
Bring my life into subjection to the plan and purpose that
You have ordained for me that I may truly be that vessel through
which you will channel your glory.
I submit everything to you, Lord, and I thank you for what will
transpire in my life, from this moment on, Amen!

Special Thanks

To my husband Lambert- If praying for a husband at the age of 12 brought a man like you, then I would encourage young girls to start praying for their husbands as soon as they can say a prayer. Thank you so much for being the husband I prayed for and desired. I will forever love you. Two precious sisters in Christ, Rose Allen, Mary Smith, thanks for being real and being there.

Those psalmist who did not sing for a recording or fame but allow the angels of God to minister through them in songs. Thank You!

Shirley Ceasar –*God's got it all in Control*

Juanita Bynum & Helen Baylor- *Numerous songs*

Marvin Sapp – *You are God*,

Maurette Brown - *Speak*,

Paul Morton – *He is here, Bow Down Songs by LA & Florida Mass Choirs* and so many other individuals that impacted my life, Thank You!!!.

About the Author:
Kim V. E Sands

Ordained Minister, Psalmist, Author, and International Speaker, but her family loves her best as wife and mother. Very early in her life, Kim saw and understood the existence of powerful God. Growing up in the Church, she came to understand the importance of having a personal relationship with the Lord. It is that relationship that propels her forward today. Through books and messages of inspiration she has touched the lives of not only those in Christian ministries, but schools, businesses, and personal relationships. The message that God has given her is one of hope and encouragement. Her passion and understanding of God's word is indeed what the body of Christ needs as we move into a time of revelation and power.

Kim Sands is married to Pastor Lambert Sands. Their union has been rewarded with a son, two daughters, and two precious grand angels. The couple ministers individually and through the Christian based ministry of Marriage Mechanics. Marriage Mechanics ministers to both the physical relationship between husband and wife, and the spiritual relationship of Christ and the body of believers through television and other medias worldwide.

In a time of worldwide chaos, never is a message of restoration, inspiration, and life more important to spiritual survival. When you meet Kim Sands you will understand why she has been placed in the body of Christ for such a time as this.

MARRIAGE MECHANICS

For more information and inspiration visit:
www.marriagemechanics.org
or our Facebook page
https://www.facebook.com/
Marriage-Mechanics-Ministries-373287776129308

OTHER BOOKS AVAILABLE:

Understanding Male Authority

The Complete Fight For Your Marriage Book

The Real Truth About Marriage, Divorce, and Remarriage

Living Single

The Noah Chronicles

The Long and Short of Choosing the Right Marriage Partner

Lightning Source UK Ltd.
Milton Keynes UK
UKHW021228171220
375421UK00008B/334